In the World of Sumer

Samuel Noah Kramer.

Samuel Noah Kramer

In the World of Sumer

AN AUTOBIOGRAPHY

Wayne State University Press   Detroit 1986

Library of Congress Cataloging-in-Publication Data

Kramer, Samuel Noah, 1897–
  In the world of Sumer.

  Bibliography: p.
  1. Kramer, Samuel Noah, 1897–   . 2. Sumerian
philology. 3. Sumerians. 4. Assyriologists—United
States—Biography.   I. Title.
PJ3164.K73A35 1986   499.95   [B]   85-22483
ISBN 0-8143-1785-5

Contents

Foreword

This is the first time, if I am not mistaken, that a cuneiformist scholar has bared his soul in a printed autobiography. With the increasing popularity of this literary genre, it was bound to happen sooner or later, but in a sense it seems fitting for the pioneer who discovered so many new Sumerian literary works and who sub-titled one of his best-known books "Thirty-nine Firsts in Man's Re-corded History" to be the first to tell the world about himself. Under a cold, almost clinically sounding label, "autobiography" covers, as a literary endeavor, quite different expressions of inner life. But, leaving aside banal cases motivated by greed, the starting point of an autobi-ography is always the awareness of history, the need to find the place of the self in the temporal flow of things, the need to find an answer to "Where do I fit?" A man who devotes his life to the study of the past is bound to feel the urge to answer this pressing question more strongly and from a wider perspective than one who by education or occupation lacks historical sense. If the scholar, like Sam Kramer, has cleared new paths and tilled new fields, the need becomes more pressing yet. Why some people keep the answer within themselves, while others are com-pelled to formulate it publicly, depends on very personal factors that contribute to making the autobiography "one of the more fascinating aspects of one of the great myths of modern western civilization, the myth of the SELF," as Philippe Lejeune has put it in his "Le Pacte au-tobiographique." No matter what weaknesses surface, no matter how much the writer's view of his own life differs from that of the reader's, the act of baring one's own soul commands always utmost respect.

In the present case, no great effort is requested from the reader to admire and to learn. Sam Kramer tells about himself in a direct, almost naive manner that casts no veils on his subject's outline. What one admires is a very personal matter which I will not presume to discuss. I will dare, however, to point out some of the lessons that may be had from the perusal of his book. These days it is not fashionable for the autobiographer to stress, as Gianbattista Vico or Benjamin Franklin did, the exemplary value of one's own life story. Exemplarity, nonetheless, continues to be, next to immortality in the cultural world, one of the main functions of autobiography. The mysterious interplay of circumstances and advocation—that Sam likes to call by its Sumerian name nam-tar, or "fate,"—can be followed in the first five chapters. Sam's narrative of his father's Talmudic school-at-home describes—in a measure of which Sam himself is perhaps unaware—the Sumerian school, é-dub-ba, "the tablet house," of old Babylonian times, as revealed by the most recent investigation, much better than the term "academy" used often in the past by Sumerologists. Sam Kramer must have felt an instinctive liking for the activities of Sumerian scribes, trained in a school not unlike his own home. His first contacts with cuneiform and specifically with Sumerian texts came at a turning point in the development of American Assyriology. A cuneiform language was first taught in American in 1879–1880. Some of the pioneers were still around when Sam, a brand new Ph.D. diploma in hand, had to make a professional choice. Cyrus Adler (1863–1940), the president of Dropsie when Sam started his graduate studies, had been the first student of cuneiform at Johns Hopkins and the first recipient of a Ph.D. in Semitic languages granted by an American school. George A. Barton (1859–1942), one of Sam's teachers at the University of Pennsylvania, had started teaching Assyriology at Bryn Mawr College forty years before. Although apparently not in direct contact with Kramer, David G. Lyon (1852–1935), the "Father of American Assyriology," was in those days still curator of the Harvard Semitic Museum after retiring from teaching. Sam, the Russian immigrant, started his academic life just in time to join the new generation of American Assyriologists. By choosing Sumerian literature, he became associated with one of the most successful American archaeological enterprises, the excavations at Nippur. The Sumerians were discovered not too long after the decipherment of cuneiform, and their traces have surfaced in many Mesopotamian sites, but most of what we know about their language and literature comes from Nippur. Without the hundreds of lexical texts and the wealth of literary and historical tablets found in the Nippur mounds, the echos of ancient Sumer would be very faint indeed.

The economic boom of the late twenties had favored the expansion of Assyriology, an expansion that found its most powerful expression in the growth of the Oriental Institute of the University of Chicago. The regrettable anti-Semitic incident related in the book might have delayed, but in the long run not interrupted, Sam's academic career. The Great Depression almost did. And therein lies one of the more important lessons of Sam's life. Captivated by the charm and mystery of the Sumerian literary texts, he pursued their study with such tenacity and selfless dedication that he was able to overcome tremendous financial difficulties that would have forced a less resolute person to abandon the field in search of more materially rewarding endeavors. Difficult times have, after all, a beneficial effect on scholarly and scientific pursuits. The ones who lack the proper priorities of values are weeded out and only the truly faithful persist. This is not easily appreciated in a culture like ours that not only has a difficult time recognizing the distinction between "making something while making money in the process" and "making money while making something in the process," but attempts on occasion to deny, on theoretical grounds, the existence or at least the legitimacy of the first attitude. Sam Kramer passed this difficult test with flying colors, and I believe that this, even more than his books, makes him a true scholar.

Another measure of the dedication of Sam Kramer as a scholar is his choice of themes for the autobiography. Except for his childhood memories—and these still deal more often than not with his education—what we have in front of us is much more a chronicle of his scholarly work than a picture of his personal life. Family, health, social life, and landscape are all left untouched or dealt with only in the most peripheral manner. One has only to read the narrative of his trip around the world in Chapter 12. Scholarly reflections and lectures are considered the only things worthy of record. This picture of professional concentration does not result from the author's selection of what to tell, as much as it reflects Sam's true priorities in life. I happen to know that he did not even want to take a camera for the trip. Only some aspects of life behind the Iron Curtain, and especially in his native Russia, seem to have impressed him deeply enough to deserve being told.

The reader will easily understand Sam Kramer's silences and respect his privacy. There is one point, however, whose omission the reader will regret with some justification. Like any scholar trying to reconstruct the past, Sam must have asked himself more than once about the value of devoting one's life to exploring the past when so many momentous events are taking place in the present. The recovery of the past represents a sheer enrichment of human thought. It is a sort of time travel in which, unlike in science fiction in which we encounter generally pitiful creations of an ethnocentric imagination in alien worlds, we make acquaintance with fellow humans who represent aspects of ourselves which temporal and cultural boundaries have made impossible to actualize. One day may come when the study of man, frustrated by the limitations implied by the study of the present man with no possible knowledge of the long-range consequences of his behavior, will focus with new interest on man as a historical being, on the behavior of the species through extended periods of time. We will know then whether the belief in progressive changes in the quality of human life, paralleled by the technical progress of mankind, is based on a mirage or on facts. Works of scholars like Kramer will allow us to answer this sort of question. Although Sam does not tell us why he did it, the readers and all students of man will all be grateful to him for what he did.

If I may be pardoned a personal note, I met Sam Kramer for the first time in Paris in his Boulevard Raspail hotel in 1958. He had invited Jean Bottéro to be his assistant in Philadelphia; Bottéro declined and suggested my name. Being a foreigner, my Assyriological future in France was rather bleak. Sam did for me what no person had done for him in the difficult times of the Depression. He saved my scholarly career. That does not mean that I was spared a trial period. He could not afford to pay me much, and more than once I was sorely tempted to quit, but his contagious enthusiasm kept me going. I want thus to add my personal thanks to those of all his readers.

Miguel Civil
Oriental Institute
University of Chicago

1
From the Talmud to Cuneiform

I was born on September 28, 1897, in Zashkov, a ghetto *shtedtel* in the district of Kiev in the Ukraine. The week of my birth happened to coincide that year with Simchath Torah, the annual Jewish festival commemorating the reading in the synagogue of the concluding portion of the Torah, the Five Books of Moses. This coincidence of birth and feast inspired my father to name me Simcha, "Joy." The *ch* in this Hebrew word, which represents a harsh Semitic guttural, later proved to be a thorn in the throats of my Philadelphia teachers when they tried to Anglicize my name. To make matters worse, the week in which I was circumcised coincided with the reading in the synagogue of the weekly portion of the Pentateuch that tells the story of the patriarch Noach, and this concurrence of *brith* and Flood hero prompted my father to give me the middle name Noach. So there I was, beginning life in the czar's Zashkov with the "begutturaled" name Simcha Noach Kramer.

The last name, Kramer, "Storekeeper," must have been acquired by the family in a German-speaking community long before my father's day. For my father was no merchant, big or little, wholesale or retail. He was a *Gemoorah-rebbi*, a teacher of the Talmud. His pupils were boys aged nine to thirteen who had finished their earlier elementary studies in the Pentateuch and the prayer book and were now ready to tackle the more difficult, complex, and deeply revered Talmud, which consists of numerous compendia of legal lore and legendary tradition.

The author's father, Benjamin, and mother, Yetta, about 1915.

Our town had no yeshivah, and the pupils who completed their talmudic studies with my father and wished to delve deeper into talmudic and kabbalistic lore would go off to some larger town renowned as a center of learning.

The number of pupils in my father's school, located in our home, was about a dozen, and the remuneration he received from the parents was, as I recollect, about 10 rubles per student per year. This annual income of approximately 120 rubles barely sufficed for our family of five—I had an older brother and an older sister—and there was little danger of our suffering from overeating. Many a meal consisted of cabbage soup and tea with a piece of hard sugar to bite on. But our little house with plastered walls and straw roof was our own, and there was a goat to provide us with milk and cheese. And then there was the Sabbath, glorious and holy, that lit up our home once a week and turned it into a palace. On Friday night we gorged ourselves on fish and meat, on *kugel* and *tzimes,* and sang our hearts out to Jahweh and his goodness.

On my fourth birthday, my older brother brought me to the *dardeki-*

rebbi (elementary teacher) in our town to begin my studies in bible and prayer. I was not a bad student, and by the time I was eight, I had covered the reading and translating into Yiddish of a good part of the Bible, including the commentary of the venerated medieval French-Jewish scholar Rashi which was printed in small type below the biblical passages. The teaching was by rote, and there was many a biblical sentence whose meaning I knew only superficially and from memory. But it imbued me with profound faith in Jahweh's love for his suffering people, and I had no doubt that one day the Messiah would appear and turn things around.

My special heroes were Judah, son of Jacob, who dared talk back to Joseph, whom he took to be second only to Pharaoh in power and station; Moses, the man of God and leader of his people; the brave Joshua, who made the sun stand still until "the people had avenged themselves upon their enemies"; David, the valiant, generous singer of psalms; and Solomon, the wisest of men. King Solomon was a great favorite in our house, since, as every believing Jew knew, he was the author of the Song of Songs. My father cherished this book, so much so that from time to time, when in a happy mood, he would seat me on his knee and ecstatically intone its voluptuous words redolent with lust and desire. Its two ardent lovers, he assured me, were none other than Jahweh and the people of Israel, and their rapturous speech was but an avowal of their tender love and yearning. Little did I dream that one day, with innocence gone and faith departed, I would write a learned monograph to demonstrate that the Song of Songs echoed the pagan fertility rite of a Sacred Marriage between a ravishing goddess of sexual love and her blissful royal acolyte.

Heroes were certainly needed in the dark, bitter days of the early part of the twentieth century, when both the czarist court and the Russian church were inciting the populace to organize pogroms and massacre Jews. No pogrom had yet actually violated our *shtedtel,* but neighboring towns had been ravaged, and terror was at our doors. A number of the more daring Zashkovites had now departed for America. Some had settled in Philadelphia and were doing well as merchants. There was plenty to eat and drink and much material comfort, but they were deeply worried about their children, who were being well educated in the public schools but were learning nothing of Hebrew tradition. From time to time they wrote to my father, with whom some of them had studied in Zashkov, urging him to leave pogrom-ridden Russia and come to Philadelphia to teach their young the Bible and the Hebrew prayer book. In 1905, though in his fifties, he decided to harken to their plea. Since there was not enough money to take along the entire family, he traveled alone in order to prepare the way. The very next year, with savings from his earnings as a Hebrew teacher, he sent us *Schiffskarten* (travel tickets) to bring us from Zashkov to Philadelphia, and we were off to America, fearful and hopeful.

We almost did not make it. Like most other Jewish emigrants, we were leaving Russia without official permission and therefore had to "steal the border," to translate literally the Yiddish idiom. This was a clandestine procedure, carried out in the dark of night, in which an agent of the travel agency from which our tickets had been purchased would lead a batch of emigrants across the border, after having bribed both the border guards and the customs officials. Usually this was a smooth operation, carried out without difficulty. But the group to which we were attached ran into trouble, and we were caught and arrested on the Austrian side of the border. We were not mistreated, however, and after an anxious, frightening night, and some additional bribes no doubt, we were permitted to board a train for Rotterdam and the steamer that would take us to New York. Our journey continued without further misadventure, and after landing at Ellis Island, we left immediately by train for Philadelphia, where my father installed us in a small but not uncomfortable apartment on Bainbridge Street, in a section of the city inhabited largely by immigrant Jews and Italians. It was not far from Independence Square and the home of the American Philosophical Society that was one day to be a pillar of support to me and my research, but I had no inkling of this at the time. Here, then, in the month of June, 1906, in a South Philadelphia tenement, began the realization of one version of the American dream.

July and August were school vacation months. But in early September I was taken to the Meridith Elementary School, not far from home, and entered the first grade. Then and there began my first confrontation with the Anglo-Saxon world and the loss of some of my native identity. When my first-grade teacher, Miss Nellie, a lovely, buxom lady whom I remember with no little affection, saw in cold black ink the given names Simcha Noach, she became alarmed—these were hardly words fit for the English tongue. Simcha was changed then and there to the more commonplace Samuel, and Noach to the less exotic Nathan. And so I became Samuel Nathan Kramer, and continued to be so called throughout my school years. These are also the names on my naturalization papers, my passport, and my earliest publications. Only when my publications increased in number and weight did I become more daring, and, while hesitating to tamper with Samuel, I changed the middle name to Noah (for Noach), so that all my later publications are signed Samuel Noah Kramer. And although this is perhaps hallucination, the change from Nathan to Noah seemed to have had an effect on my academic colleagues, who began to read my published studies more respectfully and attentively.

Still, this name transformation had its darker consequences. Librarians tend to look upon me as an enemy, since every time they catalogue Kramer, Samuel Noah, they have to add: See also Kramer, Samuel Nathan. And whenever in my many travels I show my passport, with its Samuel Nathan Kramer, I do so with some trepidation, since my suitcases bear the inscription Samuel Noah Kramer, and I might be taken to be some kind of impostor.

I was eight years old on entering the first grade, while most of my classmates had begun their school careers at six. But I was moved to a more advanced grade several times, so that when I reached the last grade in elementary school I was fourteen, then the average age of elementary school graduates. I remember these early school days with much pleasure, for my teachers were dedicated and did their best to impart to us their limited knowledge and learning. In fact, throughout my school experience, I found most of my teachers sympathetic and sensitive in their attitude to the immigrant "greenhorn" pupils whom they endeavored to make part and parcel of the American scene; they believed truly and fervently in the American melting pot, and at no time denigrated the mores and customs of the diverse ethnic groups with whom they came in contact.

The Philadelphia public schools were not the sole source of my education. My father, who remained an observant Orthodox Jew to the end of his days and who absorbed and assimilated very little of either the English language or American culture, was deeply concerned about my religious education. At that time there was a yeshivah in Philadelphia, and he had me matriculated in it not long after our arrival. The hours were from about four in the afternoon to seven in the evening, and there were also sessions on Sunday morning. This did not leave me much time for play. Neverthelesss, we yeshivah students did manage to find time for baseball and other games during recesses and holidays; our bodies were not neglected altogether, although the educational emphasis was almost entirely on the intellect.

Virtually the sole discipline in the yeshivah consisted of the study of the Talmud, together with the commentaries composed by medieval scholars. Having a rather logical, analytic mind, I did not find the talmudic type of close chain reasoning from given, unquestioned, premises difficult to follow, and I rather enjoyed my talmudic experience. The pedagogy, to be sure, was at times rather bizarre: the volume on divorce, for example, was taught before the one on marriage, not to mention the fact that neither theme was very close to the hearts of youngsters barely in their teens. Nevertheless, my mental processes were stimulated by the talmudic dialectics and argumentation. It was then, too, that I made a rather interesting psychological observation of the scholarly mentality, one that was corroborated in later life by my academic experience.

Even in those early years I perceived that there were two main types of scholars. There were those whom the yeshivah professors designated as *genarniks,* a Yiddish word for the students who "fooled" themselves by reciting glibly and smoothly the assigned passage, no matter how convoluted, without understanding the underlying postulates and reasoning. On the other hand, there were students who tended to hesitate and even stutter and sputter in their recitation, because they felt the need to make sure of the validity of their data and logical inferences prior to stating their conclusions. Not infrequently, too, the glib student was the possessor of an unerring memory and could pride himself on remembering the exact page on which any given talmudic quotation was to be found, a quality that was not characteristic of the sharp analyst. Again, not surprisingly, it was the former who tended to favor the fanciful, mythic, mystic portions of the Talmud, while the latter felt more comfortable with the rational, realistic, legal sections. As I learned many years later, a similar dichotomy of attitude and predilection characterizes the academic world and is responsible for no little contention among professors, including those in my chosen discipline, the ancient Near East.

I attended the yeshivah for a good many years, all through my grammar school days and my first years of high school, and I have pleasant memories of a number of my fellow students. Several of my predecessors, whom I admired and even idolized, went on to carve out notable careers for themselves. One was Abraham Agronsky, who became a fervent Zionist and left America for Palestine, where he founded the outstanding English-language newspaper, the *Palestine Post,* and was elected one of the first Jewish mayors of Jerusalem. On the other hand, Louis Fisher became a well-known jounalist deeply sympathetic to atheistic Russian communism, only to reject it later in bitter disillusionment. Two others were Louis Leventhal, one of the first Jewish judges in Philadelphia, and Israel Goldstein, who for many years was the spiritual leader of Bene Jeshurun, one of the outstanding synagogues of Conservative Judaism. These four childhood heroes of mine graduated from the yeshivah several years ahead of me, and the only one I encountered in later life was Israel Goldstein, whom I met when I was a visiting professor at the Hebrew University in Jerusalem.

After graduating from grammar school, I attended Southern High. There were very few high schools in Philadelphia then. The most prestigious was Central High, but this institution of learning was chiefly populated by richer, more Americanized, more sophisticated students. Most of the poorer and more recently immigrated Jews lived in South Philadelphia and sent their children to Southern High, which began as a manual training center but was soon transformed into a liberal arts school. It was here that I began to get some idea of the scope and importance of secular education. The courses in mathematics, history, literature, and foreign languages opened my eyes, and I saw the parochialism of my biblical and talmudic learning. This was so much so that when I was midway through the high school years I persuaded my father to permit me to leave the yeshivah and instead attend Gratz College, a Jewish educational institution where the teachers were college graduates who taught in English rather than Yiddish.

Here, in courses scheduled for evenings and Sundays, I first learned Hebrew grammar in a systematic fashion and Jewish history from a relatively secular perspective. I was very much taken with this new approach to Jewish studies and graduated with high honors, not to mention two prizes of one hundred dollars each, a welcome contribution to the family finances. The Gratz College sojourn was not without influence on my later choice of an academic career, and when, much later,

I was invited to prepare an article for the volume commemorating its seventy-fifth jubilee, I did so with a feeling of deep gratitude. My contribution, however, dealt with a Sumerian goddess and idolatrous temples and revealed, I fear, how far I had strayed from the college's Jewish-oriented disciplines.

After my graduation from Southern High, there was no question that I would continue with some form of higher education. There was no money, however, for college tuition, and I decided to matriculate in the Philadelphia School of Pedagogy, which provided two years of free preparatory education for men who wished to become teachers in the Philadelphia elementary school system. There was a special Normal School for women, who far outnumbered men in the school system. The School of Pedagogy was a rather unusual teaching-training college, in which the liberal arts, rather than courses in education, were the center of instruction. Its head was a Dr. Brandt, who taught philosophy, and the small faculty included several mavericks who were a very real source of inspiration to the students. The one I remember best is Hugh Mearns, who, I believe, later became a professor in the Teachers' College of Columbia University. In his courses in English, he had us write compositions and short stories which he read with great care and evaluated in considerable detail in private sessions with the students. It was Mearns who aroused in me an appetite for American literature, as well as the notion of becoming a writer, a profession for which, I gradually realized, I was not at all qualified.

Another subject that influenced me profoundly was philosophy, and especially the course in Western philosophy, my favorites being Locke and Hume. Throughout my years at the school I was the diligent and enthusiastic secretary of the Philosophy Club under the aegis of Dr. Brandt. What all this did to my Jewish orthodoxy is not difficult to imagine, and it became obvious to me that I could no longer perform the daily prayers with phylacteries bound tight about head and arm. Nor could I attend synagogue or keep the Sabbath without feeling like a hypocrite. It became ever more clear that I would have to come to some compromise arrangement with my father and that sooner or later I would have to leave home.

In the year 1917, I graduated from the School of Pedagogy. The First World War was then raging, and I enlisted in the Student Army Training Corps. But the war soon came to an end, and I was almost immediately discharged when the Training Corps was disbanded. During the army training I lived in the dormitories of the University of Pennsylvania, which gave me a taste of living away from home. In the course of the next year I rented an apartment in the Bohemian center-city section, Philadelphia's Latin Quarter, as it were—I was still not free of the writer complex. Money was not a serious problem at the time, since my father's Hebrew school in South Philadelphia had become quite popular and was well attended. I now did most of the teaching.

Young, energetic, college-trained, I taught the Bible and even the Talmud in the English language, so the the pupils understood and, at least to some extent, appreciated what they were learning. It was this Hebrew school that supported my father and myself—Mother had died rather unexpectedly following a stomach operation—throughout the twenties. In fact, the school was so successful that I could employ one of my close friends, Max Scarf, who was studying medicine, as an associate.

The hours at the Hebrew school were from four to nine in the evening, which left me free during the day. I could now think of continuing my higher education. I therefore enrolled at Temple University, Philadelphia's "poor man's" college, where I obtained a bachelor of science in education after two years of study. The courses that attracted and affected me most were those concerned with the history of the novel and drama as taught by a man whose name I vaguely recollect as Robertson. He was a lean, shy professor, soft of voice and sad of face. All of which helped to bring conviction to his constantly repeated melancholy theme that great literature reflected the tragedy of life and the pathos of the human condition.

The inspiration of Mearns and Robertson kindled in me a desire to become a novelist and dramatist. Since my days were free, I read avidly the works of the current and classic American and English novelists and dramatists. At the time, the acknowledged guru of the American literary scene was H. L. Mencken, and the *Smart Set* magazine, which he and the drama critic George Jean Nathan edited, was the bible of young would-be writers. I read it assiduously. It took some years and many rejection slips to convince me that I had no literary talent and had better settle for something less creative and more suited to my rather literal, unimaginative mind. However, those groping years of unwarranted literary expectations did help me understand myself.

On looking back, I realize that some of the virtues and failings of my scholarship were already apparent in those days of literary dilettantism. For example, my favorite author was Theodore Dreiser, a novelist whose style is dense and unattractive but who was a master at depicting character. On the other hand, in spite of Mencken's encomiums, I never took to James Branch Cabell, a master of form and style. This preference for content over form has influenced my scholarship. In studying the Sumerian literary documents, I tend to stress their context and content to the neglect of their formal features, although these are also quite significant. And my predilection for character study has prompted me to search out the nature of the ancients by reading between the lines of their literary works; hence, such studies as "Love, Hate, and Fear: Psychological Aspects of Sumerian Culture."

The years passed, and I was approaching thirty. Unsuccessful as a writer, I began looking around for more practical ways of meeting the future. My good friend Herman Silver, from the yeshivah days, had been led by chance and circumstance into the printing business, where he was doing quite well. Because of our close friendship, he suggested that I join him as a partner. But it took only a year or so to realize that the business would go bankrupt if I continued as a partner; I had no business sense whatsoever. I therefore turned once again to academe. For a few weeks I tried the Law School of the University of Pennsylvania. But when the professor of torts began to lecture on his specialty, it sounded so much like the Talmud of yeshivah days, that I was loath to continue. I next tried the Department of Philosophy, but after listening to several of the professor's lectures on Kant and the *Ding-an-sich,* I lost my appetite for philosophy. Finally it came to me that I might well go back to my beginnings and try to utilize the Hebrew learning on which I had spent so much of my youth, and to relate it in some way to an academic future. And so in 1925, at the age of twenty-nine, I matriculated in one of America's unique educational institutions, the Dropsie College of Philadelphia for Hebrew and Cognate Learning.

The college building was a small, charming, many-windowed structure with a broad impressive lawn in front that I had often passed admiringly in the years when I was attending nearby Gratz College. Its president was Cyrus Adler, a well-known and highly respected leader of the German-Jewish community. Its small and distinguished faculty included one of the world's most renowned biblical scholars, Max Margolis; Solomon Zeitlin, the learned but controversial Talmudist and historian of the Hebrews at the time of the birth and growth of Christianity; the Arabist Solomon Skoss, a scholar devoted primarily to Judaeo-Arabic studies and editor of a unique Karaite commentary on the Bible; and Nathaniel Reich, an Austrian Egyptologist who had been given the newly established chair of Egyptology. These men opened new horizons for me in Hebrew studies and in their Oriental backgrounds. From Margolis, for example, I learned of the existence and importance of the Greek, Latin, and Syriac translations of the Bible. Skoss introduced me to Judaeo-Arabic manuscripts, that is, medieval Hebrew written in Arabic characters. But what attracted me most was Egyptology. For two years I studied it assiduously and enthusiastically and knew almost by heart the contents of the superb Egyptian grammar published by the British Egyptologist Alan Gardiner in 1923.

Fate, however, did not approve of my becoming an Egyptologist—

she had other plans for my future. For reasons that are trivial, the professor of Egyptology and I had a falling out, and I left Dropsie College without obtaining a doctorate in Egyptology. By this time I was no stranger to the Philadelphia halls of learning. Immediately upon my rupture with Dropsie College I matriculated in the Oriental studies department of the Graduate School of the University of Pennsylvania, which included in its faculty George Barton, a prolific but, as I learned later, not very trustworthy contributor to such facets of Oriental research as Sumerian, Egyptian, and biblical archaeology; Alan Montgomery, one of the finest American students of Hebrew and Aramaic; and the brilliant young Ephraim Avigdor Speiser, who was to become one of the world's leading figures in Near Eastern studies and would make fundamental contributions in archaeology, cuneiform, and Bible scholarship.

When I came to the department, Speiser, five years my junior, had already published several articles relating to Hebrew linguistics. But his main interest at the time lay in the cuneiform documents excavated at Nuzi, an ancient site close to the modern city of Kirkuk, in the oil-rich region of northern Iraq. Most of the tablets, dating from about 1300 B.C., had been excavated by his predecessor at the University of Pennsylvania, Edward Chiera, with whom Speiser had collaborated closely as a fellow in the Oriental studies department. These ancient Nuzi documents were written in Akkadian, a Semitic language, though the native population were not Akkadians but a non-Semitic people, the Hurrians, about whom virtually nothing was then known. Speiser devoted much of his efforts to the study of these Nuzi texts and the Hurrian language and culture. To learn more about the history and background of this mysterious people, he traveled to Iraq as a Guggenheim Fellow in the years 1926–1927, and after surveying much of the territory surrounding Nuzi, he selected two tells (mounds) in the neighborhood for possible excavations at some opportune date. When I joined the department as a graduate student in 1928, I decided to work with Speiser for my doctorate, and because of his involvement with the Nuzi tablets it was inevitable that my dissertation would be related to them.

After two years under his inspiring tutelage, I completed my dissertation, which bore the unexciting title "The Verb in the Kirkuk Tablets"; accepted and approved toward the end of 1929, it was published in 1931 in the *Annual* of the American Schools of Oriental Research. As the title indicates, it dealt with one very narrow linguistic aspect of a specialized, limited area of research. As I looked back on it in later years, I realized that it was hardly a major contribution even to that circumscribed and restricted specialty. On the other hand, some of the

later researchers on the Nuzi documents told me that they found the dissertation of considerable value, and that it helped them to make further, more significant progress in their study of the Nuzi dialect. It thus provided a dependable tool for future scholars, and this, to my mind, is the main purpose of a doctoral dissertation, at least in the humanities. A young graduate, however gifted and talented, can hardly be expected to produce the momentous synthesis for which the critics of Ph.D. programs clamor. This requires the maturity and breadth of knowledge that come only after years of scholarly dedication and effort. In my case even "The Verb in the Kirkuk Tablets," limited as it is, strained my knowledge and competence, for I knew very little about the many other diverse cuneiform documents available at the time, let alone the broader aspects of Near East history and culture. I may have been a poor example of a Ph.D. candidate. But after observing the academic scene for more than four decades I am more than ever convinced that the young would-be scholar is not prepared to produce an original, all-embracing treatise. He would be wiser to settle for a circumscribed, systematic contribution that could be used effectively by fellow scholars.

So, in 1930, I found myself the proud possessor of a doctorate in Oriental studies from the Graduate School of the University of Pennsylvania. The problem was what to do with it. There were very few universities in America with Oriental departments at that time, and available academic positions were minimal. But then there occurred the first of a series of what might be termed minor miracles—strokes of luck, if you like—that came to the rescue of my scholarly career whenever it seemed to be on the verge of collapsing. In 1919 there had come into being the American Council of Learned Societies (ACLS), a sort of central exchange of all American societies concerned with humanistic research. In 1930, the very year my postdoctoral career began, the ACLS instituted a new program of fellowship awards to young scholars, especially those who had recently graduated and were eager to broaden their studies. At the suggestion of the Oriental studies department of the University of Pennsylvania and with the warm recommendation and blessing of its faculty, I applied for and was awarded one of these postdoctoral fellowships. The amount, if I am not mistaken, was two thousand dollars, enough to keep me for a year in comfort, if not in luxury.

That same year, 1930, my erstwhile professor and mentor, E. A. Speiser, was going to northern Iraq to excavate one of the tells he had surveyed several years earlier, a mound known as Tell Billah, which he hoped would turn out to be the capital of his favorite people, the ancient

Ephraim Avigdor Speiser.

Hurrians. The ACLS Fellowship enabled me to join his expedition as epigrapher, or tablet reader, although this is hardly what Speiser needed, since he could read the tablets far better than I. It was agreed that the members of the expedition were to meet in Baghdad in the fall of 1930 and from there proceed as a group to Tell Billah, some two hundred miles to the north. But I left Philadelphia several months earlier to acquaint myself with some of the museums abroad and learn something firsthand about the archaeology of the ancient Near East before joining the expedition in Baghdad.

2
A Timid Epigraphist in Iraq

Making plans, as I had occasion to learn more than once in the course of my scholarly career, is relatively easy and painless, but carrying them out is quite another matter. Timid and shy by nature, introspective and withdrawn, I failed to take full advantage of my trip through Europe and the archaeologically informative opportunities it provided. In London, for example, I visited the British Museum several days in a row and gazed in wonder at its extraordinary collection of inscribed bas-reliefs from the palaces of Nineveh and Nimrud, as well as at the exhibits of scores of cuneiform tablets whose discovery had brought about the decipherment of the long-dead Akkadian and Sumerian languages. But I was too timorous to ring the bell of the museum's famous Student Room, where in later years I spent many a summer, and ask for the keeper or one of his colleagues to discuss with him the history and significance of the museum's archaeological and epigraphic activities.

In Paris I stood with palpitating heart before the vast collection of statues and inscriptions excavated some four decades earlier in ancient Lagash. These archaeological discoveries finally authenticated the existence of a non-Semitic people in southern Iraq who were responsible for much of the civilization of the ancient Near East, an existence that had been put in doubt by some scholars. But I dared not ask the whereabouts of the conservateurs and excavators and try to learn something of their plans and projects. I was even too shy to knock at the gates of the renowned Collège de France, not far from the Sorbonne, where was located the invaluable library of one of my archaeological heroes, Jules Oppert, the French Jew who may be said to have uncovered the Sumerians.

Only in Berlin, where I stood enthralled before the fabled Ishtar Gate of Babylon, then restored, in the Vorderasiatische Museum by the river Spree, did I have the courage to ask for an appointment with its director, Walter Andrae, the excavator of Babylon, Ashur, and Farah (ancient Shuruppak), home of the Sumerian Flood hero. Though I did not know it at the time, it was in the roofless, broken-down excavation house built at Farah by Andrae and his colleagues that I would make my bed a few months later. And how could I anticipate that one day in the distant future this renowned German archaeologist would honor me with his attendance at one of my lectures on the Sumerians delivered in that very museum, then still partially bombed out? Sick in body and almost blind, he had somehow survived the Nazis and the Second World War. In 1930, though, he was at the peak of his career. Nevertheless, he received me, nonentity that I was, with graceful courtesy, and I left his presence happy and starry-eyed.

From Berlin I journeyed to Istanbul, where I lingered some days in order to visit the archaeological museums situated beside the Bosphorus, in the palace grounds of the former sultans. (I had no inkling then that Istanbul and its Museum of the Ancient Orient, especially the rooms devoted to its tablet collections, would become a second home to me, Sumerologically speaking.) From Istanbul I hastened on to holy Jerusalem, visiting the Jewish sacred places about which I had studied in my youth, little dreaming that I would be a visiting professor in its Hebrew University, lecturing on Sumerian echoes in the Hebrew Bible. From Jerusalem I journeyed to charming, verdant Damascus, and from there by bus over the harsh desert to Baghdad.

There I was in September, 1930, in Baghdad, the fabled city of the caliph Haroun al-Rashid, in the land where the mighty empires of Assyria and Babylonia had risen, flourished, and fallen. I had come full of hopes and dreams that turned to disappointment and disenchantment as I trudged in the mud of the narrow streets of shabby Baghdad of forty years ago and along the dreary roads of its desolate hinterland. Could this sun-parched, wind-riven, desert-like land have been the home of heroic Gilgamesh, the celebrated ruler of Erech of the broad marts? Or of the ruler and statesman Hammurabi, immortalized by his pre-Mosaic law code? Or of the mighty kings of Assyria, the scourge of Jahweh, who led their conquering armies from remote, barbarous Urartu to the southernmost reaches of Egypt? Or of the powerful Nebuchadnezzar who destroyed Jerusalem and exiled Jahweh's people to carnal Babylonia? I decided that surely there must be some misunderstanding here, some error in tradition, perhaps even a fatuous hoax perpetrated by some spurious archivist or pseudo-historian.

Fortunately, I spent several weeks visiting some of the ongoing excavations in various parts of Iraq and learned about their exciting finds. There is something exhilarating and soul-stirring about digging, especially in the Near East. Days and weeks may pass with nothing to show but the tedious cataloguing of innumerable potsherds and drab, unidentifiable fragments of clay, stone, or metal. But, sooner or later, the trained archaeologist will spy the significant artifact, the revealing inscription, the telling traces of the hoped-for monument, and there is ample reward for all those dreary days.

The year 1930, as it turned out, was the approximate midpoint of a glorious decade of Mesopotamian archaeological research. In northern Iraq, the excavations begun by Edward Chiera in 1925 in Nuzi continued under various directorships to the winter of 1931, uncovering a palace, a temple, and numerous private houses, as well as hundreds of legal and administrative documents that soon made my dissertation on the Nuzi verb badly out of date. In Ur (biblical Ur of the Chaldees) Leonard Woolley conducted twelve consecutive campaigns, beginning in the fall of 1922 and ending with the winter of 1934. In the course of these excavations, to mention but one major achievement, he exhumed the amazing Royal Cemetery and its tombs dating to the third millennium B.C. that were filled with magnificent artifacts of gold, silver, and semiprecious stones—along with the remains of the gaily bedecked courtiers and servants who accompanied the buried ruler in his grave. In biblical Erech, some fifty miles northwest of Ur, a German expedition was unearthing, layer by layer and inch by inch, colorful, monumental temples on lofty, ziggurat-like platforms, dating from 3000 B.C. and earlier. Perhaps even more important for the history of civilization, they were finding among these temple ruins hundreds of clay tablets inscribed with early semipictographic signs, the forerunners of the cuneiform script which represented the oldest writing known to man.

Still farther to the north, in central Iraq, the eminent cuneiformist Stephen Langdon and his associates were excavating ancient Kish, the city to which, according to the Sumerian sages, "kingship descended after the Flood," and were unearthing monumental buildings, ziggurats, and cemeteries. In Jemdet Nasr, a modest mound close to Kish, a special contingent of the expedition unearthed several hundred tablets inscribed with semi-pictographic characters more developed than those found by the Germans in Erech, and these provided clues to the evolution of the cuneiform script from pictograph to phonetic syllable.

Less than fifty miles northeast of Baghdad, in the region of the Diyala River, Henri Frankfort of the Oriental Institute of the University of Chicago and his associates Pinhas Delougaz, Seton Lloyd, and Thorkild Jacobsen were excavating several ancient cities, of which virtually nothing had been known before, that contained temples, palaces, and private houses, as well as a remarkable group of impressionistic sculptures, the like of which had not been known from the ancient world.

These rich archaeological and epigraphic discoveries made it ever more evident to the scholarly world that ancient Iraq, or more broadly put, ancient Mesopotamia, was where much of civilization originated. It was Mesopotamia that witnessed the rise of man's first urban centers with their rich, complex, and varied life; where loyalty was no longer to the clan or tribe but to the community at large; where temples and ziggurats rose to the sky, filling the citizens' hearts with wonder and pride; where technological inventiveness, industrial specialization, and commercial enterprise found room to grow and expand. It was in the cities of Mesopotamia that a practical and efficient system of writing was invented and developed, bringing about a revolution in communications similar to that of contemporary electronic inventions, with unforeseen effects on man's economic, intellectual, and cultural advancement. Mesopotamian ideas, techniques, and inventions were diffused east and west and left their mark on virtually all ancient cultures, and to some extent even on our own. In brief, the archaeological evidence of that inspiring decade of excavations in Iraq was producing incontrovertible proof that Mesopotamia, rather than any other land or region, could be truly designated as the cradle of civilization.

My faith in the unique significance of Mesopotamian history and culture restored, I came to Tell Billah with romantic expectations of world-resounding discoveries that turned out to be baseless and deceptive. Tell Billah was not the ruined remains of the ancient capital of the Hurrians, with potentially rich archaeological and historical treasures, but of a rather poor provincial town dating back only to the second millennium B.C. During the two months of my stay there, not a single inscription was uncovered, and I began to feel like a supernumerary, a man with useless expertise, a tablet reader without tablets to read. To make matters worse, I suffered an attack of acute appendicitis, and I was taken hurriedly to the small, poorly equipped hospital in Mosul, where, fortunately for me, there was a Canadian doctor and an Armenian nurse. There was of course a much larger and better equipped hospital in Baghdad, but my condition was serious, and it was feared that the two-hundred-mile journey might prove fatal. I was operated on in a small dark room in the Mosul hospital; the doctor told me later that he had me so long under ether that he could take no more time to sew up the wound with aesthetic care. The Mosul scar across my stomach can meet any competition for size and zigzagging. After several weeks of convalescence in Mosul, I was ready to depart once again for Tell Billah, with no appendix and very little enthusiasm, when, from a quarter entirely unexpected, the second of my minor miracles came to the rescue and turned melancholy resignation into eager anticipation.

I mentioned that I traveled to Iraq as a paid fellow of the American Council of Learned Societies, but I should have added that I was also an unpaid fellow of the American Schools of Oriental Research (ASOR) in Jerusalem and Baghdad. This was a body founded in 1900 and supported largely by dues paid by American universities and divinity schools interested in biblical archaeology. In Jerusalem, the ASOR actually had a building and library; the American School in Jerusalem became world-famous under the directorship of William Foxwell Albright, who in later years became the grand old man of American Oriental research, and it is still carrying on its archaeological activities in the holy city. In Baghdad, the ASOR had no building; its presence in Iraq was manifest only by a professor appointed annually to participate in any American excavations being conducted that year. Sometimes the ASOR also appointed an honorary fellow (honorary, in this case, meaning without honorarium). For the year 1930–1931, Theophile Meek of the University of Toronto was the paid annual professor, and I had the privilege of being honorary fellow.

Meek was one of the leading Orientalists of those days, a top-rank Hebrew and biblical scholar and a cuneiformist of note. As annual professor of the ASOR he was acting as epigraphist to the Nuzi expedition and was very busy and happy there because it was unearthing hundreds of tablets dating back to the third millennium B.C., earlier by close to a millennium than the Nuzi documents known till then, for example those that would constitute the source material for my dissertation. It was a very exciting, unexpected discovery, and it took all his time to clean the tablets and to try to read and interpret their contents. In the midst of this intense and concentrated epigraphic activity, he received a telegram from Erich Schmidt that put him in a quandary. Schmidt had just begun working at Farah, the southern site that had been excavated almost thirty years earlier by Andrae and his associates. He was finding Sumerian tablets but had no one on his staff to read and study their contents. He wired Meek, asking him to come down to Farah to act as epigraphist. Reluctant to leave Nuzi and the newly discovered third-millennium tablets, Meek turned to me at Tell Billah and asked whether I would take his place. I needed no urging. Early in February 1931, I took the train from Mosul to Baghdad, hired a car to take me to Farah, some hundred miles to the South, and was welcomed by my new

"boss" with no little enthusiasm. Quite a number of Sumerian tablets had already been excavated, and, unlike Tell Billah, there was an urgent need for an epigraphist to interpret their contents and help to clarify some of the problems besetting the excavators, especially those relating to stratigraphic chronology.

Erich Schmidt, who died in 1964, was a first-generation German of considerable personal charm who came to America in 1923. After participating in archaeological excavations in Arizona and Anatolia, he organized an expedition under the joint auspices of the Oriental Institute of the University of Chicago and the Philadelphia Museum of Art for the purpose of excavating in Iran—he is best known for his excavations at the world-renowned ruins of Persepolis. His excavations at Farah were only a stopover on the road to Iran: he undertook them at the request of Horace Jayne, the director of the University Museum of the University of Pennsylvania, who was interested in sending a permanent expedition to the site, a project that never materialized.

The expedition staff lived in tents that were reasonably comfortable. Because an epigraphist had not been planned for, there was no tent for me, and I had to bed down in the roofless ruins of the expedition house built by the Germans close to three decades earlier. The sandstorms in the Farah region were so savage that when I awoke in the early morning, I was literally buried in sand up to my neck. Even eating was often a serious problem. The expedition had on its staff a competent Iranian cook, but cooking was almost impossible because of the unremitting storms, and often the food taken from the cans was no sooner placed on the plates than it became sand-covered and inedible. Still, I remember the Farah experience as one of the happiest of my life. When Friday, the Moslem day of rest, came and we took our lukewarm showers from improvised perforated cans, sipped a cocktail we hoped was free of sand, read our mail, including now and then a love letter, and reflected on the week's archaeological finds, we were a merry, contented crew. This Friday celebration was almost as hallowed as that of the eve of the Sabbath in my Zaskov youth.

Scattered over the Farah mound were ancient wells full of clay and sand, and some of these had cuneiform tablets imbedded in them. It was my job to dig out the tablets carefully, clean them, and study their contents. By the time the expedition closed, about three hundred Sumerian tablets had been excavated, and I had only a vague idea of their import. The only professor in the Oriental department who had claimed to know Sumerian really knew very little of what it was all about, and

---

The author recovering tablets in an earth-filled well at the site of Farah, ancient Shuruppak, in 1930.

I did not get much from his courses. I was therefore deeply troubled lest the reading and interpretation of these documents would prove too difficult for my limited scholarship and I fail in this, my first fully independent attempt at cuneiform research.

Therefore, when Schmidt and his associates departed for Iran, I turned my face west and journeyed once again to Istanbul and its Museum of the Ancient Orient, which had among its collections a large group of tablets from Farah excavated by the earlier expedition under Andrae. Permission to study these was given me readily by the Turkish authorities, and, after immersing myself for several weeks in the study of their contents, I acquired a deeper understanding of the nature and scope of the Farah documents in general. Now I felt ready to publish the results of my study of the newly found tablets from the Schmidt excavations.

Still, I was quite green and hesitant about some of the formal Sumerological conventions used by recognized cuneiformists in those days. George Barton's system of transliteration, for example, was not accepted by the majority of cuneiformists. From Istanbul, therefore, I decided to journey to the Leipziger Semitisches Institut, which, in those pre-Nazi days, was the world's outstanding institution for cuneiform research. Its head was Benno Landsberger, one of the keenest minds in the history of Assyriology, who attracted a group of students that in future years came to dominate cuneiform studies. Landsberger was gracious enough to give me some help in preparing the Farah material for publication, and my study "New Tablets from Farah" appeared in 1932 in the *Journal of the American Oriental Society*. It was no trailblazing contribution, but it did help to shed some light on the results of Schmidt's excavations and made me a bit more secure in my calling.

By this time my ACLS Fellowship was running out, and I had to leave Leipzig for Philadelphia to face the future. Before doing so, however, I became a small-time philanthropist. While in Baghdad I had visited several antique dealers who in those days were uncontrolled agents, buying and selling antiquities at will. One of these dealers took a fancy to me. Seeing how excitedly I was examining tablets that I did not have the money to buy, he put his hand into a baggy receptacle like that carried on the back of a donkey, pulled out about fifty small tablets that he had bought for a couple of pennies each from Arabs digging illicitly on various tells, and presented them to me with his compliments. Planning to bring them to America and to treasure them as sweet memorabilia of my first Mesopotamian archeological and epigraphic experience, I took them with me to Leipzig. There I learned that despite its fame, the Semitisches Institut had not a single cuneiform tablet in its possession. Hence, I donated most of the precious gift to it, as a token of appreciation and gratitude.

In the decades that have passed since, the Leipziger Semitisches Institut has undergone some drastic changes. First came the Nazis, and "der Jude Landsberger" had to leave Germany together with two of his best students who were half-Jews. After the Second World War, it came under the control of the East Germans, who preferred to make it a center of modern rather than ancient Near Eastern studies. But in spite of all the changes, rumor has it that the tablets I donated are still there in showcases, a dim reminder of the institute's earlier scholarly interests and achievements.

In June 1931 I returned to Philadelphia, where I could have used a bit of philanthropy myself, since the ACLS Fellowship was at an end and I was penniless and jobless. But not hopeless—it never crossed my mind to give up my scholarly career. For the next several months I boarded with my ever faithful friends, Herman Silver and his wife Gertrude. In later days Mrs. Silver willingly typed almost all my manuscripts. I continued to study on my own in the library of the Oriental department, awaiting a favorable opportunity. And, sure enough, in another of those minor miracles, I packed my bags for Chicago and its Oriental Institute. There I was to stay from 1932 to 1936 as a member of the staff of its Assyrian Dictionary project, a bittersweet experience that gave direction and focus to my scholarly future. I came to the Oriental Institute as a groping young Assyriologist and left it five years later as a specialist in Sumerology.

3
Arno Poebel and Sumerian Grammar

The Oriental Institute of the University of Chicago was and is one of the world's foremost institutions dedicated to Egyptological and Near Eastern research. It was virtually the creation of James Henry Breasted, an Egyptologist and historian who not only made many valuable specialized contributions but also produced several popular works that were widely read. He founded the Oriental Institute in 1919, with the financial backing of John D. Rockefeller, Jr., and was its director and guiding star until the day of his death. I do not recall ever meeting him in person—he was far too exalted for a rather shy and unsure novice to approach—nor do I remember ever entering his large, elegant office on the second floor of the institute building while he was director.

But I do have one treasured bit of Breasted memorabilia. On first coming to the institute, I looked about in the University bookstore for a typewriter appropriate to my new scholarly position. When the young man behind the counter asked me why I needed it, and I informed him proudly that I had just been appointed to the staff of the Oriental Institute, he brought out a portable and suggested that it might be just the right buy for me, since this was Breasted's own machine and had just been turned in as partial exchange for a new noiseless typewriter. I took this as a good omen and needed no urging; I paid the twelve dollars, if I remember correctly, and carried it to my office. In spite of its dethronement and demotion, it served me well for many years. Now that it has grown old and sluggish, like its present owner, it lies in its case, passive but in honored memory of past days.

Breasted was one of those rare scholars who combined an appreciation of minutely detailed research with breadth of vision and pragmatic imagination. Although his specialty and passion was Egyptology, he realized that the archaeology of Western Asia was quite as important for the history of man's past. In 1935, the year of his death, four of the nine expeditions sponsored by the Oriental Institute were in that area; one each in Palestine, Syria, Iran, and Mesopotamia. Moreover, he recognized that, epigraphically speaking, Mesopotamia was more significant by far than any other land or region. Cuneiform documents of diverse character had been unearthed by the tens of thousands in the nineteenth century, and their numbers were continuing to multiply at a staggering rate in the early decades of the twentieth. The translation and interpretation of their contents, he realized, were an absolute must for historians and anthropologists. But this could not be achieved without adequate dictionaries, and these were unavailable, as he learned from the noted Orientalist Daniel Luckenbill, who was his advisor in matters pertaining to cuneiform research. In 1921, Breasted conceived and created the Assyrian Dictionary Project and put Luckenbill in charge of its administration and execution.

The goal of the project was to prepare a comprehensive up-to-the-minute dictionary that included all known Assyrian words, together with whatever text quotations were necessary to determine and define their meaning. Begun with a small staff of senior scholars, resident and nonresident, and a few graduate students, in the first two enthusiastic years over two hundred thousand word cards were collected and filed. This initial burst of productivity prompted the expectation that in another decade or so the dictionary would be ready to go to press. But the editors had utterly underestimated the vast quantity of cuneiform source material to be perused and analyzed, and this, together with several unanticipated mishaps and some serious dissension among the members of the editorial board, delayed the appearance of the first volume till 1956, thirty-five years after the commencement of the project. And though volume after volume has since appeared at irregular intervals, the end is still not in sight.

The initial misfortune was the death of Luckenbill, the dictionary's editor, in 1927. Fortunately, Breasted found a successor that very year in the person of Edward Chiera, of Nuzi fame, whom he recruited from the University of Pennsylvania. Chiera was not only a fine Assyriologist but a capable and energetic administrator as well. Immediately upon assuming his duties as editor, he realized that there were two facets of the dictionary preparation that had not received attention in the preceding years. One was the absence of a Sumerologist on the staff. For while it was true that this was an Assyrian dictionary—that is, a dictionary concerned primarily with the Assyrian language—it was a well-known fact that this language, though it belonged to the Semitic family, was full of Sumerian loan words and phrases. Moreover, a large number of cuneiform texts which were absolutely essential for the preparation of the dictionary were bilinguals, written in both Sumerian and Assyrian, and many of the Assyrian words and phrases could be understood only with the help of their Sumerian counterparts. In 1930, therefore, Chiera, whose title was managing and scientific editor, invited Arno Poebel, then professor at the University of Rostock, in Germany, to become his associate on the Assyrian Dictionary staff, with the somewhat less imposing title of scientific editor.

Second, it became clear to Chiera as the work progressed that the translation of much of the Assyrian textual source material could not be accomplished by the resident senior staff. He therefore turned over this basic task to nonresident cuneiformists, most of them foreign, who were paid a specified honorarium for their labor. And since the perusal and analysis of the incoming manuscripts, and the production of the tens of thousands of word cards, turned out to be far more complex and time-consuming than had been anticipated, he more than doubled the resident junior staff by inviting some younger cuneiformists from various institutions to become assistants on the Assyrian Dictionary Project. One of these was the unemployed but hopeful novice from Zashkov and Philadelphia, the jobless Ph.D. from the University of Pennsylvania.

On arrival in Chicago, I immediately went to the newly built and impressive Oriental Institute structure, where I was interviewed by Chiera and Poebel. I must have expressed a strong predilection for the Sumerian role in the Assyrian Dictionary, minor though that was. In any case I soon found myself under the guidance and tutelage of Poebel rather than Chiera and was assigned an office, usually shared with another young colleague, close to Poebel's office and to the large "dictionary" room where the innumerable word cards were maintained.

The work Poebel assigned me, though very specialized and limited, proved to be interesting, informative, and even exhilarating. The ancient Assyrian men of letters, when inscribing their various compendia such as omens or incantations, would often utilize Sumerian logograms to represent Assyrian words, just as, for example, we write *etc.* (the Latin *et cetera*) but usually pronouce it as "and so forth." It was my task to go through the transliterations and translations of these documents prepared by the senior scholars from America and abroad, to examine carefully their renderings of the Sumerian logograms into As-

Arno Poebel, who taught the author how to read a Sumerian text.

syrian, and to note these on cards, making sure of their consistency and accuracy before they were utilized in any passage quoted in the dictionary. I found real joy in working on this material, which provided training in both Sumerian and Assyrian. In addition, the contents of these documents were new to me, thus greatly enriching my knowledge of a number of aspects of Mesopotamian culture.

As if this gratifying scholarly labor was not enough to fill my days and nights—my evenings were often spent in the institute office—I was further enriched, Sumerologically speaking, with an unexpected bonus that determined the scholarly focus of my career. The two editors of the Assyrian Dictionary, Chiera and Poebel, were also teaching members of the Department of Near Eastern Languages and Literatures, which was part of the Humanities Faculty of the University of Chicago. Poebel, who was professor of Sumerology, the only such chair in the world, to my knowledge, taught classes in Sumerian grammar and in the translation of Sumerian texts. The junior members of the Assyrian Dictionary staff were permitted, and even encouraged, to attend these classes. Pedagogically speaking, Poebel was a terrible teacher, no better in some ways than my Talmud teachers of yeshivah days who chose to teach the laws of divorce before those of marriage. But in other respects he was stimulating and inspiring, at least for me—and I was at times the only one attending his classes. His speech was rather slow and monotonous; his English was far from idiomatic; he was given to numerous and prolonged digressions and tended to be repetitive and diffuse. But none of these pedagogical failings were defects as far as I was concerned. Not blessed with a quick mind or a superior memory, I found that Poebel's repetitions, digressions, and *obiter dicta* were just what I needed to help me understand and digest the principles of Sumerian grammar underlying the intricate and often misleading cuneiform system of writing, as well as the methodology of transforming the dead inscriptions into living informants.

Arno Poebel was in some respects a self-made Sumerologist. In his early years he studied theology and philosophy in Germany and Switzerland. In 1905 he was awarded a Harrison Research Fellowship to the University of Pennsylvania, where he acquired his Ph.D. under the supervision of Professor H. V. Hilprecht, an eminent Assyriologist but hardly a Sumerologist of note. In 1907 Poebel returned to Germany and continued his research, but without a university affiliation. In 1911 he was invited to be a teaching fellow at Johns Hopkins University, which provided him with the opportunity to spend much time in nearby Philadelphia at the University Museum. There he copied many Sumerian literary, historical, lexical, legal, and administrative texts in one of the most fruitful experiences of his career. In 1914 he returned to Germany and became a professor at the University of Rostock. There he stayed until 1930, when he was called to the Oriental Institute at the recommendation of Edward Chiera, who knew of his pioneering Sumerological research from their personal contact at the University Museum, where Chiera, too, had been copying cuneiform documents.

In 1923, one of those bitter postwar inflationary years in Germany, Poebel had published his *Grundzüge der sumerischen Grammatik,* and at his own expense, since he could find no publisher who would accept it. Based on a painstakingly thorough and minutely detailed study of the Sumerian inscriptions of all periods, from the classical of the third millennium B.C. to the late post-Sumerian of the first millennium, it set

38

down with compelling logic the fundamental rules and principles that govern Sumerian grammar and illustrated them profusely and pertinently whenever possible. Subsequent grammatical studies by Poebel and other scholars have resulted in a number of additions and corrections. But by and large, Poebel's *Grundzüge* has stood the test of time and has continued to be the cornerstone of all constructive research in the area of Sumerian grammar.

Now it might seem reasonable to expect that a fundamental and comprehensive grammar of this caliber would be received with deep appreciation by cuneiformists the world over. Not at all! It was not welcome or even accepted by European scholars and was ignored in America. There were several reasons for this rejection, but the decisive one was the manner in which Poebel cited his evidence, which consisted of innumerable phrases and sentences culled from scores of different inscriptions. These inscriptions make use of a syllabic and logographic script that tends to blur the grammatical form of the relevant work complexes, and unless this is clearly understood and intelligently reckoned with, the resulting grammatical analysis and translation will be misleading and erroneous. Since most cuneiformists were unaware of this discrepancy between the written and grammatical form, or only had some vague notion of its existence, Poebel, when citing his evidence, for the sake of clarity should have given both the written and grammatical form for each word complex in the citations. But this would have been very repetitive, and quite expensive to print. He therefore devised and made use of a shortcut that combined the two, enclosing in parentheses the grammatical elements omitted in the written form, which was left unchanged. It was this rather bizarre shorthand system of transliteration that confused most scholars; the majority were on very shaky ground when it came to Sumerian, and it was simpler to ignore Poebel's novel transliterations and conclusions than to try to understand their import and value. As a result of assiduously attending Poebel's classes, I had learned his grammar virtually by heart and had mastered its intricacies and peculiarities. Over the next several years I published several articles explaining its methodology and significance, and gradually it came to be recognized for the valuable contribution that it is.

One of Poebel's most creative grammatical contributions was a monograph published in 1931, a year before I came to the Oriental Institute, bearing the unalluring title *The Sumerian Prefix Forms e- and i- in the Time of the Earlier Princes of Lagash.* In this study Poebel demonstrated, from inscriptions dated to the twenty-fourth century B.C., that the Sumerian language had six vowels, three "close" and three "open" and that the vowels of some of its grammatical elements oscillate accordingly: they are subject to vowel assimilation not unlike that which occurs in a modern agglutinative tongue, such as Turkish. Bearing in mind that we are dealing with a language dead for some four thousand years, this was a brilliant insight and discovery by any standard. Through a penetrating application of logical analysis to mute, soundless symbols inscribed in the far-distant past, Poebel demonstrated that the vowel system of living, spoken Sumerian was not subject to irrational, haphazard changes, as had been generally accepted until then, but was based on rational principles organically interrelated.

No sooner had the monograph appeared, however, than it was attacked rather viciously by several reputable scholars. This moved me to prepare a paper entitled "A Matter of Method in Sumerology" in which I explained and demonstrated the significance of Poebel's grammatical contributions. Moreover, Poebel's monograph on the *e- i-* prefix forms inspired me to trace a parallel development in the case of another prefix that seemed to vacillate without reason, and the resulting monograph bearing the Poebellian title *The Sumerian Prefix be- and bi- in the Time of the Earlier Princes of Lagaš,* appeared in 1936. These two contributions were not uninfluential in creating a favorable climate for Poebel's Sumerological work and helped steer Sumerologial research on the right path.

As is evident from all that has been said above, my relationship to Poebel evolved into that of a disciple to his master, and on the scholarly level there developed a friendly intimacy between us that was a source of gratification to both of us, though I profited most. But in 1933 Hitler came to power in Germany, and our relationship deteriorated. I cannot say whether Poebel ever became a true Nazi, but there is no doubt that he was a German superpatriot ready to accept whatever anti-Jewish feelings this implied, and the tension between us became unbearable. Not only did I no longer attend his classes but we also tried to avoid each other as much as possible. If by accident we met in the hallway, we lowered our eyes and passed without greeting.

It was not until long after the Second World War that our relationship warmed up once again, though by this time we were separated by the distance between Chicago and Philadelphia. When my first popular work, *From the Tablets of Sumer,* was published in 1956, I deemed it a privilege to be permitted to dedicate it "To the Master of Sumerological Method, My Teacher and Colleague, Arno Poebel." When Poebel died in 1957, I traveled to Chicago to bid him good-bye forever, but only physically. On the spiritual level, Poebel's hesitating, stuttering voice still haunts my memory, and my heart is filled with deep gratitude for the debt I owe this unassuming, pioneering scholar.

The rupture of scholarly collaboration with Poebel was a serious blow to me, and I was gravely troubled about my Sumerological future in consequence. But then, to lift me out of depression, occurred the third of those minor miracles that played so decisive a role in promoting my career, although unfortunately this one began with a tragic event; the unexpected death of Edward Chiera in 1933.

4
Edward Chiera and Sumerian Literature

I have already mentioned Chiera as a pioneer in Nuzi archaeology and epigraphy. But long before his Nuzi contributions, he had published four volumes of texts copied by him in the University Museum between 1914 and 1922. Most of these were administrative and legal documents written in the Sumerian language. Chiera was no Sumerologist, and it is not surprising to read in the preface to his first volume that he had received many valuable suggestions from Arno Poebel. In 1923, Chiera was awarded a traveling fellowship by the Crozer Theological Seminary that enabled him to spend the summer in the Istanbul Museum of the Ancient Orient, where he copied fifty well-preserved tablets inscribed with Sumerian literary texts. These tablets excavated at Nippur, Sumer's cultural center, by a University of Pennsylvania expedition toward the end of the last century inspired Chiera's interest in Sumerian literature, which in turn was responsible for the direction of my own scholarship and its almost total concentration in that specialized area of cuneiform research. In order to appreciate the significance of Chiera's pioneering contributions to the recovery and restoration of the Sumerian belles lettres, it is essential that the reader have some idea of the difficulties involved in the reading, copying, and translating of Sumerian literary documents, and this necessitates in turn a background sketch of the discovery that a Sumerian people and language once existed, an archaeological event in which the Nippur excavations played a vital role.

Edward Chiera and Sumerian Literature

Prior to the middle of the nineteenth century, the existence of a Sumerian people and language was altogether unknown. The scholars and archaeologists who began excavating in Mesopotamia were not looking for Sumerians but the Assyrians and Babylonians, about whom they had considerable mention in Greek and Hebrew sources. Of Sumerians, there was no recognizable trace of the land, or its people and language, in the available biblical, classical, and postclassical literature. The very name had been erased from the memory of man for over two thousand years. Hence, the progress of Sumerological research was rather slow and troubled.

The decipherment of Sumerian came about through the decipherment of Assyrian, a Semitic tongue which, like the Sumerian, is written in cuneiform script. In the case of Assyrian, the key was found in a group of trilingual cuneiform inscriptions that included Old Persian, an Indo-European tongue, and the still obscure Elamite language. These trilingual texts, a sort of Mesopotamian counterpart of the Egyptian Rosetta Stone, became available to Western scholars between A.D. 1750 and 1850. Since they came from sites located in western Persia, it was not unreasonable to assume that they belonged to the kings of the Persian Achaemenid dynasty, well known from classical and biblical sources; that the first version of each inscription was therefore in the Persian language; and that the two other versions were translations of it. Fortunately Old Persian was becoming known to Western scholars at about this time, and some of the frequently repeated key words in the inscription, such as those for "king" and "son" could be identified and read. This fact, together with some keen manipulation of the Achaemenid proper names as handed down in Hebrew and Greek sources, made possible the decipherment of the Persian version of the trilingual inscriptions in the first half of the nineteenth century, primarily by a German high-school teacher, Georg Friedrich Grotefend, and an English military offier, Henry Creswicke Rawlinson.

Long before the final decipherment of the first, or Persian, version, great interest had been aroused in Western Europe by the third version. For it had been recognized that this was the script and language found in numerous inscriptions on bricks, clay tablets, and cylinders which were finding their way into European collections from Khorsabad, Nineveh, and Nimrud, sites in the Mesopotamian region known in Greek and biblical sources as Assyria. Since there were good reasons to assume that the Assyrians were Semites, it followed that the third version of the trilingual inscriptions represented a Semitic tongue such as Hebrew and Arabic. Indeed, the first Assyrian word deciphered was the first person pronoun *anaku* (I), which is virtually identical with its Hebrew counterpart. This identification, together with the fact that some proper names as well as a number of contextual details were known from the Persian version, facilitated its decipherment, although it was not until 1857 that the decipherment of Assyrian was fully accepted and established. The key figures in this accomplishment were Rawlinson; an Irish savant, Edward Hincks; and a German-French Jew, Jules Oppert.

So far, nothing had been heard of Sumer and the Sumerians. As early as 1850, however, a number of scholars had begun to doubt that the Semitic inhabitants of Assyria had invented the cuneiform system of writing, since the syllabic values of the signs seemed to go back to words for which no Semitic equivalent could be found. Moreover, in the Nineveh excavations of 1851–1852, there were unearthed a number of tablets inscribed with bilingual texts and syllabaries, and while one of the languages was Assyrian, the other showed no Semitic characteristics whatsoever. As was soon realized, it was not an inflected language like the Semitic languages but an agglutinative type. In addition, a number of bricks and tablets were discovered in several southern Mesopotamian sites, mostly from surface scratchings, and these, too, were found to be inscribed in the cuneiform script but in a non-Semitic tongue. It seemed reasonable to conclude, therefore, that the invention of the cuneiform system of writing went back to the speakers of this non-Semitic tongue, and that the Assyrians borrowed it from them. Various names were then suggested for this hitherto unknown language and people. In 1869, Oppert, on the basis of the royal title "King of Sumer and Akkad" found in some of the royal inscriptions, rightly concluded that Akkad referred to the land inhabited by a Semitic people, while Sumer was the land inhabited by the non-Semitic people who originated the cuneiform system of writing. Thus after more than twenty centuries of burial and oblivion, the Sumerian people and language began to see once again the light of day.

This insight was only a beginning, however, for Oppert's indentifications were not readily accepted by the scholarly world. Virtually all the source material for the study and decipherment of the so-called Sumerian language came from Assyrian sites and from the first millennium B.C., and it was difficult to believe that a Sumerian people, who seemed to have left no archaeological remains of their own, had preceded the Semites anywhere in Mesopotamia, north or south. But then, in 1877, the French began major excavations at Telloh (Ancient Lagash) and soon found assorted Sumerian monuments, statues, steles, and plaques of the rulers of Lagash dating from the third millennium B.C., as well as thousands of Sumerian tablets and fragments. The great majority of these were administrative archives, but some were votive inscriptions full of significant historical and sociological information.

The existence of the Sumerians was no longer in doubt. There they were, materialized and immortalized in stone and clay.

But there was more to come. In 1889, a second major excavation was begun in Mesopotamia, this time at Nippur, nearly a hundred miles northwest of Lagash. Here were uncovered the Sumerian literary documents in which Chiera became so deeply interested, and to which I have devoted almost all of my scholarly career. The sponsor of this first American excavating expedition to Mesopotamia was the University of Pennsylvania. All through the 1880s, discussions had been going on in American university circles about the feasibility of sending an American expedition to excavate in Mesopotamia, where the British and French were making such extraordinary archaeological discoveries. It was not until 1887, however, that John P. Peters, professor of Hebrew at the University of Pennsylvania, succeeded in obtaining moral and financial support from various individuals associated with the university for the purpose of equipping and maintaining an expedition. Nippur was chosen primarily because of its large size and impressive contours, and four campaigns were conducted there between the years 1889 and 1900, first under the direction of Peters, then under J. H. Haynes, originally the photographer of the expedition, and finally under the Assyriologist H. V. Hilprecht, who had been its epigrapher in the first campaign and who later became the Clark Research Professor in the Graduate School of the University of Pennsylvania, an endowed chair that later I was privileged to hold.

The expedition underwent severe hardships and discouraging mishaps. One young archaeologist died in the field and there was hardly a year in which one or another of its staff did not suffer serious illness. In spite of these obstacles, however, the excavating continued, and the expedition achieved magnificent, and in some respects, unparalleled results, at least in the inscriptional field. It succeeded in excavating some thirty thousand tablets and fragments, the majority of which were inscribed in the Sumerian language, ranging over two millenniums, from the second half of the third to the last half of the first millennium B.C. Among this vast treasure were more than three thousand tablets and fragments inscribed with Sumerian literary works: myths, epic tales, hymns, laments, songs of love, proverbs, disputations, dialogues, essays. About half of these went to Istanbul, since Iraq was then part of the Ottoman Empire, and were deposited in the recently created Istanbul archaeological museum. The other half was deposited in the newly built University Museum in Philadelphia.

At the time of the excavations there was no way of knowing the nature and importance of these whole and fragmentary tablets. Only later, when Hilprecht and his assistants began to catalogue and study their contents, did they become aware, to a limited extent, of their extraordinary significance. In 1909 there appeared the first twenty-one copies of Sumerian literary texts from Nippur, published by Hugo Radau, a young cuneiformist and protégé of Hilprecht who later abandoned academe altogether. Between 1909 and 1924, when Chiera returned from Istanbul and published the fifty pieces he had copied there under the title *Sumerian Religious Texts,* some two hundred of the approximately three thousand Nippur literary pieces had been copied and published by one scholar or another.

But the copying of the texts, while laborious and time-consuming, was only the first, and relatively easier, stage in the recovery and restoration of the Sumerian literary works. The more difficult and complicated aspect was the translation and interpretation of their contents in order to make it possible to penetrate and evaluate the ideas and ideals of the Sumerians, their spiritual values, religious aspirations, and aesthetic norms. But this essential task was impossible to achieve at the time, though several scholars attempted to do so. The primary reason for this failure was not so much the grammatical uncertainties and lexicographical obscurities, though these were serious enough, but rather the physical characteristics of the excavated source material. The clay tablets on which the Sumerian literary compositions are inscribed are unbaked and almost never came up whole from the ground; usually they are partly broken and at times are in a very fragmentary condition. But there is the compensating circumstance that the ancient scribes made more than one copy of any given literary work. The breaks and lacunae in one framentary tablet may therefore frequently be restored from duplicating pieces that may themselves be mere broken fragments. There are cases where more than fifty tablets and fragments were utilized to restore the text of a single composition, and at least one where it took more than a hundred to do so. But to take full advantage of these duplications and the resulting restorations, it is essential to have as much as possible of the extant Sumerian literary material identified, copied, or made available in one form or another.

The first to perceive this need clearly and to grasp its implications was Edward Chiera, and he decided to do something about it. In 1923, on his return to Philadelphia from Istanbul, he began to devote every minute he could spare to the study of the literary pieces in the Nippur collection of the University Museum. Between 1924 and 1927 he succeeded in preparing admirable copies of 270 tablets and fragments inscribed with an assortment of Sumerian literature, identified the contents of a good many more that he intended to copy at some future date, and began to prepare a glossary of key Sumerian words to enable him to recognize additional crucial duplications that could lead to the restoration of the texts of quite a number of the compositions to which these belonged. In short, Chiera may be said to have laid the groundwork for the recovery and restortion of Sumerian literature, and had he not died unexpectedly he might well have played a leading role in this ongoing process.

In 1927, when he was called to the Oriental Institute to become the editor of the Assyrian Dictionary, Chiera carried with him the copies of the Sumerian literary pieces on which he had labored in the University Museum, and Breasted agreed to have the Oriental Institute publish them in one of its series. But death came suddenly, before Chiera was able to complete his notes and prepare the introduction to the books. His copies were thus left stranded, and the institute staff in charge of publications was in a quandary. George Allen, the Egyptologist who was head of the editorial department, asked me, as a budding Sumerologist, to undertake the preparation of the two volumes for publication.

At the time, I actually knew very little about Sumerian literature and its significance or of the complex problems relating to its recovery and restoration since I had been working with Poebel on Sumerian grammar and various other aspects of cuneiform research. I therefore began to read avidly everything I could lay my hands on that had been said on this subject by earlier scholars, especially those who had already copied and published some of the Nippur literary pieces from Istanbul and Philadelphia. But I soon realized that this area of cuneiform research was almost entirely untouched. Not only had relatively few Sumerian literary texts been copied and published but hardly any of the attempts at translation and interpretation of their contents were reasonably trustworthy or enlightening. This condition of Sumerian studies inspired me to work day and night trying to read and understand the documents copied by Chiera which I had undertaken to edit. I looked upon this as a scholarly task that must not be allowed to fail. I had to make at least enough sense out of Chiera's copied material to enable me to arrange it meaningfully and intelligibly for publication and to prepare an introduction which would be of some help to future researchers. The list of duplicates that Chiera had prepared when working on the Nippur material in the University Museum proved to be most helpful, as did his scattered notes and provisional glossary. In June 1934, *Sumerian Epics and Myths* and *Sumerian Texts of Varied Contents* appeared, and I breathed a sigh of relief.

But not for long! I was now hooked on Sumerian literature, totally and obsessively, and there was so much to learn and to do in this virtually unknown field of humanistic research. Copies of tablets, such as those in the Chiera volumes, were only the roots of the tree; its trunk and branches were the translations and interpretations that would make the contents available to interested humanists the world over. Therefore, as soon as I had finished preparing Chiera's copies for publication, I concentrated all my attention and efforts to piecing together, with the help of Chiera's list of duplicates, the extant text of several Sumerian literary compositions that seemed to be of unusual significance and to attempting to translate and interpret their contents.

First came a myth which I entitled "Inanna's Descent to the Nether World," a rather melancholy tale of the gods that was nevertheless responsible for one of the happier events of my scholarly career. What made this study possible at the time was Chiera's discovery that a tablet inscribed with the first half of this myth had been broken either before or during the Nippur excavations, and that one half had gone to Istanbul and the other to Philadelphia. This long-distance join provided a partially preserved text of almost two hundred lines and enabled me to place in their correct position in the story eight other published pieces, including three that appeared in *Sumerian Epics and Myths*. The resulting edition of the extant text, still quite incomplete, consisting of transliteration, translation, and commentary, eventually was published in the *Revue d'assyriologie* in 1937.

The second text on which I concentrated was part of an epic tale that I published under the title *Gilgamesh and the ḫuluppu-Tree* in 1938, though I had begun working on it as early as 1934. At the time eight pieces of tablets inscribed with parts of this poem had already been published, but I was unable to place them in their proper position in the text until I gradually learned to utilize certain stylistic clues. Years later I realized that the initial lines of this epic tale provided the first insight into the Sumerian conception of the creation of the universe, and this in turn augmented our understanding of Sumerian religion and myth.

One of the more somber genres of the Sumerian literary repertoire is the lamentation type of composition that bewails and bemoans the sporadic destruction of Sumer and its cities. Among the Nippur pieces copied by Chiera were eight inscribed with parts of a composition that I entitled "Lamentation over the Destruction of Ur." In 1930 the French scholar Henri de Genouillac had copied and published a large tablet in the Louvre which was originally inscribed with the entire text of this composition but now had a considerable number of breaks that left large gaps in the body of the poem. By piecing together the texts of these nine pieces, I was able to reconstruct the contents of the lamentation almost, but not quite, in their entirety. This work was ready for publication in 1937, but it did not appear until 1940, after I had returned from Istanbul, where I had identified a number of additional

Milly Tokarsky Kramer, some years before her marriage.

duplicates that made the text of the lamentation, consisting of more than four hundred lines, virtually complete.

The Sumerian literary research that began in 1933 with the preparation of Chiera's posthumous volumes filled me with joy. My personal life, too, was fulfilled by my marriage, in that same year, to Milly Tokarsky, a Chicago schoolteacher, and the birth of our son Daniel in the following year. The future looked promising, and in my imagination I saw myself traveling as a member of the Oriental Institute staff to the University Museum of Philadelphia and to the Museum of the Ancient Orient in Istanbul, in order to identify, copy, and study their unpublished Nippur literary tablets and fragments, and thus bring to fruition Chiera's inspiring vision. But devious Fate had other plans. I did travel to Philadelphia and Istanbul, and I did bring Chiera's vision to fruition, at least to a considerable extent. But not as a member of the Oriental Institute. My connection with that institution was severed in 1936, after I had suffered one humiliating blow after another. The days that had begun there in sweet hope ended in despair.

The first blow came toward the end of 1934. As I had occasion to note in the preceding chapter, the Department of Near Eastern Languages and Literatures, part of the Humanities Faculty of the University of Chicago, had its offices in the Oriental Institute, and most of its professors were connected in one way or another with that institution. As a junior member of the Assyrian Dictionary staff, I was part of the institute, but not of the department, although I did teach a course in introductory Sumerian without stipend. The chairman of the department was the Arabist Martin Sprengling, a rather blunt, direct, not overly sensitive or subtle academic. One day he summoned me to his office, and after a rather warm and expansive greeting told me, in effect: "Sam, we all like you here and think highly of your scholarship. We have therefore decided to appoint you as an instructor in the department." At this point my heart began to beat with excitement and my face to shine with joy, then I heard his booming voice continue: "But I must warn you, Sam, that as a Jew you cannot rise in the department above the position of assistant professor. What's more, to balance your appointment, we shall also appoint a gentile as instructor in the department."

I could hardly believe my ears, and fearing that I would lose control of my emotions, I hurriedly said good-bye and rushed out of the office. That night my wife and I spent many an hour discussing this bitter development, and we decided that I should "take it on the chin," go along as before and try not to let this matter interfere with my research. This was easier said than done, however. The institute was no longer a Promised Land, and I walked its bare and gloomy hall with averted eyes. The denouement to this crude bit of anti-Semitism was even more disheartening. When the appointments to the department were announced, the gentile was appointed an instructor while I simply continued as a research assistant on the Assyrian Dictionary staff.

But a more severe blow struck in 1936. Breasted had died in December 1935, and the Oriental Institute was in dire financial difficulty. This was only in part because of his death. The troubles had begun earlier in 1935, when, as a result of the Depression, Mr. Rockefeller and the

Rockefeller Board, the financial angels of the institute, had decided to withdraw their support from almost all its activities, except for one large terminal grant. With Breasted gone, the terrible burden of cutting the annual budget by two-thirds fell on the shoulders of the young and relatively inexperienced acting director John Wilson, who had been secretary of the institute at the time of Breasted's death. To quote Wilson's *Thousand Years:*

> There had to be drastic surgery. In place of nine field expeditions, there were only two, the Epigraphic Survey at Luxor with a reduced staff and a small excavation to test some clearly restricted problem in some other country. Some expeditions were cancelled summarily. Others were put on notice that they would have to resolve their major problems in one or two more years. In every case there was an attempt to retain those scholars who were needed to see the work through to publication. Of the approximately one hundred and twenty staff members at home and abroad, more than forty-five had to receive notice of termination, immediately or in the near future.

As one of the lowest men on the institute's hierarchical totem pole, I knew virtually nothing of this turmoil until some weeks before the end of the academic year of 1935–1936, when I received a notice of immediate dismissal from the staff. I was among the very last hired, and it was therefore not unreasonable that I should be among the first to be fired. But what made this action seem to me most unfair, and even illegal, though the university lawyers did not think so, was the fact that I had not received the dismissal notice in sufficient time to look for another academic position, or even to apply for a grant from a foundation. My wife was pregnant with our second child at the time, making the situation so intolerable that I decided I must do something about it. As I recollect it, I wrote a letter to Wilson stating my case with no little anger and indignation and vowed to picket the institute with an explanatory sign on my shoulder unless I was appointed for one more year and given the opportunity to look about for some other academic opening.

To this day I cannot decide whether I would have had the temerity to carry out this one-man demonstration. I am not an activist by nature and far from aggressive—"Your arms are broken at the elbows," said one dear friend to me—and I might never have been able to lift and hold the accusing wooden post. But fortunately it did not reach that embarrassing stage. From some friends in the university I learned that there was a chapter of the American Association of University Professors on the campus, and that its chairman was the distinguished scientist Anton Carlson. I turned to him with my complaint, and he arranged a meeting with Wilson that resulted in the withdrawal of the dismissal notice, with the understanding that this was to be my terminal year. I immediately applied to the Guggenheim Foundation for one of its fellowships, to enable me to travel to Istanbul and copy some of the Sumerian literary tablets and fragments in the Museum of the Ancient Orient. Miracle of miracles, the application was acted upon favorably, and I was awarded a grant of about two thousand dollars for the year 1937–1938. And so in June 1937, the Kramer family—my wife, Daniel, aged four, and Judy, aged one—pulled up stakes and left by freighter for Istanbul.

Lest the reader gain a mistaken and unfavorable impression of the University of Chicago of those days, and of its Oriental Institute, from the two painful incidents recorded above, let me add a more pleasant epilogue. Although no longer a paid member of the institute, I continued to be listed in the catalogue with the title research associate, rather than research assistant, which was helpful whenever I applied to a foundation for a grant.

Two of my monographs concerned with Sumerian literature were published by the institute in its Assyriological Studies series, and this bolstered considerably my scholarly reputation. The institute also made several minor financial contributions that I was happy to acknowledge in the preface to my *Sumerian Mythology*. John Wilson, the man who "fired" me, was a scholar whom I respected and admired; we became quite good friends and often met and talked at the annual affairs of the American Philosophical Society. As for the University of Chicago, it is only fair to stress that by and large it was one of the more liberal institutions of higher learning in the 1930s, even though a few pockets of bigoted anti-Semitism did exist among its faculty. To relate my unfortunate experience of nonappointment in the Department of Near Eastern Languages and Literatures was difficult for me to decide. But I recognize that it was an episode not indicative of the university's policy as a whole and that it is also an instructive bit of academic Americana which I hope is inconceivable in today's university climate.

5
The Gods: Sumerian Mythology

The freighter took about a month for its leisurely journey to Istanbul, making several stops in the Mediterranean before docking at the Golden Horn. The weather was summery and pleasant. The Kramer family of four constituted more than half the passenger list, and the crew had made a special effort to please. The two children were their favorites, and the sailors took time out to teach Judy to walk the deck on her wobbly little legs. In Istanbul we rented a comfortable apartment in Bebek with a Greek family. There was, of course, no central heating—Istanbul can be quite cold and nasty in winter—and the bathroom and toilet facilities were hardly up-to-date. The house was situated high up on a hill that had to be climbed several times a day, but the view of the Bosphorus was breathtaking. I traveled to work by ferry, on a boat that meandered dreamily from continent to continent.

Not long after our arrival, I paid a courtesy call on the director of the Archaeological Museums, a building complex that is beautifully situated in a part of Istanbul known as Saray-burnu, or "Palace-Nose," where the Sea of Marmara branches out into the gulflike Golden Horn and the winding Bosphorus. Here, in the shelter of impenetrable walls, Mehmed the Second, the conqueror of Constantinople, built his palace and residence almost five hundred years ago. In the centuries that followed, sultan after sultan added to the palace complex, building new kiosks and mosques, installing new fountains, and laying out new gar-

The Kramer family in Salonika, en route to Istanbul in 1937. Daniel and Judith are traveling in their Radio Special.

dens. In the attractively paved courts and terraced gardens sloping uphill from the sea wandered the ladies of the harem and their attendants, the princes and their pages. Few were privileged to enter the palace grounds and fewer still were permitted to witness their inner life.

But gone are the days of the sultans, and "Palace-Nose" has now taken on an altogether different aspect. The high-towered walls are broken down in large part. The private gardens along the sea have been turned into public parks to provide shade and rest during the hot summer months. As for the buildings, the forbidding and forbidden palaces and secretive kiosks situated on the high ground of Saray-burnu have virtually all been transformed into museums.

The director of the Archaeological Museums was then Aziz Bey, a member of a distinguished Turkish family; his uncle was the eminent Halil Bey, who was largely responsible for the metamorphosis of the caliph palaces and kiosks into archaeological treasure houses. Aziz Bey received me cordially. I had of course written to the Turkish Directorate of Antiquities in some detail about the nature and purpose of my visit and had received permission to carry on my research in the Museum of the Ancient Orient. What worried me deeply, however, was how to do so effectively and without too many delays. The tablet collection of the Istanbul museum is enormous, second only to that of the British Museum. From ancient Lagash alone it had in its cupboards more than fifty thousand tablets, and, in addition, it had many thousands from Nippur and other sites that had been excavated in Iraq. I was interested only in a tiny fraction of this vast collection, the Sumerian literary tablets from Nippur, which at the time could be estimated to be not much more than a thousand or so. Where were these stored? Would I have to examine thousands upon thousands of tablets in order to locate them? If so, this task in itself would be immense and laborious and might well consume the entire year of the Guggenheim Fellowship. With these disturbing thoughts, I followed the guard whom Aziz Bey had instructed to take me to the small building alongside the Museum of the Ancient Orient that housed the tablet collections. There I was met by the young cuneiformist from Leipzig, Rudolph Kraus, and I soon realized that my troubles were over, at least with regard to the location and partial identification of the source material for my research. But first a word to explain the surprising presence of a Leipzig cuneiformist as an official in a Turkish museum.

In the 1930s, there was an immense brain drain from Germany to the rest of the world, and Turkey was one of the major beneficiaries. The founder of the Turkish republic, the broad-faced, sad-eyed Kemal Atatürk, who in some ways was one of the most remarkable figures of that period, had invited there a large number of refugees from Nazism, most of whom were Jews or half-Jews, or married to Jewesses. These scholars brought about a veritable explosion in the climate of Turkish cultural and academic institutions. One who came was Benno Landsberger, the head of the Leipziger Semitisches Institut, whom I had met on my way back from Iraq to America in 1931 and who was recognized as one of the world's leading Orientalists. In spite of his heroic service during the First World War, he was stigmatized after Germany came under Nazi domination as "der Jude Landsberger," even by a former student or two. The handwriting was on the wall, and when he received a call from Atatürk to come to teach in Turkey, he accepted with alacrity.

Atatürk was more interested in developing the newly established University of Ankara than the University of Istanbul, and Landsberger was appointed to a cuneiform chair at Ankara. He had brought along with him two of his former students who were half-Jews. The young Hittitologist Hans Güterbock was also given an appointment at the University of Ankara, while Rudolph Kraus, his last and youngest Leipziger Ph.D., was appointed curator of the tablet collection of the Istanbul Museum of the Ancient Orient. During their stay in Turkey, these three scholars inspired a considerable number of Turkish students to specialize in cuneiform studies, which are now full-fledged humanistic disciplines in both Turkish universities. After the Second World War, when Thorkild Jacobsen became director of the Oriental Institute, Landsberger and Güterbock were invited to come to Chicago, where they have contributed enormously to the development of cuneiform studies in America. Kraus was then invited to become professor of Assyriology at the Univesrity of Vienna, and later at the prestigious University of Leiden.

Returning to the year 1937, let me explain why Kraus's presence in the museum was so fortunate for me. When he became curator of the tablet collection, Kraus decided to catalogue its myriad tablets and fragments to let cuneiformists the world over know the nature of their contents, a laborious but essential task which would have taken him many years. Fortunately for me, he began with the Nippur collection, and when I arrived at the museum I was happy to learn that he had already identified roughly, and set aside, several hundred Nippur literary pieces which I could begin to study and copy at once.

Before I did so, however, it was agreed between us that there was a rather unappealing but very useful scholarly chore to perform in connection with the museum's Nippur literary tablets, the task of collation, that is, the correction of copies made by earlier scholars who for one reason or another had misread or missed altogether some signs on the original. In 1914, almost a quarter of a century before my arrival in Istanbul, the eminent Anglo-American scholar Stephen Langdon had copied and published some fifty of the Nippur literary pieces in the Istanbul museum. Langdon was an energetic and enthusiastic cuneiformist who made numerous important contributions to the discipline. But he was a fast and careless copyist, and many misreadings crept into his copies, errors that were to confuse and bedevil future translators and interpreters of the texts. I therefore spent several months collating his copies with the originals, and the resulting additions and corrections were published in 1940 in the *Journal of the American Oriental Society*. In the course of my scholarly career I have made it my business to prepare a number of such collations, the last one as late as 1973. Copyists are only human, and even the best make some errors, which the collator, perched on the shoulders of his predecessor, is able to correct. This is also true of my own copies, which will no doubt be collated and corrected in due time.

The collation of Langdon's copies proved useful in another respect; it helped to prepare me for the main task of copying originals. Until this time, the Sumerian literary texts that I had studied were copies, published or unpublished, prepared by other scholars, and these are much easier to read than the original tablets and fragments. Unlike Poebel and Chiera, I was not blessed with particularly good handwriting, and it took weeks of concentrated practice to learn to copy adequately and accurately. Time was passing and I was becoming somewhat panicky, for soon the year of the Guggenheim award would come to an end, and I had made only a few copies of the original tablets. I therefore applied to the Guggenheim Foundation for a renewal of the fellowship, and to my surprise the application was again acted upon favorably. The grant was even increased by five hundred dollars to help pay our traveling expenses!

Encouraged by this show of faith in such an esoteric and specialized project, I continued my work with renewed energy, and by the end of the second year of the fellowship, in June 1939, I had copied 167 tablets and fragments whose contents ranged over the entire spectrum of Sumerian literary genres. These were not published, however, until 1944, when they appeared under the title *Sumerian Literary Texts from Nippur,* with an introduction in English and Turkish. The Turkish translation had been prepared as a labor of love by two young Turkish co-workers. I returned to Philadelphia after my two Guggenheim years in Istanbul, almost penniless and without a job, or the prospects of one. My wife's father, a retired carpenter, had bought a small farm near Niles, Michigan, and she and the children left immediately for that welcome haven. I stayed in Philadelphia with my friends the Silvers, whose generous hospitality was extended to me at all times and in all seasons. My object in Philadelphia was twofold: to see if I could get permission from University Museum authorities to study, copy, and publish the Nippur literary pieces in the tablet collection of its Babylonian Section and to try to obtain some financial support for this research. So it came about in the fall of 1939 that I climbed with fluttering heart the majestic steps of the University Museum and knocked timidly on the door of the office of its director, Horace Howard Furness Jayne.

The founding of the University Museum in 1891 was sparked by the anthropologically oriented Department of Archaeology and Paleontology that was created in the university "to provide instruction in archaeology, ethnology, and paleontology and to extend scientific inquiry by means of original investigation"; by the formation of the University Archaeological Association consisting of prominent Philadelphians who were interested in archaeology and who undertook to raise the necessary funds; and last, but by no means least, by the prestigious discoveries of the Nippur expedition, especially its inscriptional finds that were attracting worldwide attention. Financially speaking, the University Museum is largely the creation of the Philadelphia Main Line and its more cultured bankers and merchants. They provided most of the funds for its impressive buildings, donated a large part of its outstanding collections, and sponsored and supported many of its excavations and expeditions. By 1962, the year of its seventy-fifth anniversary, the museum could boast that it had sponsored alone or jointly 220 expeditions to 160 sites scattered over the globe.

The museum did not fare so well, however, with its annual operational budget, and there were repeated financial crises when personnel and salaries had to be cut. This was especially true in the 1930s, when the university, its own finances critically depressed, found it necessary to suspend its annual allocation to the museum budget. In fact, until quite recently, the relationship between the museum and the university blew hot and cold; there were times when members of the museum staff had no teaching posts in the university and when university professors of archaeology and anthropology rarely visited the museum and its collections. But I did not learn of these internal problems and relationships until a much later day; none of this was known to me as I hesitantly opened the door of the director's office.

Almost immediately I realized that my qualms were quite unfounded. Horace Howard Furness Jayne ("Hoddy" to his friends), a specialist in Chinese art and archaeology, was a warmhearted and, despite his impressive prenomen that indicated high Philadelphia lineage, unpretentious man. He received me cordially, listened sympathetically to my enthusiastic description of the projected research and its importance, and responded favorably to my request. Most of the Nippur tablets, he informed me, were numbered and arranged in metal cases in a room in the basement. A desk and chair would be provided for me, and I could carry on my research there to my heart's content. The matter of a stipend, or any other source of financial support, was not mentioned throughout our conversations.

I next proceeded to the office of Leon Legrain, the curator of the Babylonian Section, Hilprecht's successor as Clark Research Professor of Assyriology, to obtain his blessing for the project. He, too, was favorably disposed. In the 1930s he had represented the museum in the joint British-American excavations at Ur, and at the moment was concentrating on preparing copies, indices, and glossaries of about eighteen hundred Ur tablets, virtually all administrative in content. He had lost all enthusiasm for the Nippur material and was only too happy to have it studied by a younger cuneiformist who seemed to be deeply immersed in it.

I had thus achieved my first objective and immediately began to work in the tablet-lined basement that was destined to be my happy workshop for the next four years. As for the second objective, someone in the museum suggested that I apply to the American Philosophical Society for one of its research grants. Rumor had it that this august society had recently come into some millions, and that it was awarding small grants to scholars in need of limited financial help. I filled out an application form in which I described the project, as well as my qualifications for carrying it out, and asked for the modest stipend of eighteen hundred dollars for the year 1939–1940. To my delight, the grant came through. Solvent once again, I immediately rented an apartment, and the family joined me in Philadelphia, which became our permanent home.

The American Philosophical Society awarded me grants ranging from fifteen hundred to three thousand dollars for the next four years, enabling me to continue my work without interruption. It was not until much later, after I had been elected a member of the society, that I learned which member had been the Sumerological Santa Claus. The society is virtually run by committees, one of the most important of which is the Committee on Research. It consists of a dozen or more scholars, each representing a major scientific or humanistic discipline. The scholar responsible for the archaeology of Bible Lands, which included Mesopotamia, was William Foxwell Albright, whose popular books, such as *From the Stone Age to Christianity* and *The Archaeology of Palestine* had made his name a household word. Although he had devoted his career to Palestinian archaeology, as he confided to me after we had become good friends, his earliest ambition had been to study Sumerian and work on the Sumerian literary texts. He had had to give up that dream because of his poor eyesight. In a sense I was his surrogate.

Albright, I realized later, was not the only member of the society to put in a good word for me. The executive secretary, and later president, Edwin Conklin, he of the Scopes trial fame, was also in my corner when needed. Although a biologist by calling, he had a passion for the humanities, and he recognized that the recovery and restoration of the Sumerian literary documents was a humanistic contribution of major import. Another of my supporters, one whom I hardly knew at all, was Roland Morris, a one-time ambassador to Japan who also served as president of the American Philosophical Society. The Nippur tablets were about fifteen thousand in number. But only a small fraction of these were inscribed with Sumerian literary texts; the vast majority consisted of Sumerian and Assyrian documents of diverse content, not germane to my research. First, therefore, it was necessary to work my way through this immense mass of tablets and fragments, to handle each individual piece and scan its contents in order to identify and put aside for later study those inscribed with texts belonging to one or another of the Sumerian literary works. This was a slow process, though not especially difficult, since the Sumerian literary pieces could often be recognized at first glance by their shape and script. After several months of this preparatory labor, I succeeded in identifying 675 pieces as literary. Of these, approximately 175 were inscribed with parts of myths and epic tales; about 350 were hymns and laments; 150 were "wisdom" texts of one sort or another. I now had to decide on which of these literary categories to start working in earnest. But this quandary was soon resolved for me by an unexpected source.

In the early 1940s, the Department of Oriental Studies in the Graduate School of the University of Pennsylvania, one of the largest and most distinguished in America and abroad and whose courses covered the entire ancient Orient from the Mediterranean to the Pacific, instituted an Interconnection Seminar. Attended by more professors than students, it had as its goal the bridging of the gap between the various separate Oriental disciplines, as well as the developing of a comparative approach that might uncover some underlying principles applicable to the study of ancient man in general. Every year, a central, pivotal theme was chosen for investigation, and each of the distinguished professors participating was committed to prepare a comprehensive survey of whatever was known about it in his own geographical area, including and stressing the results of his most recent relevant research.

I was not a member of the department at the time, but as one of its former graduates and a guest researcher in the museum, not to mention my continued tenuous connection with the Oriental Institute as honorary, that is, unsalaried, research associate on the Assyrian Dictionary staff, I was invited to participate in this seminar. The theme selected for the year 1940–1941 was cosmogony and cosmology: the concepts

In more recent years, just to keep the record up-to-date, two more Inanna myths have been recovered. One relates how the goddess puts to death a crone-like deity named Bilulu and turns her corpse into a waterskin to serve the wanderer in the desert steppes where Dumuzi had had his sheepfolds. The death-dealing aspect of the goddess is also apparent in the second myth, which can be entitled "Inanna and Shukalletuda: The Gardener's Mortal Sin." This tale relates that one day a gardener, Shukalletuda, took advantage of the goddess and raped her as she lay asleep under one of his shade trees, resting from a wearisome journey over heaven and earth. Upon waking and realizing what had happened to her, she pursued Shukalletuda relentlessly. When she finally caught up with him, she put him to death but comforted him with the promise that he would be commemorated in story and song.

The other mythological compositions available for presentation to the seminar were one concerned with the marriage of the Bedu god Martu; another depicting the journey of the moon god Nanna to holy Nippur in order to obtain a blessing for his city, Ur, from his father Enlil; a third, about the destruction of mankind by a Deluge from which only the forewarned Ziusudra, the Sumerian counterpart of the biblical Noah, was saved, thus preserving the seed of man from total annihilation. Added to these were two "disputations," one between Winter and Summer, the other between Cattle and Grain, which contained significant mythological material in their introductory passages.

With so many myths at my disposal, one might conclude that I had no problems with the Sumerian cosmogonic and cosmological thought, the major themes for the seminar discussions. Not so! Actually, the myths, at least on the surface, tell very little about Sumerian cosmogony and cosmology, since their authors were not systematic theologians concerned with the formulation of theories and postulates. The Sumerian mythographers were poets whose main objectives were to glorify the gods and their deeds by composing narrative poems that would be inspiring and entertaining. Their literary tools were not logic and reason but imagination and fantasy, and these were hardly conducive to a methodical exposition of the Sumerian cosmogonic views and cosmological dogmas. These had to be inferred, surmised, and ferreted out from diverse inscriptional sources, a task that proved to be time-consuming and often quite frustrating.

At long last, however, a solution came to me, thanks largely to a between-the-lines reading of a mythological passage that introduced, not a myth, but an epic tale, that is, a narrative poem in which mortal heroes rather than immortal gods are the protagonists. The contents of this epic tale of "Gilgamesh, Enkidu, and the Nether World" are out-

lined later. Here are only the initial lines that provided the clue for the detection and unraveling of some Sumerian ideas and preconceptions relating to the origin of the universe and the creation of the cosmos.

> In days of yore, in distant days of yore,
> In nights of yore, in distant nights of yore,
> In years of yore, in distant years of yore . . . ,
> After heaven had been moved away from earth,
> After earth had been separated from heaven,
> After the name of man had been fixed,
> After An had carried off heaven,
> After Enlil had carried off earth . . .

A paraphrase is: Heaven and earth, originally united, were separated and moved away from each other, after which the creation of man was ordained. An, the heaven god, then carried off heaven, while Enlil, the air god, carried off the earth. All that could be learned from this passage, therefore, was that at one time heaven and earth had been united; that some of the gods existed before the separation of earth from heaven; and that after the separation, it was, as might have been expected, the heaven god An who carried off heaven, but, rather surprisingly, it was the air god Enlil who carried off earth.

Among the crucial cosmological ideas not stated or implied in these lines were such questions as: Were heaven and earth conceived as created, and if so by whom? How did the Sumerians conceive the shape of the united heaven and earth? Who separated heaven from earth? The answers to these three questions could be gleaned from several other texts. In a tablet inscribed with a list of Sumerian gods, a goddess by the name of Nammu, the name written with the ideogram for "sea," is described as "the mother, who gave birth to heaven and earth." Judging from this statement, heaven and earth were conceived by the Sumerians as the created product of a primeval sea. The disputation "Cattle and Grain" mentioned earlier begins with the following two lines:

> After on the mountain of heaven and earth,
> An had caused the Anunnaki [his followers] to be born . . .

It was not unreasonable to assume, therefore, that the united heaven and earth were conceived as a mountain whose base was the bottom of the earth, and whose peak was the top of heaven. The myth "Enlil and

---

The ziggurat at Aqar Quf, west of Baghdad, 1946. On the right, Najr-al-Asil, then director of antiquities of Iraq; next to him is the author and Taha Bagir, then director of the Iraq Museum and former student of Kramer at the Oriental Institute.

the Creation of the Pickax," referred to earlier, is introduced by the following passage:

> The lord brought into existence that which is needful,
> The lord whose decisions are unalterable,
> Enlil, who brings up the seed of the land from the earth,
> Hastened to move away heaven from earth,
> Hastened to move away earth from heaven.

Here, therefore, we have the explicit statement that it was the god Enlil who separated heaven and earth.

Combining the cosmogonic data provided by, or inferred from, all these passages, the creation picture that emerged could be sketched as follows: First was the primeval sea. Nothing is said of its origin or birth, and it is not unlikely that it was conceived as having existed eternally. This primeval sea engendered the cosmic mountain consisting of heaven and earth. Conceived as gods in human form, An (heaven) was the male and Ki (earth) was the female. Their union produced the air god Enlil, who proceeded to separate heaven from earth, and while it was his father An who carried off heaven, he himself carried off his mother Ki, earth. The union of Enlil with Mother Earth set the stage for the organization of the universe, the creation of man, and the establishment of civilization.

With some of the major cosmogonic ideas now abstracted from diverse sources, I found it possible to arrange the myths in a meaningful order and to present them to the seminar. It took seven two-hour sessions to do so, and these lectures served as a framework for the first draft of a manuscript that later became *Sumerian Mythology: A Study of Spiritual and Literary Achievement in the Third Millennium B.C.*, a small monograph-like volume that for the first time made available to scholar and humanist alike the contents of almost a score of myths from clay "books" that had lain buried in the ruins of Sumer for four thousand years. The spontaneous and enthusiastic response of both professors and students attending the seminar was of considerable support in the complex and at times heartbreaking effort to penetrate the meaning of texts that were often ambiguous and elusive.

Sumerian Mythology appeared only after several other auspicious events, all connected in one way or another with the American Philosophical Society. In April 1941 I read a twenty-minute paper before the annual meeting of the society on a translation of the myth "Inanna's Descent to the Nether World." When I had first pieced together the text, there still remained quite a number of breaks and gaps that obscured the meaning of several crucial passages and made the interpretation of even the extant part of the myth rather dubious. But now in 1941, I had

The temple wall at Harmal, near Baghdad.

unpublished copies of five more pieces belonging to the myth, three
that I had identified in the Museum of the Ancient Orient and two in
the University Museum. These additional pieces filled most of the more
serious gaps in the earlier reconstruction, so that only the end of the
poem was still missing and had to await later discoveries. Briefly put,
the plot of the myth, as I was able to present it to society, was as
follows.

Inanna, queen of heaven, the goddess of light and love and life, had
set her heart upon visiting the Nether World, perhaps in order to free
her lover. She gathered together all the appropriate divine decrees,
adorned herself with her queenly robes and jewels, and was ready to
enter the "Land of No Return." The queen of the Nether World was her
elder sister and bitter enemy Ereshkigal, the goddess of darkness and
death. Fearing lest her sister put her to death in the Nether World,
Inanna instructed her messenger, Ninshubur, who was always at her
beck and call, that if after three days she had not returned, he was to

The Iraqi excavations at Eridu, the ancient center of worship of Enki, the Sumerian god of water and wisdom.

go to heaven and set up a hue and cry for her in the assembly of the gods. From there he was to go to Nippur (the very city where our tablets have been excavated) and there weep and plead before the god Enlil to save Inanna from Ereshkigal's clutches. If Enlil should refuse, he was to go to Ur (whence, according to biblical tradition, Abraham migrated to Canaan) and there repeat his plea before Nanna, the great Sumerian moon god. If Nanna also refused, he was to go to Eridu, the city in which Sumerian civilization is said to have originated, and weep and plead before Enki, the god of wisdom. Surely the latter, "who knows the food of life, who knows the water of life," would restore her to life.

Having taken these precautions, Inanna descended to the Nether World and approached Ereshkigal's palace of lapis lazuli. At the gate she was met by the chief gatekeeper, who demanded to know who she was and why she had come. Inanna concocted an excuse for her visit, and the gatekeeper, upon instructions from his mistress Ereshkigal, led her through the seven gates of the Nether World. As she passed through each of the gates, part of her robes and jewels were removed, in spite of her protests. Finally, after entering the last gate, she was brought naked and on bended knee before Ereshkigal and the seven Anunnaki, the dreaded judges of the Nether World. These latter fastened upon Inanna their "look of death," whereupon she was turned into a corpse and hung from a stake.

So passed three days and three nights. On the fourth day Ninshubur, seeing that his mistress had not returned, proceeded to make the rounds of the gods in accordance with his instructions. As Inanna had foreseen, both Enlil of Nippur and Nanna of Ur refused all help. Enki, however, devised a plan to restore her to life. He fashioned the *kurgarra* and *kalatur,* two sexless creatures, and entrusted to them the "food of life" and the "water of life," with instructions to proceed to the Nether World and to sprinkle this food and this water sixty times upon Inanna's suspended corpse. This they did, and Inanna revived. As she left the Nether World to ascend to the earth, however, she was accompanied by the shades of the dead and by the bogies and harpies who had their home there. Surrounded by this ghostly crowd, she wandered from city to city through Sumer.

My presentation made a deep impression on the gathered immortals, as the members of the American Philosophical Society are often facetiously called. The response was enthusiastic. William Albright was visibly stirred. He rose and pointed out the significance of the myth—to take but one instance, the parallelism of Inanna's resurrection after three days and nights with aspects of the Christ story. Covering the meeting for the *New York Times* was Lawrence E. Davies, who devoted two full columns to a detailed account of my paper. But even more crucial for my future was the presence at the meeting of John Story Jenks, then president of the Board of Managers of the University Museum. He was so impressed with my paper and the response of the audience that he decided to see about regularizing my tenuous position at the museum. It was largely through his influence that I was appointed associate curator of the Babylonian Section in 1943, a position I held until 1948, when, on the retirement of Leon Legrain, I was appointed curator of the tablet collection and Clark Research Professor of Assyriology on the recommendation of then director F. G. Rainey.

At last I was in a relatively secure academic post, upgraded from my basement workshop in the museum's lower depths to a window-lit office alongside fellow curators. Who was responsible for starting my ascent, the rise in my Sumerological fortune? No one other than the bright, white goddess Inanna! No wonder Inanna became my guardian angel, and I have clung to her throughout my career, even when to my dismay I learned that she had a destructive, death-dealing side to her character.

Since I read that paper in 1941, a dozen more tablets and fragments inscribed with parts of "Inanna's Descent to the Nether World" have been uncovered and copied by various scholars, and these provided the missing denouement. The interested reader will find a fully revised version of the myth in my *The Sacred Marriage Rite*. Here let me only stress that the end of the story revealed the goddess as a rather hottempered, vindictive deity who sent her spouse Dumuzi to his death as soon as he showed any signs of marital independence. Inanna is the one goddess in the Sumerian pantheon whose deeds and powers should serve as soothing balm to the wounds of liberated women the world over. Brave, crafty, ambitious, aggressive, awesome, but also desirable, lovable, and passionate, she was glorified and extolled throughout Sumer's existence in myth, epic, and hymn. No one, neither god nor man, dared oppose her, stand in her way, say her nay. And neither can I.

In 1970, when I was visiting professor of Sumerology in the Sorbonne-related Ecole Pratique des Hautes Etudes, I encouraged one of my best and most mature students, a Swiss lady from the University of Geneva named Françoise Bruschweiler, to take the goddess as the theme for her doctoral dissertation. The last I heard she was making good progress, and it is my fond hope that her study will see the light of day before I join Dumuzi, Inanna's love-hate victim, in the Nether World.

Although papers read at the meetings of the American Philosophical Society are usually quite short, it is the generous policy of the society to encourage their expansion for publication in its *Proceedings*. I took full advantage of this and transformed the short paper into a long article entitled "Sumerian Literature: A Preliminary Survey of the Oldest Literature in the World." It included a survey of the results of my research in the University Museum, as well as an edition of the available text of "Inanna's Descent to the Nether World," with transliteration, translation, and commentary. As a direct result of this paper, I was invited in the spring of 1942 to deliver the annual lectures of the Jayne Memorial Foundation under the auspices of the American Philosophical Society. The Jayne Memorial Foundation also provided the financial support for the publication of *Sumerian Mythology* in 1944, which earned for me the Lewis Prize: three hundred dollars and a diploma, awarded "to the American citizen who shall announce at any general or special meeting of the Society, and publish among its papers, some truth which the Council of the Society shall deem worthy of the award."

In 1944, when the book was published, there was little interest in Sumerian mythology. In 1961, however, Harper and Brothers asked for permission to republish it as a Harper Torchbook and even paid me a modest royalty. In 1971, the University of Pennsylvania Press invited me to prepare a revised edition which it published the following year. For this edition, I reexamined the sketches, inferences, and conclusions propounded in the earlier two editions and could claim in good conscience that on the whole, the book has stood the test of time, although the accumulation of new texts and deeper insights during the three decades that had elapsed since its first publication made necessary some corrigenda and addenda, and these I treated in some detail in the newly prepared preface.

Before leaving this chapter dedicated to the gods of Sumer responsible for my good fortune, let me mention two other important publications resulting from my sojourn in the University Museum basement. One concerns a literary catalogue, prepared by an ancient Sumerian academic, that lists the titles of sixty-eight compositions, including "Inanna's Descent to the Nether World." It is not quite certain what induced the author to prepare this list of incipits, but it is probable that he was recording the literary tablets in the library of the school where he was teacher. If so, this would be one of man's oldest library catalogues. I had first published it in 1942. Since then, half a dozen such catalogues have been uncovered, and one of these, in the Yale Babylonian collection and published by William Hallo, may turn out to be a century or more older than the Nippur piece. In the summer of 1973, I was privileged to copy two catalogues inscribed with more than a hundred titles of Sumerian psalms of lament that had been lying for close to a hundred years in the cupboards of the British Museum until they were resurrected and identified by Edmond Sollberger, former keeper of the Western Asiatic Antiquities Section of the museum; these appeared in 1975 in the Festschrift dedicated to the eminent Finnish cuneiformist Armas Salonen.

The second publication, *Enki and Ninhursag: A Sumerian Paradise Myth,* appeared in 1945, although the manuscript was prepared several years earlier. This study provided a new translation and interpretation of a myth published in 1915 by Stephen Langdon under the title *Sumerian Epic of Paradise, the Flood, and the Fall of Man.* His translation and interpretation of this myth was so faulty and misleading that it seemed to me imperative to prepare a new translation based on a careful collation of the tablet, which was in the University Museum, to correct many of Langdon's misreadings. Moreover, in 1930, the French scholar Henri de Genouillac had published a small tablet from the Louvre that duplicated part of the myth and was useful for the restoration of the text. My study of the poem demonstrated that the myth had nothing to do with the Flood or the Fall of Man, and that while it did concern a paradise-land, its protagonists were not mortals, like Adam and Eve, but divine beings. To demonstrate the vast difference between Langdon's interpretation of the myth, which had found its way into virtually all handbooks and encyclopedias utilized by students and scholars, and that which I published in 1945, let me present here the two synopses of its contents, Langdon's and mine, a juxtaposition that might well serve to illustrate the sad plight of Sumerian mythology before the appearance of my book in 1944.

LANGDON: The theme which inspired this epic is the Fall of Man. Enki the water god and his consort Ninella, or Damkina, ruled over mankind in paradise, which the epic places in Dilmun. In that land there was no infirmity, no sin, and man grew not old. In a long address to her consort, Ninella glorifies the land of Dilmun, praising its peace and bliss. And all things were so.

But for some reason which is all too briefly defined, Enki, the god of wisdom, became dissatisfied with man and decided to overwhelm him with his waters. This plan he revealed to Nintud, the earth mother goddess, who with the help of Enlil, the earth god, had created man. According to one passage Nintud under the title Ninhursag assisted in the destruction of humanity. For nine months the flood endured and man dissolved in the waters like tallow and fat. But Nintud had planned to save the king and certain pious ones. These she summoned to the river's bank, where they embarked in a boat. After the flood, Nintud is represented in conversation with the hero, who had escaped. He is here called Tagtug and dignified by the title of a god. He becomes a gardener for whom Nintud intercedes with Enki and explains to this god how Tagtug escaped his plan of universal destruction. This at any rate is the natural inference to be made from one of the broken passages. Enki became reconciled with the gardener, called him to his temple, and revealed to him secrets. After a break we find Tagtug instructed in regard to plants and trees whose fruit the gods permitted him to eat. But it seems that Nintud had forbidden him to eat of the cassia. Of this he took and ate, whereupon Ninharsag afflicted him with bodily weakness. Life, that is, good health in the Babylonian idiom, he would no longer see. He loses the longevity of the prediluvian age.

Such is the Sumerian conception of the Fall of Man. His great loss consists in being deprived of extreme longevity and good health. The fall from primeval sinlessness is not mentioned here. But we infer from one of the passages that sin had already entered into the souls of men before the flood and caused Enki to send the great catastrophe. In a real sense, therefore, our epic contains both the fall from purity and the fall from longevity. The latter is brought about by the eating of the tree, and this was considered the greater disaster. We now find that man is fallen on toil and disease. Wherefore the gods sent him patrons of healing, of plants and various arts, to comfort him and aid him in his struggle for existence.

KRAMER: This Enki myth tells an intricate and as yet somewhat obscure tale which involves the paradise-land Dilmun, perhaps to be identified with ancient India. Briefly sketched, the plot of this Sumerian paradise myth, which treats of gods, not humans, runs as follows.

Dilmun is a land that is "pure," "clean," and "bright," a "Land of the Living" which knows neither sickness nor death. What is lacking, however, is the fresh water so essential to animal and plant life. The great Sumerian water god Enki, therefore, orders Utu, the sun god, to fill it with fresh water brought up from the earth. Dilmun is thus turned into a divine garden, green with fruit-laden fields and meadows.

In this paradise of the gods eight plants are made to sprout by Ninhursag, the great mother goddess of the Sumerians, perhaps the original Mother Earth. She succeeds in bringing these plants into being only after an intricate process involving three generations of goddesses, all conceived from the water god and born, so our poem repeatedly underlines, after only nine days of gestation and without the slightest pain or travail. But probably because Enki wanted to taste them, his messenger, the two-faced god Isimud, plucks these precious plants one by one and gives them to his master Enki, who proceeds to eat each in turn. Whereupon the angered Ninhursag pronounces upon him the curse of death. Evidently to make sure that she does not change her mind and relent, she disappears from among the gods.

Enki's health begins to fail; eight of his organs become sick. As Enki sinks fast, the great gods sit in the dust. Enlil, the air god and king of the gods, seems unable to cope with the situation, when up speaks the fox. If properly rewarded, says the fox, he will bring Ninhursag back. As good as his word, the fox succeeds in some way—the relevant passage is destroyed—in having the mother goddess return to the gods and heal the dying water god. She seats him by her vulva, and after inquiring which eight organs of his body ache, she brings into existence eight corresponding healing deities, and Enki is brought back to life and health.

As can be seen from my synopsis of the myth, there is not a word about the fall of man from primeval sinlessness, or of a flood that raged for nine months and caused man to dissolve in the waters "like tallow and fat." But although the myth depicts events in a divine paradise, not a human one, it does have a number of parallels to the biblical story, as well as a possible explanation for the creation of Eve from the rib of man; the interested reader can follow the relevant demonstration in *The Sumerians*.

6
The Heroes: Sumerian Epics

Though most of my scholarly efforts in the 1930s and 1940s were devoted to the gods of Sumer, I did not neglect its heroes. As early as 1936, I had published the first half of a Gilgamesh tale, and in the years that followed I prepared tentative reconstructions and translations of several more Gilgamesh poems. But Gilgamesh was not the only Sumerian hero; he was preceded by at least two others who with their bold deeds had captured the imagination of the Sumerian bards. In fact, as I came to realize in the course of this concentrated research on their epic tales, the Sumerians very early in their history had passed through a political and literary stage of development generally known as a Heroic Age, and this shed new light on the "Sumerian problem" that has troubled historians of Mesopotamia for many a decade.

Generally speaking, I am not one who likes to depend on the theories of fellow academics. Regarding Sumerian epic poetry, however, I have found the work of the British scholars H. Munro Chadwick and Nora Kershaw Chadwick both stimulating and illuminating. In their monumental three-volume *Growth of Literature,* published during the years 1932–1940, the Chadwicks' conclusions, based on a close examination of the more important world literatures, written and oral, ancient and modern, primitive and advanced, are convincing and dependable, though they are stated in a low key that tends to disappoint readers who prefer more impassioned writing. The Chadwicks knew nothing, of course, of Sumerian epic poetry, and yet their scholarly research has proved invaluable for a clearer understanding of its place in man's literary and cultural history. This is especially true of Sumer's Heroic Age, whose existence would probably never have been detected were it not for the Chadwicks. But before turning to the Heroic Age, let me first sketch briefly what is known of Sumerian epic literature, and my role in its recovery over the years.

In 1933–1934, when I was editing Chiera's *Sumerian Epics and Myths,* I had occasion to study his copies of some thirty tablets and fragments inscribed with parts of quite a number of epic tales whose protagonists were the heroes Enmerkar, Lugalbanda, and Gilgamesh. Of the first two, almost nothing was known. Gilgamesh, on the other hand, was then one of the most celebrated and attractive figures in cuneiform literature. His very name had cast a spell on more than one cuneiformist, and his character, adventures, and frustrations were analyzed in great detail. Gilgamesh's popularity, however, did not stem from Sumerian literary sources but from a long, loosely integrated poem commonly known as the "Epic of Gilgamesh," the text of which had been pieced together over the decades from tablets and fragments inscribed in the Semitic Assyrian language.

As early as 1862, the Englishman George Smith, who had been studying the thousands of tablets and fragments brought to the British Museum from the mounds covering ancient Nineveh, read a paper before the then recently organized Society of Biblical Archaeology in which he announced the discovery and decipherment of a version of the Deluge myth which showed marked resemblances to the biblical Flood story. Not long after this announcement, Smith realized on further study that this Deluge myth was but a small part of a long poem that the tablets referred to as the Gilgamesh cycle. According to the ancient scribes, it consisted of twelve songs or cantos of about three hundred lines each. Each of the cantos was inscribed on a separate tablet in the Nineveh library of King Ashurbanipal. The Deluge story formed the major part of the eleventh tablet.

Since the days of George Smith quite a number of new pieces of the Semitic "Epic of Gilgamesh" have been excavated and identified, some dating back to the seventeenth and eighteenth centuries B.C., more than a millennium earlier than the Nineveh tablets. Ancient translations of parts of the poem into Hurrian, as well as into the Indo-European Hittite language, have been found on tablets excavated in Asia Minor that date to the second half of the second millennium B.C. It is thus evident that the Assyrian "Epic of Gilgamesh" was studied, translated, and imitated in ancient times all over the Near East. Today, more than half of its approximately thirty-five hundred lines have been recovered, and a superb edition of all the material available at the time was published in 1930 by another Englishman, R. Campbell Thompson. Several English translations of the poem have been published in the past four decades: one of the more perceptive and trustworthy is that of Ephraim Speiser in *Ancient Near Eastern Texts*.

Although the "Epic of Gilgamesh" is written in the Semitic Assyrian language, it has long been evident to cuneiformists that some of its contents were of Sumerian origin. The names of the two protagonists, Gilgamesh and Enkidu, have a Sumerian ring. The parents of Gilgamesh bear good Sumerian names. Virtually all the deities who play a significant role in the epic belong to the Sumerian pantheon. Moreover, between the years 1911 and 1930, when Thompson published the Assyrian "Epic of Gilgamesh," eleven tablets and fragments inscribed with portions of Sumerian Gilgamesh tales had been copied and published by several scholars. Though at the time little could be made of their meager contents, it was nevertheless apparent that several of the episodes in the Gilgamesh epic were of Sumerian origin. Indeed, most cuneiformists had come to the conclusion that there had existed a Sumerian original for the work in its entirety, that sooner or later we could expect to recover a long Sumerian poem which, in spite of some variation in form and content, would so closely resemble the Semitic epic that it would be readily recognized as its Sumerian precursor. In the 1930s, when I began the intensive study of the Sumerian Gilgamesh material, I was of the same opinion, and it took almost a decade of concentrated research to realize that this was not so, that while some of its episodes were of Sumerian origin, the "Epic of Gilgamesh" as a whole was largely a Semitic creation.

What led me to this conclusion was not a sudden flash of profound insight or brilliant perception but the slow, steady accumulation of new inscriptional data and evidence. In addition to the eleven Sumerian Gilgamesh pieces known to earlier scholars, there were at my disposal about seventy-five tablets and fragments, the majority of which were still unpublished: fifteen identified and copied by Chiera that were published in *Sumerian Epics and Myths* and sixty still unpublished pieces that I had identified and studied, in large part copied in Istanbul and Philadelphia. These new texts provided a much fuller picture of the Sumerian Gilgamesh material than that previously envisioned, and it became possible to compare the Sumerian and Assyrian poems in much greater detail and with more promising results. This I did in a paper published in 1944 entitled "The Epic of Gilgamesh and Its Sumerian Sources," a comparative study that provided literary historians and critics with the oldest known example of literary borrowing, together with a detailed analysis of the editing procedures utilized by poets who were also creative redactors.

I began the comparison of the Sumerian and Semitic Gilgamesh material with a carefully prepared analysis of the contents of the Assyrian "Epic of Gilgamesh." The poem begins with an introductory passage that portrays Gilgamesh as an all-knowing, world-wandering king who had built the walls of Erech, one of Sumer's renowned cities, and who eulogizes these walls in a rhetorical address to the reader or hearer. Then begins the narrative proper. Gilgamesh, king of Erech, is a restless hero, unrivaled and undisciplined, who tyrannizes the citizens of his city. Especially oppressive are his demands for the satisfaction of his Rabelaisian appetite for sex. The Erechites cry out in anguish to the gods, who, realizing that Gilgamesh acts the tyrant because he has still to find his match among his fellow humans, direct the mother goddess Aruru to put an end to this intolerable situation. She proceeds to fashion from clay the powerful Enkidu, who, naked and long-haired, innocent of all human relations, spends his days and nights with the wild beasts of the steppe. It is Enkidu, more brute than man, whom the gods have destined to subdue Gilgamesh's arrogance and discipline his despotic spirit. First, however, Enkidu must be humanized, a process that is primarily a woman's task. An Erechite courtesan arouses and satisfies his sexual hunger. As a result he loses in physical stature and brute strength but gains immensely in intellect and spirit. The sexual experience has made Enkidu wise and knowing; the wild beasts no longer recognize him as their own. Patiently the courtesan proceeds to guide him in the civilized arts of eating, drinking, and dressing.

The humanized Enkidu is now ready to meet Gilgamesh, who had already learned in his dreams of the coming of Enkidu. Eager to display his unrivaled position in Erech, he arranges a nocturnal orgy and invites Enkidu to attend. But Enkidu is repelled by Gilgamesh's sexual cravings and blocks his way to prevent him from entering the house appointed for the unseemly gathering. Thereupon the two titans join in combat: Gilgamesh the sophisticated townsman and Enkidu the simple plainsman. Enkidu seems to be getting the best of his rival when, for some unstated reason, Gilgamesh's wrath leaves him, and the two heroes kiss and embrace. Out of this bitter struggle is born a deep friendship, loyal, lasting, and rich in heroic achievement, a comradeship that has been echoed in Hebrew, Greek, and medieval literature.

Enkidu, though, is not happy in Erech; its carefree, sensuous life is making a weakling of him. Gilgamesh, too, has become disaffected with his effete existence and reveals to Enkidu an adventurous plan to journey to the far-distant cedar forest, to kill its terrifying guardian

Huwawa, fell the cedars, and "destroy all that is evil from the land." Enkidu, who in his early savage days had wandered freely through the cedar forest, warns Gilgamesh of the mortal danger of the undertaking. Gilgamesh mocks his fears; it is enduring fame that he longs for, not a prolonged but unheroic existence. He confers with the elders of Erech, obtains the approval of the sun god, the patron deity of all travelers, and has the smiths of Erech forge gigantic weapons for himself and Enkidu. Thus prepared, they set out on their adventure. After a wearisome journey they arrive at the dazzlingly beautiful cedar forest, kill Huwawa, and fell the cedars.

Adventure leads to adventure. Upon their return to Erech, Ishtar, the tutelary deity of the city, the goddess of love and lust, becomes infatuated with the well-formed, physically attractive Gilgamesh. With the promise of many rich favors, she attempts to induce Gilgamesh to satisfy her sexual desires. But Gilgamesh is no longer the undisciplined tyrant of former days. Well aware of her promiscuity and faithlessness, he mocks her offer and spurns it, whereupon Ishtar, deeply offended, tries to persuade An, the heaven god, to send down the Bull of Heaven to destroy Gilgamesh and his city. An at first refuses, but when Ishtar threatens to bring up the dead from the Nether World, he consents. The Bull of Heaven descends to earth and begins to lay waste the city of Erech, slaughtering its warriors by the hundreds. Gilgamesh and Enkidu battle the beast and in a mighty concerted effort succeed in killing him.

The two heroes have now reached the pinnacle of their career, and the city of Erech rings with songs celebrating their exalted deeds. However, inexorable fate brings a sudden and cruel end to their happiness. Because of his part in the killing of Huwawa and the Bull of Heaven, Enkidu is sentenced by the gods to a premature death. Following a twelve-day illness, Enkidu breathes his last while his friend Gilgamesh looks on helplessly, stunned with grief. His anguished spirit becomes obsessed with one doubly bitter thought: Enkidu, his dear companion, is dead, and he is destined to meet the same fate. He now finds little comfort in the fame and glory of his past heroic deeds. It is tangible, physical immortality which his tormented spirit craves. He must seek and find the secret of eternal life.

As Gilgamesh may have learned from the sages of Erech, there was but one individual who succeeded in obtaining immortality. This was Utanapishtim, the wise and pious king of ancient Shuruppak, and he had been transported by the gods to the far-distant divine land that no mortal could hope to reach. Gilgamesh, determined to make his way to Utanapishtim to try to persuade him to reveal his precious secret, wanders long and far over mountain and steppe, ever exposed to wild beasts and famine. He crosses the primeval sea and the "waters of death." Finally, weary and emaciated, his hair long and shaggy, his filthy body covered with raw animal hides, the once-proud ruler of Erech stands before Utanapishtim, eager to learn the secret of eternal life.

But Utanapishtim's words are far from reassuring. The immortal king of Shuruppak narrates at great length the story of the destructive Deluge that the gods had sent against the earth in order to exterminate all living creatures. He, too, would surely have perished, had it not been for the sheltering boat he had built on the advice of the water god Ea, the god of wisdom. As for the gift of eternal life, it was the gods who willed its bestowal upon him. But there was no god who would do the same for Gilgamesh, and he, Utanapishtim, could do nothing for him. Despairing of his fate, Gilgamesh is about to return empty-handed to Erech when a ray of hope appears. At the urging of his wife, Utanapishtim reveals to Gilgamesh the whereabouts of the plant of eternal youth lying at the bottom of the sea. Gilgamesh dives to the floor of the sea, brings up the plant, and proceeds joyfully to Erech. But while he is bathing in a well, a snake carries off the plant of eternal youth. Exhausted and bitterly disappointed, he returns to Erech to find what comfort he can in its enduring walls.

So much for the contents of the first eleven cantos of the Assyrian "Epic of Gilgamesh." (The ancient scribes tacked on a twelfth canto, which is described later.) On close examination it is clear that the episodes recounted between the prologue eulogizing Erech's impressive walls and the epilogue depicting Gilgamesh's melancholy return to these same walls form a fairly well-integrated plot structure: the tyranny of Gilgamesh, the creation of Enkidu as his match and peer, the sexually motivated humanizing of the beast-like savage, the forging of the bond of friendship between the two heroes, the adventurous journey to the cedar forest, the struggle with the Bull of Heaven, the death of Enkidu, Gilgamesh's perilous journey to Utanapishtim in quest of the secret of eternal life, the Flood story, the loss of the plant of eternal youth. Before me was a problem: How does all this compare with the Sumerian Gilgamesh texts? Did the Sumerians have an "Epic of Gilgamesh," with an integrated plot structure between an introductory prologue and a concluding epilogue? If not, could any of the episodes and tales recounted in the Assyrian poem be traced to Sumerian prototypes? To try to answer these questions, I turn to the Sumerian Gilgamesh material.

Between the years 1934 and 1943, I pieced together the available text of five Sumerian Gilgamesh tales varying in length from just over one hundred lines to more than four hundred: "Gilgamesh and Agga of Kish," "Gilgamesh and the Land of the Living," "Gilgamesh and the

Bull of Heaven," "Gilgamesh, Enkidu, and the Nether World," and "The Death of Gilgamesh." Each of these tales consists of a plot built around a single central episode, and there is not a trace of any connection between them. The answer to the first question was therefore self-evident: there was no Sumerian original for the Assyrian "Epic of Gilgamesh" in its entirety. The answer to the second question, whether there were Sumerian prototypes for any of the individual episodes in the Assyrian epic, was much more complex and necessitated a thorough examination of the plots of each of the Sumerian Gilgamesh poems.

"Gilgamesh and Agga of Kish" is a poem of 115 lines that tells the following story. Gilgamesh, the king of Erech, has just received an ultimatum from Agga, the king of Kish, that he and his city must submit to Agga as their overlord or take the consequences. Before giving his answer, Gilgamesh goes before the assembly of the elders of his city with an urgent plea to take up arms rather than yield to Agga's demands. The elders, however, are of a different mind: they would rather submit to Kish and enjoy peace. Their decision displeases Gilgamesh, who then goes before the assembly of the young arms-bearing males of Erech and repeats his plea. This assembly decides to fight rather than submit. Gilgamesh is delighted and seems confident of victory in the expected struggle. Soon Agga besieges Erech, and the Erechites are dumbfounded. The meaning of the remainder of the poem was not clear to me at the time, but it seemed that Gilgamesh in some way succeeded in gaining the friendship of Agga, and the siege was lifted without a struggle. There is not a trace of this tale in the Assyrian epic of Gilgamesh; one must conclude that it was either unknown to or deliberately ignored by the authors of the Semitic poem.

"Gilgamesh and the Land of the Living," a poem whose initial 174 lines I pieced together, has as its motivating theme man's anxiety about death and its sublimation in the notion of an immortal name. In brief, the lord Gilgamesh, as he is designated throughout this poem, realizing that like all mortals he must die sooner or later, is determined to "raise up a name" for himself before he meets his destined end. He therefore sets his heart on journeying to the unnamed far-distant "Land of the Living" with the intention of felling its cedars and bringing them to Erech. He informs his loyal slave and constant companion Enkidu of his proposed undertaking. The latter advises him first to acquaint the sun god Utu with his plan, for it is Utu who has charge of the cedar land.

Acting on this advice, Gilgamesh brings offerings to the sun god and pleads for his support of the contemplated journey to the "Land of the Living." At first Utu seems skeptical of Gilgamesh's qualifications, but

Gilgamesh repeats his plea in more persuasive language, and Utu mercifully decides to help him by immobilizing the seven vicious weather demons that might menace him on his way. Overjoyed, Gilgamesh gathers fifty volunteers from his city Erech, unattached men who have neither house nor mother and who are ready to follow him no matter how grave the danger. After weapons of bronze and wood have been prepared for him and his companions, with the help of Utu they cross the seven mountains that separate Erech from the Land of the Living.

Just what happened immediately after the crossing of the seven mountains was not clear to me at the time, since the relevant passage was very fragmentary. When the text is intelligible again, Gilgamesh has fallen into a heavy sleep from which he is awakened only after considerable time and effort. Thoroughly aroused by this delay, he swears by his mother, the goddess Ninsun, and by his father, the deified hero Lugalbanda, that he will enter the "Land of the Living" and brook no interference from either man or god. Enkidu pleads with him to turn back, for the guardian of the cedars is the fearful monster Huwawa whose destructive attack none can withstand. But Gilgamesh will have none of this caution. Convinced that with Enkidu's help no harm can befall either of them, he bids his servant to put away fear and go forward with him to achieve their goal.

Spying Gilgamesh, Enkidu, and their fifty followers from his cedar house is the monster Huwawa, who makes frantic efforts to drive them off. But in vain. After cutting down seven trees, Gilgamesh and his band arrive at Huwawa's inner chamber. At the very first and seemingly light blow by Gilgamesh, Huwawa is overcome with fright and appeals to Gilgamesh not to kill him. Gilgamesh would like to act the generous victor and in riddle-like phrases suggests to Enkidu that Huwawa be set free. But Enkidu is fearful of the consequences and advises against such action. Following an indignant rebuke by Huwawa of Enkidu's meanness, the two heroes cut off the monster's head and bring his corpse before the god Enlil. At that time, the end of the poem was still missing, and the final outcome was unknown.

It was quite obvious that this Sumerian tale was the prototype of the cedar forest episode in the Semitic poem. But when the two versions are put side by side, it becomes clear that they have only the bare skeleton of the story in common. In both versions Gilgamesh decides to journey to the cedar forest; he is accompanied by Enkidu; he seeks and obtains the protection of the sun god; they arrive at their destination; the cedars are felled; Huwawa is killed. But the two versions differ greatly in detail, arrangement, and emphasis.

"Gilgamesh and the Bull of Heaven" relates how the goddess Inanna (the Semitic Ishtar) made passionate love proposals to Gilgamesh, promising to shower him with gifts and favors, but he rejects her advances. Offended, the goddess goes before the heaven god An demanding to be given the Bull of Heaven. An finally yields to her request after she threatens to go before the other gods. Inanna sends the Bull of Heaven to ravage the city of Erech. The end of the poem is missing, but I have little doubt that it describes the victory of Gilgamesh and Enkidu and the death of the monster.

The contents of this Sumerian poem and its Semitic counterpart show an unmistakable resemblance in the broad outlines of the plot: the goddess's wooing of Gilgamesh, his rejection of her, the giving of the Bull of Heaven reluctantly, the despoiling of Erech, and the slaying of the beast. In details, however, the two versions vary almost beyond recognition. The gifts offered by the goddess are quite different in the two versions. Gilgamesh's rejection speech in the Assyrian epic is full of learned allusions to myths and proverbs, but it is much shorter in the Sumerian version. The conversations between the goddess and the heaven god bear little similarity in the two versions. Nor is there reason to doubt that the now lost concluding details of the Sumerian poem had but little in common with those of the Semitic epic.

"Gilgamesh, Enkidu, and the Nether World," the poem whose initial lines helped me unravel some of the Sumerian cosmogonic ideas, is one of the more complex Gilgamesh tales. It depicts the hero as a chivalrous knight, an oppressive bully, a despairing whiner, a counseling sage, a loyal master, and also a melancholy mortal worried about life in the Nether World. From the tablets and fragments available to me at the time, I reconstructed the plot as follows. Once upon a time a *huluppu*-tree (perhaps a willow) planted on the bank of the Euphrates and nurtured by its waters was violently attacked by the South Wind and flooded by the waters of the Euphrates. The goddess Inanna, walking by, took the tree in her hand and brought it to her city Erech, where she planted it in her holy garden. There she tended it most carefully, for she planned that when the tree had grown big she would make of its wood a chair and a couch.

Years passed, and the tree grew large, but Inanna found herself unable to cut it down, for at its base the snake who "knows no charm" had built its nest; in its crown the monstrous *Imdugud*-bird had placed its young; in its middle Lilith had built her house. And so Inanna, the lighthearted and ever joyful maid, shed bitter tears.

As dawn broke, and her brother, the sun god Utu, came forth from his sleeping chamber, Inanna tearfully repeated to him all that had befallen her *huluppu*-tree. Immediately Gilgamesh, who presumably had overheard her plaint, came to her aid. He donned his armor, weighing fifty minas, and with his ax that weighed seven talents and seven minas, he slew the snake at the base of the tree. Whereupon the *Imdugud*-bird fled with its young to the mountain, while Lilith tore down her house and fled to the desolate places. Gilgamesh and the men of Erech who accompanied him then cut down the tree and gave it to Inanna for her chair and couch.

What did Inanna do? From the base of the tree she fashioned a *pukku* (perhaps a drum), and from the crown a *mikku* (drumstick). There followed an obscure passage that seems to describe certain tyrannical acts performed by Gilgamesh with the *pukku* and the *mikku,* which brought suffering and woe to the citizens of Erech. When the story became intelligible once again, it continued with the assertion that "because of the outcry of the young maidens," the *pukku* and the *mikku* fell into the Nether World. Gilgamesh put in his hand and his foot to retrieve them but was unable to reach them. He then seated himself at the gate of the Nether World and lamented his lost *pukku* and *mikku,* crying in despair for someone to bring them up. At this, his servant Enkidu volunteered to descend to the Nether World and retrieve the lost objects but was warned by Gilgaemsh about a number of taboos that he must guard against, lest the "cry of the Nether World" seize him. But Enkidu, disregarding the instructions of his master, transgressed the taboos and, held fast by the cry of the Nether World, was unable to ascend to earth. The distressed Gilgamesh now went to Nippur and asked Enlil for help, but in vain. He then repeated his plea, at Eridu, to Enki, who responded favorably and commanded the sun god Utu to open a vent in the Nether World to allow the shade of Enkidu to ascend to earth. Master and servant embraced, whereupon Gilgamesh questioned Enkidu in great detail about what he had seen in the Nether World. With this depressing colloquy, the tale that began with the joyous days of creation comes to a melancholy end.

On comparing this poem with the Assyrian "Epic of Gilgamesh," I noted that there was not a trace of it in the first eleven Assyrian cantos. In fact, there is a serious divergence between the Sumerian and Assyrian tales, the Sumerian work attributing the death of Enkidu to his breaking the taboos of the Nether World and thus contradicting the Assyrian version that ascribes the death of Enkidu to his role in the killing of Huwawa and the Bull of Heaven. But when I turned to the twelfth canto, I was amazed to find that it was simply a verbatim translation into Assyrian of the second half of the Sumerian poem. Its contents are totally out of keeping with Assyrian epics as a whole; it was tacked on to the preceding eleven cantos probably for no better reason than the predilection of the ancients for the number twelve, a favorite number to the Sumerians as well as to the other peoples of the ancient Near East.

The fifth of the available Sumerian Gilgamesh tales, "The Death of Gilgamesh," is still very fragmentary. From its meager extant contents, only the following is recognizable: Gilgamesh still seems to be in quest of immortality. He is informed, however, that eternal life is impossible to obtain. Kingship, prominence, heroism in battle—all these have been decreed for him, but not immortality. Fragmentary as it is, this part of the poem shows an indubitable source relationship to the episode in the Assyrian epic concerned with Gilgamesh's vain quest for immortality. The Sumerian poem, however, concludes with a poignant depiction of the death of Gilgamesh, an event that has no counterpart in the Assyrian version.

So much for a comparison of the Assyrian and Sumerian Gilgamesh epic tales. Clearly a number of episodes in the former had their counterpart in the latter: the journey to the cedar forest, the struggle with the Bull of Heaven, the quest for immortality theme. But the Assyrian versions are no slavish reproductions of their Sumerian prototypes; only the broad outlines of the plot are held by the two in common. Moreover, the Semitic editors of the epic, in their efforts to construct a unified but variegated plot structure, did not confine themselves to the Sumerian epic tales but felt free to turn to other Sumerian literary genres in their search for theme, motif, and story.

Take, for example, the Flood story that constitutes the major part of the eleventh canto of the "Epic of Gilgamesh." This is a replica of the Sumerian Flood story that is part of a myth that has no connection whatever with Gilgamesh. But the Assyrian writers deemed it appropriate for their epic and found a suitable location for it in the eleventh canto. The manner in which they did this can be followed step by step and provides us with a valuable clue for determining some of the procedures employed in ancient literary borrowing. The Sumerian myth actually consists of two parts: the introduction, which includes passages concerned with the creation of man, vegetation, and animals, the origin of kingship, and the founding of at least five antediluvian cities, is followed by the Flood story and the immortalization of the divinely favored Ziusudra, the Sumerian prototype of the Semitic Utanapishtim. It is the second half of the myth which the Assyrian poets fitted into the eleventh canto of their epic, when the weary Gilgamesh comes before Utanapishtim and questions him concerning the secret of eternal life. They therefore omitted altogether the introductory passages of the Su-

Before the Ishtar Gate at Babylon.

merian poem as not germane to their theme and retained only the Flood and immortalization episodes. But since in their epic it was Utanapishtim himself, rather than some anonymous author, who was reciting these events, they had to change all relevant grammatical forms from third person to first. In addition, they introduced numerous variations of detail. In the Sumerian poem, Ziusudra is depicted as a humble, god-fearing man, but his Semitic counterpart, Utanapishtim, is not so described. The Assyrian version is much more lavish with details concerning the building of the boat and the nature and violence of the Flood than its Sumerian counterpart. The latter also omits the motif of the sending of birds to test the degree of water abatement that is recorded in the Assyrian version, and has its biblical echo.

Nor, in all probability, is the Flood story the only case of a Sumerian episode or theme in no way connected with Gilgamesh that has found its way into the Assyrian Gilgamesh epic; no doubt others will be uncovered in the course of time. On the other hand, there are quite a number of themes, motifs, and stylistic features that are certainly Semitic rather than Sumerian in origin: the introductory passage with its rhapsodic description of the walls of Erech; the interrelated chain of events following the creation of Enkidu that culminated in the friendship between the two heroes; the death and burial of Enkidu that motivated dramatically Gilgamesh's despairing quest for immortality. Above all, the integrated climactic plot structure of the epic as a whole, the forceful and fateful episodic drama of the restless, adventurous hero and his inevitable disappointment and disillusionment, is definitely a Semitic rather than a Sumerian development and achievement; Sumerian narratives tend to ramble rather disconnectedly and monotonously, with little variation in emphasis and tone, and virtually no sense of climax. In a very deep sense, therefore, the "Epic of Gilgamesh" may be characterized as a Semitic rather than a Sumerian creation.

Since 1944, the year of the publication of "The Epic of Gilgamesh and Its Sumerian Sources," quite a number of additional Sumerian Gilgamesh tablets and fragments have become available. I stayed several months in Istanbul in 1946 as Annual Professor of the American Schools of Oriental Research and for the better part of 1952 worked as Fulbright Research Professor in Turkey. During the course of these two sojourns I identified and copied close to two hundred Sumerian literary pieces from the Nippur collection of the Museum of the Ancient Orient, among which were twenty-eight inscribed with parts of one or another of the Gilgamesh tales. In 1952–1953, a joint Oriental Institute-University Museum expedition to Nippur, then in its third season, excavated hundreds of Sumerian literary tablets and fragments, and among these were a half dozen dealing with Gilgamesh. In 1957 I traveled to Jena, in East Germany, to study Sumerian tablets in the Hilprecht collection of the Friedrich-Schiller University, which included two pieces inscribed with parts of "Gilgamesh and Agga," but more of that later. Several consecutive summers, beginning in 1960, were spent at the British Museum collaborating with C. J. Gadd, one of its former keepers, identifying the contents of several hundred Sumerian literary tablets and fragments excavated at Ur, most of which he had copied before the outbreak of the Second World War. Among these were eleven of Gilgamesh. With this new material at my disposal I was able to revise my earlier translations for *The Sumerians: Their History, Culture, and Character,* published in 1963. As for the definitive edition of the Gilgamesh epic tales, as the years passed and the shadow of retirement began to loom, I realized that I would be unable to accomplish this highly detailed, time-consuming task. I therefore turned over all my copies, notes, and tentative transliterations and translations to my former student Aaron Shaffer at the Hebrew University in Jerusalem, who will no doubt produce in the course of time a Gilgamesh *magnum opus* that will make some of my Gilgamesh contributions outdated. All in all, however, it is my conviction that the conclusions and suggestions proposed in "The Epic of Gilgamesh and Its Sumerian Sources" will stand the test of time.

But enough of the brave, adventurous Gilgamesh and his poignant fate; after all, he was not the only Sumerian hero celebrated in story and song. Two other heroes, Enmerkar and Lugalbanda, who preceded Gilgamesh as kings of Erech, inspired the Sumerian poets to compose at least four fairly long poems exalting their deeds and prowess, although the Semitic poets of later days seem to have completely ignored them. I first made their acquaintance in 1934, when I read among Chiera's copies twenty tablets and fragments that he had identified as belonging to epic poems concerned with Enmerkar and Lugalbanda; also among his notes I found a list of Enmerkar and Lugalbanda texts published by several earlier scholars, as well as the museum numbers of some duplicating pieces that he had identified in the University Museum but had not had time to copy. In 1938–1939, when working in Istanbul, I identified two small fragments that were part of Enmerkar and Lugalbanda texts, and, studying the Nippur tablets in the basement of the University Museum in the years 1940–1943, I identified, with the help of Chiera's list of duplicates, another score of tablets and fragments inscribed with Enmerkar and Lugalbanda epic poems. Now I was in a position to make tentative transliterations and translations of the relevant material, published and unpublished.

In 1946 I published in the *Proceedings of the American Philosophical Society* an article which provided the first survey of the contents of four Enmerkar and Lugalbanda epic tales. Since it was the recovery of these four heroic poems that, together with the five Gilgamesh tales, led me to postulate the existence of a Sumerian Heroic Age, let me sketch briefly their contents as I reconstructed them at that time.

"Enmerkar and the Lord of Aratta" probably consisted of over five hundred lines, of which only two hundred were well preserved. Obviously, the sketch of its contents in 1946 was quite tentative in character, to be filled out and corrected as new material was uncovered. The action of the poem centers about Enmerkar's successful efforts to obtain submission and allegiance from a lord of Aratta who remains unnamed throughout the poem. To achieve his end, Enmerkar wins the favor of the god Enki with the promise that if Aratta submits to Erech, he will have the inhabitants of Aratta transport stones from the mountains to build a great shrine for him and that in numerous other ways he will exalt the god and his shrines. He then dispatches a herald to the lord of Aratta with instructions to prevail upon him to recognize Enmerkar as his overlord. He is to achieve this by extolling Enmerkar as the favorite of Enki, and especially by reciting to him the "spell of Enki."

The herald, after a long journey involving the crossing of seven mountains, finally arrives in Aratta and presents Enmerkar's demands to its lord. The latter at first refuses, since such action would result in a loss of prestige for the goddess Inanna, whose protégé he seems to be, but the herald overcomes his reluctance with the promise that his patron deity, Inanna, will be made queen of the temple Eanna in Erech, whereupon the lord of Aratta is ready to yield. This is not the end of the poem, however. After a considerable break in the text, we find the lord of Aratta addressing his own herald and instructing him to go to Enmerkar and invite him to visit Aratta, for before actually bowing down to Enmerkar as his overlord, he would first like to meet him face to face and debate the issue between them. And so Enmerkar starts on his long journey, accompanied by a considerable retinue. Before his actual arrival, however, Enmerkar once again dispatches his herald to the lord of Aratta with a message which seems to consist of a eulogy of his scepter and rule. The herald returns from Aratta with a reply whose import is obscure. Here the text breaks off altogether, with the end of the poem not yet in sight.

The next tale, "Ernmerkar and Ensukushsiranna," is also concerned with the submission of a lord of Aratta to Enmerkar. However, in this poem it is not Enmerkar who makes the first demands on his rival but the lord of Aratta who issues the challenge that leads to his own discomfiture. Moreover, since throughout this second Enmerkar poem the lord of Aratta is referred to by his actual name, Ensukushsiranna, it is not quite certain whether he is to be identified with the lord of Aratta who remained unnamed throughout the first Enmerkar poem. In 1946 only approximately one hundred well-preserved lines at the beginning and twenty-five lines at the very end of the text were extant. I reconstructed its contents as follows. Ensukushsiranna, the lord of Aratta, having decided to issue a challenge to Enmerkar, dispatched a herald to him with the demand that he submit to his overlordship. If he does so, the herald is to continue, he will be allowed to dwell with the goddess Inanna and lie with her on a fruitful couch; also, he will be allowed to eat of the *kurku*-bird with the other princes who recognize Ensukushsiranna as their suzerain. The herald delivers his message to Enmerkar, who promptly returns the challenge and contemptuously rejects the promised rewards. Upon hearing this, Ensukushsiranna gathers his council and informs them of Enmerkar's insolent attitude. The rest of the poem was almost entirely destroyed except for the very end that relates how Ensukushsiranna, for some unknown reason, is only too ready to take second place to Enmerkar, whom he extols as the beloved of Inanna and as a mighty lord who knows no rival.

"Lugalbanda and Enmerkar" is a poem of over four hundred lines whose contents I tentatively reconstructed. Lugalbanda, perhaps because he has set his heart on journeying to far-distant Aratta, is determined first to win the friendship of the fabulous *Imdugud*-bird which decrees the fates and utters "the word that none may transgress." While the bird is away, therefore, Lugalbanda goes to his nest and presents his young with fat, honey, and bread, paints their faces, and puts crowns on their heads. The *Imdugud*-bird, upon returning to his nest, is most gratified with the god-like treatment of his young and proclaims his readiness to bestow friendship and favor upon whatever god or man had done this gracious deed, whereupon Lugalbanda steps up to receive his reward. Accordingly, the *Imdugud*-bird, in a eulogistic passage replete with blessings, bids him go with head high to Aratta. Upon Lugalbanda's request he decrees a favorable journey for him and adds some pertinent advice which he is to repeat to no one, not even his most faithful followers. The bird now returns to his nest, while Lugalbanda goes back to his friends and informs them of his imminent journey. They try to dissuade him, claiming that it is a journey from which none return, since it involves the crossing of high mountains and the dreaded river of the Nether World. However, Lugalbanda is adamant and eagerly awaits his opportunity.

Now, in Erech, Lugalbanda's suzerain Enmerkar is in great distress. For many years past, the Semitic Martu had been ravaging the land and were now laying siege to Erech itself. Enmerkar therefore decides that he must get through a call for help to his "sister," the goddess Inanna of Aratta. But try as he will, he can find no one to undertake the dangerous journey to Aratta to deliver his message. This, then, seems to be Lugalbanda's moment; he bravely volunteers for the task. Upon Enmerkar's insistence, moreover, he swears that he will make the journey alone, unaccompanied by his followers. After receiving from Enmerkar the exact wording of the message, Lugalbanda again informs his friends of his impending journey. Again they try to dissuade him, but to no avail. He takes up his weapons, crosses the seven mountains that separate Aratta from Erech, and finally arrives with joyful step at his destination. He is welcomed warmly by the goddess Inanna of Aratta, and, upon her query as to what brought him all alone from Erech to Aratta, Lugalbanda repeats verbatim Enmerkar's message and call for help. Inanna's answer, which marks the end of the poem, is most obscure: it seems to involve a river and its rather unusual fish which Enmerkar is to catch; also certain water vessels which he is to fashion; and finally workers of metal and stone that he is to settle in his city. But just how all this will remove the threat of the Martu from Sumer or lift the siege of Erech is far from clear.

"Lugalbanda and Mt. Hurrum" probably also ran well over 400 lines. But in 1946, only about 350 lines were extant, and the beginning and end of the poem were missing altogether. From its fragmentary text I reconstructed the contents. In the course of a journey from Erech to Aratta, Lugalbanda and his followers arrive at Mt. Hurrum. There Lugalbanda falls ill. His companions, believing that he is soon to die, decide to leave without him, planning to pick up his dead body upon their return and carry it back to Erech for burial. To take care of his immediate wants, they leave him with a considerable quantity of food, water, and strong drink, as well as his weapons. Alone, sick, and forsaken, Lugalbanda prays to the sun god Utu, who sees to it that his health is restored by means of the "food of life" and the "water of life." Upon regaining his health, Lugalbanda appears to wander alone over the highland steppe, hunting its wildlife and gathering its uncultivated plants. Once, he dreams that he is commanded, perhaps by the sun god, to take up his weapons, hunt and kill a wild bull, and present its fat to the rising Utu; also to slaughter a kid and pour out its blood in a ditch, and its fat on the steppe. Upon awaking, Lugalbanda does exactly as bidden and, in addition, prepares a banquet for An, Enlil, Enki, and Ninhursag, the four leading deities of the Sumerian pantheon. The approximately 100 lines of extant text that follow seemed to contain a eulogy of the seven heavenly lights which help the moon god Nanna, the sun god Utu, and the planet Venus illuminate the cosmos.

Now that I had before me the contents of nine Sumerian epic tales revolving about three heroic figures, it became clear to me that early in their history the Sumerians experienced a period of social, political, and literary development deserving to be called a Heroic Age. I, therefore, began looking for parallels in the history of civilization, and in the Chadwicks' *Growth of Literature* mentioned above I found the answer. The Chadwicks had analyzed three ancient Indo-European Heroic Ages that seemed to me strikingly like that of the Sumerians: one which flourished on the mainland of Greece toward the very end of the second millennium B.C.; that of India, which probably dates only a century or so after the Greek; and the Teutonic Heroic Age, which dominated much of northern Europe from the fourth to the sixth century A.D. All three reveal a marked resemblance in social structure, governmental organization, religious concepts, and aesthetic expression; obviously they owe their origin and being to very similar social, political, and psychological factors. The Heroic Age of the Sumerians as revealed in their epic literature follows with remarkable closeness the culture pattern of the three Indo-European Heroic Ages, although it flowered about a millennium and a half before that of the Greeks, in the third millennium B.C.

As the Chadwicks concluded from their research, the Greek, Indian, and Teutonic periods, to judge from the relevant literary records, are essentially barbaric and have a number of salient features in common. The political unit consists of a petty kingdom ruled by a king or prince who obtains and holds his rule through military prowess. His mainstay in power consists of a comitatus, a retinue of armed, loyal followers who are prepared to do his bidding without question, no matter how foolhardy and dangerous the undertaking. There may be an assembly, but it is convened at the ruler's pleasure and serves only in an advisory and confirmatory capacity. The ruling kings and princes of the separate principalities carry on among themselves a lively and at times friendly and even intimate intercourse; they thus tend to develop into what may be termed an international aristocratic caste whose thoughts and acts have little in common with those of their subjects.

On the religious side, the three Indo-European Heroic Ages are characterized by the worship of anthropomorphic deities which to a large extent seem to be recognized everywhere throughout the various states and principalities. These gods form organized communities in a specially chosen locality, though, in addition, each god may have a special abode of his own. There are few traces of chthonic or spirit worship; at death, the soul travels to some distant locality which is conceived as a universal home and is not reserved for members of any particular community. Some of the heroes are conceived as descending from gods, but there is no trace of hero cults. All these features are shared to a large extent by the Heroic Age of Sumer as revealed in the Sumerian epic tales.

But the parallelism among the four Heroic Ages extends even further; indeed it is particularly revealing on the aesthetic plane, especially in the field of literature. For one of the notable achievements of all four ages consisted of the creation of oral heroic narratives in poetic form, which reflect and illuminate the spirit of the time and its temper. Impelled by the thirst for fame so characteristic of the ruling caste during a Heroic Age, the bards and minstrels attached to the court were moved to improvise and compose narrative poems or lays celebrating the adventures and achievements of those kings and princes whose experiences lent themselves to imaginative and sympathetic treatment. These epic tales, whose primary objective was to provide entertainment at the frequent court banquets and feasts, were recited no doubt to the accompaniment of harp and lyre.

Obviously, these early heroic lays have not survived in their original form, since their first composition took place during the Heroic Age itself when writing was either unknown or of little concern to the illiterate minstrel. The written epics we have of the Greek, Indian, and Teutonic Heroic Ages date from much later times, and consist of highly complex literary reworkings in which only a selected number of the earlier lays are imbedded, and these in greatly modified and expanded form. In Sumer there is good reason to believe that at least some of the early oral heroic lays were first inscribed on clay, some five to six centuries following the close of the Heroic Age, and then only after they had undergone substantial transformation at the hands of the literate poets.

As is well known, the written epics relating to the three Indo-European Heroic Ages show a number of striking similarities in form and content. In the first place, all the poems are concerned primarily with individuals—the deeds and exploits of the individual hero are the prime concern of the poet, not the fate or glory of the state or the community. Moreover, while no doubt a few of the experiences and adventures celebrated in the poems have some historical basis, the poet does not hesitate to introduce many unhistorical motifs and conventions, such as exaggerated notions of the hero's powers, ominous dreams, and the presence of divine beings with whom the heroes can communicate. Stylistically, the epic poems abound in static epithets, lengthy repetitions, and recurrent formulas, and certain types of descriptions tend to be overleisurely and unexpectedly detailed. Particularly noteworthy is the fact that all the epics devote very considerable space to speeches.

In all these respects the Sumerian heroic poetry follows closely the pattern of the Greek, Indian, and Teutonic epic material. Since it is rather improbable that a literary genre so individual in content, style, and technique was created and developed independently, and at different time intervals, in Sumer, Greece, India, and northern Europe, and since the Sumerian is by all odds the oldest of the four, it is not impossible, or perhaps not even improbable, that it is to Sumer that we may look for the origin of epic poetry—a possibility that is of some importance for the history of world literature.

As is often the case in scholarship, the advancement of a new, well-grounded, meaningful hypothesis may help to illuminate and resolve problems that at first glance seem totally unrelated to its substance. This turned out to be true of the Heroic Age hypothesis that I adduced from the Sumerian epic tales: it shed new light on a historical quandary that had plagued cuneiformists and archaeologists for many a decade and that on the surface seems to have no connection whatever with either the Sumerian Heroic Age or Sumerian epic literature. This is the so-called Sumerian problem, which may be briefly stated as follows: Were the Sumerians the first people to settle in lower Mesopotamia, or were they preceded there by one or more ethnic groups? There is general agreement that the Sumerians were in the region about 3000 B.C., when writing was introduced there. It is with respect to the earlier preliterate, that is, prehistoric, period that we find a serious conflict of views. To be sure, in the course of the past hundred years, the prehistoric levels of quite a number of important lower Mesopotamian sites have been excavated, and a very considerable quantity of early, preliterate remains have been brought to light. Unfortunately, these prehistoric finds have not resolved the Sumerian problem; rather they posed a new dilemma for the excavators, who had to decide whether these prehistoric remains belonged to the Sumerians or some pre-Sumerian ethnic group.

Theoretically, the solution of this dilemma might seem quite simple: all the archaeologist has to do is to compare these prehistoric remains with those known to be Sumerian and see if they are more or less identical. If they are, they belong to the Sumerians; if not, they belong to some prehistoric people who inhabited the land before the arrival of the Sumerians. In practice, however, this comparative analysis turns out to be so ambiguous and equivocal that it leads to two antithetical views which divided archaeologists into two diametrically opposite camps. One group, upon examining the material remains of the earlier, prehistoric period, concluded that while these remains differ considerably from those of the Sumerians, they can nevertheless be identified as prototypes from which the latter had developed over the centuries, and that therefore the Sumerians first settled in lower Mesopotamia. Another group, after analyzing the very same remains, arrived at exactly the opposite conclusion, claiming that although there were certain similarities between the prehistoric and the Sumerian artifacts, the differences between them are so significant that the former cannot possibly be attributed to the Sumerians and must belong to people who had preceded them—hence the Sumerians were not the first in the land.

As a result of the unavoidably subjective interpretation of the archaeological evidence, the solution of the Sumerian problem had more or less reached an impasse. To break the deadlock, it was essential to uncover evidence based on sources other than the ambiguous material remains dug up by the excavators. It was just such new, fresh evidence that was provided by the hypothesis of the existence of the Sumerian Heroic Age, which involves purely literary and historical sources, and not material artifacts. A comparative analysis of the factors responsible for the genesis and growth of the Sumerian Heroic Age with those of the three Indo-European Heroic Ages demonstrated beyond reasonable doubt that the Sumerians were not the first in the land but were preceded by a people who were more advanced culturally than the invading Sumerians. And once again the key to the solution came from the Chadwicks, who knew nothing about the Sumerians but a great deal about the ancient Indo-Europeans.

The Chadwicks, after establishing the salient features that characterized the Greek, Indian, and Teutonic Heroic Ages, turned their attention to the origin and development of these ages and came to the conclusion that they were the product of two significant historical events and cultural situations. In the first place, these Heroic Ages coincided with a period of national migrations, a *Völkerwanderungszeit*. Secondly, and more significantly, the peoples responsible for the Indo-European Heroic Ages—the Achaeans, the Aryans, and the Teutons—while still on a relatively primitive tribal level, had each come in contact with a civilized power in the process of disintegration. Particularly, they served as mercenaries in the military service of this power during its struggle for survival, they absorbed the military technique and, to a superficial extent, some of the cultural accomplishments of their far more civilized neighbors. It was when they finally broke through the frontiers of these civilized states and carved out kingdoms and principalities for themselves within their territories, amassing considerable wealth in the process, that they developed that rather adolescent cultural stage known as a Heroic Age.

With this Chadwickian analysis in mind, I turned to the Sumerian Heroic Age for comparable factors responsible for its genesis and growth. In the first place, it is reasonable to surmise that the Sumerian

Heroic Age must have coincided with a period of national migrations. But more important for the Sumerian problem is the postulate that analogous with the Indo-European Heroic Ages, the occupation of lower Mesopotamia by the Sumerians, which gave birth to their Heroic Age, must have marked the culminating stage in a historical process that had begun several centuries earlier, when lower Mesopotamia was still part of a power with a far more advanced civilization than that of the Sumerians living somewhere along its outer fringes. It is from this more civilized power that the relatively primitive Sumerians, no doubt largely as mercenaries, had absorbed some of the essentials of its military technique and its more superficial cultural attainments. Finally the Sumerians succeeded in breaking through the frontiers of this power, occupied much of its territory and amassed considerable wealth in the process. This period marks the flourishing of their Heroic Age. In short, not only were the Sumerians not the first settlers in lower Mesopotamia, they must have been preceded by a civilized power of some magnitude, one far more advanced culturally than the Sumerian invading hordes. As for what is generally spoken of as Sumerian civilization, that outstanding cultural composite which played so predominant a role in the ancient Near East, it resulted from five to six centuries of intellectual and spiritual growth following the rather callow Sumerian Heroic Age and was due no doubt to the fruitful application of the Sumerian genius to the material and spiritual heritage of the pre-Sumerian civilization.

More than a quarter century ago, in 1948, in a paper titled "New Light on the Early History of the Ancient Near East," I presented my Chadwickian views about the genesis of the Sumerian Heroic Age and its significance for the solution of the Sumerian problem. Since then much new material has accrued for the restoration of the texts of the four Enmerkar and Lugalbanda epic poems, primarily in the form of copies of tablets and fragments from the Nippur tablet collections of the Museum of the Ancient Orient and the University Museum, and from the 1951–1952 season of excavations at Nippur.

In 1952 I published a monograph entitled *Enmerkar and the Lord of Aratta: A Sumerian Epic Tale of Iraq and Iran* containing the text of the poem, over six hundred lines pieced together from twenty tablets and fragments, the most important of which was a twelve-column tablet I copied in Istanbul. Although it took me about a month to copy this single tablet, I remember it to this day with no little wonder and admiration. Roughly square and only nine inches by nine in size, smaller in area than a standard sheet of typewriter paper, the ancient scribe, writing in a minute but quite legible hand, succeeded in inscribing on its two sides over six hundred lines, ten times the number of lines contained in two ordinary typewritten pages. By utilizing all the new material that had become available before the year 1963, it was possible for me to prepare revised versions of all four Enmerkar and Lugalbanda poems and to publish them in *The Sumerians*. Since 1963, several new studies related to the two heroes have been published; fortunately, Sumerian epic literature has aroused the interest of younger cuneiformists. But none of the resulting corrections and additions have adversely affected the Heroic Age hypothesis and its historical significance. I am confident that these will stand the test of time.

7
The Kings: Sumerian Hymns

"After kingship had descended from heaven" begins a Sumerian document known to cuneiformists as the King List, which then proceeds to name five cities that existed before the Flood together with their eight fabulous kings that had ruled no less than 241,200 years. This King List, a panoramic compilation of the Sumerian royal dynasties from antediluvian days to about 1800 B.C., was edited in masterful detail by Thorkild Jacobsen, my colleague and contemporary, a "heroic" figure in cuneiform research; a translation of the document based on Jacobsen's study appears in *The Sumerians*. Its contents are a bizarre mixture of fact and fantasy, and it is often difficult to decide where the one begins and the other ends. But the King List is the only document that provides an overall dynastic framework, and if used with discrimination and understanding, it is a valuable historical tool.

The need for vigilant discrimination becomes evident from its very first words: "After kingship had descended from heaven," which seem to say that kingship had come full-blown on the political scene and had taken spontaneous root in one of the antediluvian city centers. Now that may well be what the unhistorically oriented pundits of those early credulous days actually believed to be true, but the modern scholar has good reason to assume that the institution of kingship did not come to Sumer till about 3000 B.C., when the struggle for power between the rival city-states grew ever more bitter and violent, and when the pressure from the "barbarians" to the east and west of Sumer made the selection of a "big man"—the literal meaning of the Sumerian word for king, *lugal*—a compelling necessity. Before that, and for some time after, political power was vested in the hands of the free citizens who in case of crucial decisions met in something like a bicameral assembly consisting of an upper house of elders, "senators" in our parlance, and a lower house of younger arms-bearing males.

A graphic example of this political procedure is found in the epic tale "Gilgamesh and Agga of Kish." When Gilgamesh, king of Erech, was confronted with an ultimatum by the king of Kish, rejection of which meant war, he felt bound first to obtain the approval of the citizenry as represented by the assembly of elders as well as the assembly of younger men. Here then in Erech—and no doubt this is true of other Sumerian cities for which no evidence is available at present—the king felt that in case of so grave a decision as war or peace, he had to consult its free citizens, and it is unlikely that he would have taken the drastic step of rejecting Agga's ultimatum had there been total disapproval. Kingship with its vast privileges and prerogatives only gradually became a hereditary institution, the very hallmark of civilization.

Returning to the King List, following the reigns of the kings of the five antediluvian cities, we find: "The Flood swept over everything. After the Flood had swept over everything, and kingship had [once again] descended from heaven, the city of Kish became the seat of kingship." Little did the ancient scholar who inscribed these lines dream that this innocent-sounding passage would provoke heated controversy among his colleagues working nearly four thousand years after he had departed for the Land of No Return. For what he seemed to say was that he knew of a real, historic, universal, catastrophic Deluge that had overwhelmed and destroyed not only Sumer but mankind as a whole, a statement that most modern historians hardly accept as credible. Still, there are a few who, especially in view of the biblical account of the Deluge that has been part of the Judaeo-Christian tradition for close to three thousand years, would like to think of it as an authentic event in the far distant past. Even among the sceptics, there are some who feel that there must be at least a kernel of truth in the Flood motif; it seems to have played too large a role in Near Eastern myth and legend for it to have been nothing but a fanciful fabrication.

To be sure, as far as Sumerian literature is concerned, up to the year 1964 the only significant inscriptional evidence bearing on the Flood was the Flood myth that culminated in the immortalization of Ziusudra, the pious king of Shuruppak. But in the summer of 1964, I was working in the Student Room of the Western Asiatic Antiquities Section of the British Museum when Edmond Sollberger, then assistant keeper of the section, brought me some sixty tablets bought by the museum many decades ago that were inscribed with a number of hitherto unknown Sumerian compositions. Among these were two beginning with Flood passages of considerable length. The first is inscribed with a myth concerning the birth of the *numun*-plant, the reedy rush that was utilized in many ways in the daily life of the Sumerians. Its initial lines, which set the scene for the tale as a whole, take us back to the days of the Flood:

> After the storm had brought the rains,
> After (all) built walls had been destroyed,
> After the raging tempest had brought the rains,
> After a second man had been raised up as rival against man,
> After the seed had been implanted—yes implanted,
> After the grain had been engendered—yes engendered,
> After the storm had said: "I will bring the rains,"
> After it had said: "I will bring down the rains on the built walls,"
> After the Flood had said: "I will wipe out everything—"
> Heaven commanded, Earth gave birth,
> Gave birth to the *numun*-plant,
> Earth gave birth, Heaven commanded,
> Gave birth to the *numun*-plant

Much of the remainder of this poem is still unintelligible. It seems to tell of the earth's desolation after the Flood; of the killing of the creature *kingia* (perhaps a personification of Labor) by the *numun*-plant; of the seizing of a raven by the goddess Inanna; of her husband Dumuzi, the shepherd god, whose stalls and sheepfolds were destroyed by the Flood.

The second document is even more intriguing—it purports to sketch in outline the history of the growth and development of the city of Lagash from earliest times to the days of Gudea, who began his reign about 2150 B.C. The introductory passage of this pseudo-historical composition concerns the Flood:

> After the Flood had wiped out everything,
> After the destruction of the lands had been completed,
> After mankind was made (to endure) forever,
> After the seed of mankind had been saved,
> After the blackheaded people (the Sumerians) had of themselves been
>   lifted high,
> After An and Enlil had called man by name,
> After *ensi*-ship had been established,
> But kingship . . . had not yet descended from heaven.

With this new Flood documentation added to the long-known Flood myth, it is justifiable to conclude that the Sumerian bards and poets knew of a catastrophic deluge that had done immense damage to the land and its people but from which they had eventually recovered, and that it was this unforgettable disaster with its "happy ending" that inspired them to compose a universal Flood myth that was appealing, entertaining, and in accord with their religious views. That this took place in lower Mesopotamia where Sumer was situated is not surprising, for this is a region where torrential floods are common. There was one such appalling disaster for example, in 1954, when an exceptionally rainy spring, combined with the melting snows of Armenia and Kurdistan, so swelled the waters of the Tigris that they submerged the low-lying plain for hundreds of miles, and all Baghdad was in imminent danger of destruction. Sir Max Mallowan, the distinguished British archaeologist who excavated with Leonard Woolley, reported that from 1925 to 1930 "there was hardly a season, either in the spring or autumn, when the desert did not at least for a few days assume the appearance of a lake, and quite often Eridu (some twelve miles to the southeast of Ur) was cut off from us. I remember a day in the month of November, either 1925 or 1926, when in a torrential downpour we had to use our two hundred workmen to complete a dyke across the courtyard of our expedition house in order to save it from being swept away; within a few minutes of this cloud-burst, we were standing chest-deep in water outside our own front door."

There are historical references to violent floods in southern Mesopotamia going back to the Abbasid days of the seventh and eighth centuries A.D., as well as to the tenth, eighteenth, and twentieth centuries, and there were certainly many more of which we have no record. The date of the catastrophic event on which the Sumerian Flood myth is based will obviously depend on the date ascribed to its main protagonist, Ziusudra, who, as one version of the King List expressly states, was the king of Shuruppak immediately before the Flood. As yet, however, no contemporary records of his life and times have been recovered, and his date must therefore be inferred indirectly from circumstantial evidence. I suggested in an essay published in *Expedition* in 1967 that the clue to Ziusudra's date may be found in his reputation in Sumerian literary tradition as a ruler and sage who, like King Solomon of a much later day, was revered for his wisdom and perspicacity. Thus there is a Sumerian wisdom document which may be entitled "The Instructions of Shuruppak to His Son Ziusudra" that begins with the lines:

> Shuruppak gave instructions to his son,
> Shuruppak, the son of Ubartutu,
> Gave instructions to his son Ziusudra:
> "My son, I would instruct you, take my instruction,
> Ziusudra, I would utter a word to you, give heed to it.

Do not neglect my instruction,
Do not transgress the word I uttered,
The father's instructions, the precious, carry out diligently."

Until recently these lines were known only from tablets inscribed about 1800 or 1700 B.C. and were therefore no help whatever for the dating of Ziusudra. But somewhat more than a decade ago, an expedition of the Oriental Institute, while excavating the ruins of Tell Salabih, a site not far from Nippur, whose ancient name is still unknown, discovered several fragments inscribed with the same passage, and these can be dated with reasonable certainty to about 2500 B.C. Since, therefore, Ziusudra had become a venerable figure in literary tradition by the middle of the third millennium B.C., it is reasonable to conclude that he lived some centuries earlier, and we may therefore date his reign as well as the Flood that had presumably occurred in his days to about 3000 B.C., not long after kingship came into vogue.

But if so, if a catastrophic deluge of immense destructive force had actually come upon the land about 3000 B.C., there should be some corroborating archaeological evidence from the more important excavated cities in Sumer. And there is! In the past fifty years quite a number of notable discoveries relating to the "archaeology of the Flood" have been reported, but their interpretation has been a source of persistent controversy.

The key figure in the archaeological Flood debate, the excavator who staked first claim to the discovery and identification of a Flood stratum in Sumer, is Leonard Woolley. In 1929, after he had completed excavating the Royal Cemetery at Ur with its extraordinary finds, he sank a small shaft, not more than five feet square at the top, and no more than about three feet square at the bottom, into the underlying soil. For about three feet, this shaft penetrated a layer of mixed rubbish typical of inhabited sites: decomposed mud brick, ashes, and broken pottery. But then, to quote Woolley, "It all stopped—there were no more potsherds, no ashes, only clean, water-laid mud, and the Arab workman at the bottom of the shaft told me that he had reached virgin soil; there was nothing more to be found, and he had better go elsewhere" (*Excavations at Ur*). But Woolley noted that this so-called virgin soil was not nearly as deep down as he had expected; he told the workman to keep on digging. He did so rather grudgingly and went through eight feet of absolutely clean soil, without a sign of human activity. Suddenly, immediately below the empty stratum, there appeared pottery vessels and stone implements readily recognizable as belonging to a prehistoric period dated roughly to about 4000–3500 B.C. Woolley was convinced then and there that he had the "Flood." And since he could scarcely argue convincingly for his identification of a Flood from a pit only a yard square at the bottom, the following season he dug a rectangle seventy-five feet by sixty and went down sixty-four feet. To his satisfaction, here too he found a deposit of clean, water-laid soil, this time eleven feet thick, above the earliest prehistoric remains. All in all, Woolley sank fourteen pits at various points down to virgin soil, or approximately so, and in almost every case he encountered some clean water-laid soil overlying the same early remains. He therefore concluded that he had found the Flood myth archaeologically verified at Ur.

The matter was not as simple and clean-cut as Woolley assumed, however. He judged his Flood deposits at Ur to go back to 3500 B.C., far too early for the Ziusudra Deluge. Moreover, the year before Woolley staked his claim for Ur, Stephen Langdon and L. Watelin, who were then excavating Kish, had discovered a Flood layer there that is chronologically closer to Ziusudra's date, since it overlaid prehistoric remains dating from about 3000–2800 B.C. Even more intriguing and germane was a similar discovery in 1931 by Erich Schmidt in Farah (ancient Shuruppak), Ziusudra's own city. All in all, therefore, it is justifiable to conclude from the present evidence, as does Max Mallowan in his thoughtful article "Noah's Flood Reconsidered," that the Mesopotamian Flood story and the Old Testament version based on it were inspired by an actual, catastrophic, but by no means universal, disaster which took place some time about 3000 B.C. and left its archaeological traces in Ur, Kish, Shuruppak, and probably in a good many other places yet to be discovered.

But Flood or not, there is little doubt that Kish was the first important capital of Sumer. The dynasty that reigned in Kish, according to the eccentric and capricious King List, consisted of twenty-three kings who reigned an unbelievable 24,510 years, three months, and three and one-half days—if, as is rather unlikely, the author had some historical and traditional support for this bizarre chronological summation, we are quite unable to grasp it at present. One of the outstanding rulers of this dynasty was Etana, a king of whom the King List says "stabilized all the lands," a statement that seems to imply that he held sway not only over Sumer but over some of the neighboring lands as well. That this early Sumerian ruler was a remarkable and impressive figure in Sumerian history is evidenced by the legend that he ascended to heaven, a theme that was very popular with the ancient seal cutters.

Following Etana, Kish was beginning to have a rival for power in Erech, about a hundred miles to the southeast, the city closely identified with the Sumerian Heroic Age. The founder of the heroic Erech dynasty was a king by the name of Meskiaggasher, designated in the King List as the "son of Utu (the sun god)," and as one who "entered the sea and ascended the mountains." Nothing else about him is known as yet, though he must obviously have been a remarkable ruler. He was followed on the throne by his son Enmerkar, the first Heroic Age protagonist, who was succeeded in turn by his knightly herald Lugalbanda, the second of the Heroic Age trio. Lugalbanda was so memorable a figure that he was deified after his death, and some of the later kings of Sumer, including mighty Gilgamesh, claimed him as their divine father.

Lugalbanda was followed by Dumuzi, a ruler whose life and character left so deep an imprint on the people that he became the central figure in the impressive Sumerian Sacred Marriage rites and the related dying-god myths which played a prominent role in the religious life of the entire ancient Near East. Dumuzi, according to the King List, was followed by Gilgamesh, the hero par excellence of the ancient world, the forerunner of the Greek Herakles, whose very name may be etymologically related to Gilgamesh. Though celebrated in song and story, we still have no contemporary historical records of Gilgamesh's life and reign, and we can only hope that future excavations will be more productive in this respect than those past. However, at least some light has been shed recently on the political turmoil of his days by the initial lines of a later quasi-historical document inscribed on a Nippur tablet now in the Hilprecht collection of the Friedrich-Schiller University.

The text purports to record the names of the rulers who restored the Tummal, a Nippur shrine dedicated to Ninlil, the wife of the Sumerian air god Enlil, and its contents indicate that in the days of our hero there was a bitter three-cornered struggle for the hegemony of Sumer which involved Agga, the last ruler of the First Dynasty of Kish; Mesannepadda, the long-lived founder of the First Dynasty of Ur; and Gilgamesh of Erech, his younger contemporary. The victor in these internecine hostilities that probably took place early in the third millennium B.C. was Gilgamesh. But it was an empty triumph. These bloody civil wars so weakened Sumer that it became a vassal state of the Elamites to the east, and kingship was carried off to such foreign cities as Awan and Hamazi.

In the course of the years that followed, efforts were made by one or another of the Sumerian cities to regain control over the land. But it was not until the reign of Lugalannemundu, whose capital was the city of Adab, about a century after Gilgamesh, that Sumer recovered from its plight. Lugalannemundu, to judge from a hymnal document of later days, was a mighty conqueror and successful military leader. He defeated a confederation of thirteen kinglets who between them controlled much of the ancient Near East, reunified Sumer, and restored it to its former glory. But his military victories and patriotic achievements did not bring lasting unity and enduring peace. After his death, the chronic rivalry between the city-states came once again to the fore, and the ensuing years witnessed a disastrous struggle for power that came to an end only with the appearance of the Semites as rulers of the land.

The dominating military and political power in the divided Sumer of those troubled days was Lagash, a city-state that was hardly heard of in earlier times. This we learn from contemporary documents written by man's first historiographers, a group of Lagashite archivists whose inscriptions show a profound respect for historical truth, despite their religious phraseology and pious circumlocutions. I have prepared translations of these extraordinary historical documents, based largely on the studies of my teacher and colleague Arno Poebel, in *The Sumerians,* under "Votive Inscriptions." Here very briefly sketched is the history of this Lagash dynasty as revealed by its own inscriptions. Its founder was Ur-Nanshe, an ambitious and energetic ruler who built numerous temples, fashioned quite a number of statues and steles, and dug several large irrigation canals—he even carried on extensive commercial trade with Dilmun, the Sumerian paradise-land, "the place where the sun rises."

But it was Ur-Nanshe's grandson, Eannatum, whose aggressive military conquests raised Lagash to the pinnacle of political power. He began his upward climb with a successful attack against Elam, Sumer's perennial enemy to the east. He next turned to neighboring Umma, the city with which Lagash had an interminable bitter dispute over irrigation rights, leading to repeated fratricidal wars that bled both cities white. After defeating the Ummaites, he commemorated his victory on an important monument known in archaeological circles as the Stele of the Vultures and inscribed on it the peace terms that brought the war to a temporary end, thus providing us with the first recorded diplomatic treaty in history. Encouraged by his victories over Elam and Umma, Eannatum proceeded to attack Erech, Ur, and finally Kish, the city with the longest kingship tradition, so that for at least a brief period, he could claim suzerainty over all Sumer. But his defeated enemies gave him no respite, and in spite of his proud title of "Prostrator of all the Lands," he died in battle, and the political power of Lagash shrank to its former narrow limits.

We next hear of a conflict between Eannatum's nephew, Entemena, and the rulers of Umma, who were not slow in taking advantage of Lagash's weakness. This struggle ended in a compromise which still left the Ummaites disaffected and vindictive. Their opportunity came when some years later Lagash underwent a palace coup that brought into power a peace-loving, idealistic reformer by the name of Urukagina. This was the moment when Lugalzaggesi, an ambitious, contentious, and aggressive governor of Umma, found it opportune to attack Lagash and burn and loot virtually all its holy places. The luckless Urukagina, who failed to "keep his powder dry" and so doomed Lagash to military defeat and temporary political oblivion, left behind him two documents that will keep his memory ever green in the hearts of men: a moving record of social reform in which the word "freedom" is mentioned for the first time in man's written history, and a touching account of his city's defeat and his own downfall that ends with a statement of his profound conviction in the rightness of his cause and his faith in the ultimate triumph of divine justice.

Lugalzaggesi's career that began with the conquest of Lagash, and for a time was crowned with such phenomenal success that he could boast of controlling all the lands "from the Lower Sea to the Upper Sea," came to an ignominious end, as Urukagina had indeed predicted, in a neck stock at the gates of Nippur, reviled and spat upon by all who passed by. His conqueror was the mighty Sargon, a Semitic ruler who was a military leader of genius and an outstanding organizer and administrator. Little is known of his youth. According to a Moses-like legend, his mother launched the baby on the Euphrates in a pitch-covered basket which was drawn up to safety by a gardener named Akki. But whatever his origin, we can follow most of his far-ranging conquests from his own contemporary inscriptions. Not that we actually have the statues and steles on which these are inscribed; they seem to have perished, or in any case have thus far eluded the modern archaeologist.

Fortunately for us there were also ancient archaeologists of a sort, and one of these was farsighted enough to carefully copy many of the inscriptions on Sargon's monuments, even taking pains to note the exact spot where the inscription was located in such phrases as "inscription on the statue," or "inscription on the pedestal," or even the negative remark "the pedestal is uninscribed." The tablets prepared by this archaeologically oriented scholar were excavated primarily in Nippur close to a century ago, and most were copied, translated, and interpreted by Arno Poebel during his stay at the University Museum some seventy years ago.

Like the biblical Joseph, Sargon for some time held the high office of cupbearer in a "foreign" court, that of the powerful Sumerian potentate, Ur-Zababa of Kish. Just how he rose to this office and what his true feeling towards his suzerain were is unknown. It must have been this Ur-Zababa who was dethroned by Lugalzaggesi when the latter embarked on his path of conquest. Sargon's first objective, therefore, was to avenge his king and eliminate Lugalzaggesi as a political force, a feat that he accomplished by making a successful surprise attack against Erech, the city chosen by Lugalzaggesi as his capital, and carrying off the defeated ruler into captivity. He then turned his attention to Erech's allies, the cities Ur, Lagash, and Umma, and thus completed the conquest of Sumer, only one of his triumphs; according to his inscriptions his armies reached the Amanus and Taurus ranges to the north and perhaps even such distant lands as Egypt, Ethiopia, and India. To control his vast empire he stationed military garrisons in key outposts and everywhere appointed fellow Semites in the highest administrative posts—the effective Semitization of the Sumerian cities began in his days. He built a new capital for himself named Agade (biblical Akkad), a city that for a brief span became one of the most prosperous and resplendent in the ancient world.

As is so often the case with mighty conquerors, their empires tend to fall apart after their deaths, and Sargon's two sons, Rimush and Manishtushu, had their hands full trying to preserve Sargon's dominions, at least in part. His grandson Naram-Sin, to be sure, at first proved himself to be a worthy successor of the great empire builder. His conquests, too, ranged all over the ancient world, and one of his victory steles that can still be seen by the traveler in the Zagros ranges commemorates in eloquent stone his military achievements and political ambition. But then came an overwhelming catastrophe that virtually wiped Agade from the face of the earth and threatened to engulf Sumer: a destructive invasion by ruthless, barbaric Gutians from the mountains to the east which was long remembered by the Sumerians as one of the most humiliating experiences in their long and checkered history. All this became known in 1956 from a Sumerian historiographic document that may be entitled "The Curse of Agade: The Ekur Avenged." Prior to that year, a score of published and unpublished pieces inscribed with one part or another of this composition had been identified, but its true character eluded the cuneiformist, especially since the second half of the document was preserved in small part only. But in 1946 I identified among the tablets in the Hilprecht collection of the Friedrich-Schiller University seven pieces belonging to it, one of which was a well-preserved four-column tablet inscribed with the last 138 lines of the text; all these pieces have since been copied by Dr. Bernhardt and published in a joint Bernhardt-Kramer volume of texts in 1961. This new material enabled my eminent Heidelberg colleague the late Adam Falkenstein to publish an excellent transliteration and translation of the document. There were still quite a number of gaps in the text, however, and most of these could be filled in and corrected with the help of still unpublished Nippur material that I identified in more recent years. A decade ago I turned these identifications over to Adele Feigenbaum, a graduate student at the University of Pennsylvania, as part of her dissertation. Based upon her careful transliteration of the entire text, I prepared a translation of this melancholy composition that was published in the third edition of *Ancient Near Eastern Texts* in 1969. In 1983, a superb edition of the composition based on ninety-nine tablets and fragments, including many only recently identified, was published by Jerrold S. Cooper.

Throughout the dark days of Gutian domination, only the city of Lagash seems to have prospered, perhaps because its governors, such as the prince Gudea, whose numerous statues and inscriptions have made him one of the better known figures of Sumerian history, were not above collaborating with the invading Gutians. But after less than a century of Gutian overlordship, there arose a savior in Sumer, a king of Erech by the name of Utuhegal. Or, as the happy recorder of this event put it:

> Enlil, the king of all the lands, commissioned Utuhegal, the mighty man, the king of Erech, the king of the four quarters, the king whose command none can gainsay, to destroy the name of Gutium, the snake and scorpion of the mountain, who raised his arm against the gods, who carried off the kingship of Sumer to a foreign land, who filled Sumer with enmity, who tore away the wife from him who had a wife, who tore away the child from him who had child, and set up enmity and rebellion in the land.

These are the initial lines of a historiographic document inscribed on two duplicating tablets of unknown provenance, now in the Louvre, copied and edited with admirable skill and acumen by the eminent French savant François Thureau-Dangin. The document then goes on to describe vividly Utuhegal's victorious campaign against the Gutian king Tirigan, who was taken prisoner and brought fettered and blindfolded before Utuhegal to "put his foot upon his neck."

But despite his resounding victory, Utuhegal did not long hold power over Sumer. While he may have been a courageous warrior, he was not very discriminating in his choice of subordinates, and only seven years after the beginning of his reign, his throne was usurped by Ur-Nammu, one of his more ambitious generals whom he had appointed governor of Ur. This Ur-Nammu was an energetic ruler noted for his building activities throughout Sumer, and especially at Ur, where the remains of his lofty ziggurat, excavated with dedicated care by Woolley, still stand as an enduring monument to his memory; scenes relating to the building of this remarkable structure are depicted on one of his steles restored by Leon Legrain when he was the curator of the Babylonian Section of the University Museum, where the stele now stands.

Ur-Nammu was also the first "Moses" in man's recorded history, for he promulgated a law code that predated the long-known Code of Hammurabi by more than three centuries, and the Mosaic laws by over a millennium. Ur-Nammu's code became known from a tablet in the Istanbul Museum of the Ancient Orient that I was privileged to copy in 1952. I might never have come upon this tablet among the thousands in the museum had it not been for an opportune letter from Rudolph Kraus of the University of Leiden. Hearing that I was once again in Istanbul, he wrote me in a letter of reminiscences and shoptalk, that in the course of his duties in the Istanbul museum he had come upon two fragments of a tablet inscribed with Sumerian laws and had made a join of the two pieces, which he catalogued as no. 3191 of the museum's Nippur collection.

There it lay, a sun-baked tablet, 20 centimeters by 10 in size. More than half the writing was destroyed, and what was preserved seemed at first quite unintelligible. But after I had spent several days of concentrated study, its contents began to become clear, and I realized with no little excitement that this unimpressive piece of clay which I held in my hand was a copy of the oldest law code as yet known to man, one that had been promulgated by Ur-Nammu after he had established his capital at Ur, defeated Ur's archenemy, the city of Lagash, and instituted a number of social and moral reforms. In 1965, Oliver Gurney of Oxford and I published in a Festschrift dedicated to Benno Landsberger two new fragments containing part of the Ur-Nammu code, and after that an excellent revised translation of the laws of Ur-Nammu was published by my former student J. J. Finkelstein of Yale in the third edition of *Ancient Near Eastern Texts*.

Ur-Nammu reigned for sixteen years, during which he brought stability and prosperity to Sumer and served the gods so faithfully that he came to be designated as the "righteous shepherd." In spite of his good deeds, however, he was killed in battle. This bereavement, so arbitrary and unjust, which left the Sumerians desolate, moved one of the more reflective poets to compose a document that is part historiographic, part funereal, and part bitter diatribe against the inscrutable, hardhearted gods who manipulated man's fate. A portion of the text was known as early as 1917, but its contents remained quite obscure until 1967, when, with the help of eight duplicating pieces copied by the curators of the Istanbul tablet collection and of the Hilprecht collection, I was able to prepare a reasonably adequate rendering of its approximately 240 lines of text and to publish this in a Festschrift for the late Yale cuneiformist Albrecht Goetz.

Ur-Nammu was followed to the throne by his son Shulgi, who proved to be one of the most distinguished and influential kings of ancient times: an outstanding military leader, a punctilious administrator, an energetic builder of monumental temples, and a lavish patron of the arts, particularly of literature and music, who claimed to have founded two major Sumerian academies in Nippur and Ur. The Sumerian poets and men of letters outdid themselves in composing hymns of exaltation and glorification in his honor. The texts of two of these, pieced together from some seventy tablets and fragments scattered in the collections of Istanbul, Jena, Philadelphia, and London, were published in 1972 by G. R. Castellino of the University of Rome, who had worked with me in Philadelphia for some months and to whom I turned over all the relevant material available to me at the time. One of these hymns is of outstanding importance for its vivid portrayal of Shulgi as a rare combination of sage, soldier, sportsman, diviner, diplomat, and patron of learning—a blessed provider of all good things to his land and people.

In 1968, the year of my retirement, Jacob Klein, of Bar-Ilan University, prepared a dissertation under my guidance that included an overview of all available Shulgi hymns, together with a detailed edition of one of them. Since then he has been working on the publication of several more Shulgi hymns. It is a justifiable hope that in due time he will come to be known in cuneiform circles as Mr. Shulgi (just as Aaron Shaffer of the Hebrew University is on his way to becoming Mr. Gilgamesh) and will provide us with a well-rounded portrait of this extraordinary ruler, whose outstanding achievements were a source of joyous inspiration to the Sumerian bards and poets, and no doubt to the Sumerian people as a whole.

Shulgi reigned for over half a century. He was succeeded by his two sons Amar-Sin and Shu-Sin. These two kings each reigned for nine years, barely managing to keep their people united and independent. But time was running out for the Sumerians, and when Shu-Sin's successor Ibbi-Sin came to the throne, he found himself under attack by both the Elamites from the east and the nomadic Amorites from the west. At the same time his generals and governors, sensing doom in the air, began to throw off their loyalty to their monarch and his capital, Ur, and to fend for themselves.

The key figure in the betrayal of Ibbi-Sin was the king's most trusted confidant, Ishbi-Erra, a man "not of Sumerian seed" who made himself master of two important cities, Isin and Nippur, and subverted the governors of other cities by the use of force or threats. The true nature of the political turmoil of this period, and especially Ishbi-Erra's Machiavellian role in it, was brought to the attention of scholars in 1964 when my former student, Fadhil Ali, who became a professor in the University of Baghdad, completed his dissertation on two collections of Sumerian letters, an outstanding original contribution to Sumerian political history during the reigns of Shulgi and Ibbi-Sin. In more recent

years, Oliver Gurney and I, in the course of preparing for publication
the Sumerian literary tablets and fragments in the Ashmolean Museum,
came upon five letters that further illuminated the political history of
these two reigns, and especially the crafty behavior of Ishbi-Erra,
whose letters to Ibbi-Sin are masterpieces of duplicity, interweaving
comforting promises with honeyed words of flattery, in order to lull the
rather obtuse king into a false sense of security and keep him from
suspecting the traitorous intrigues that eventually led to his downfall
and to Ishbi-Erra's rise to kingship over Sumer in a new capital, Isin.

Despite Ishbi-Erra's treacherous successes, Ibbi-Sin held on to some
of his royal prerogatives and powers, at least in prestigious Ur, until the
twenty-fifth year of his reign, when the Elamites sacked and destroyed
Ur and its renowned temple, the Ekishnugal, and carried the king into
the foreign captivity from which he was never to return. This overwhelming catastrophe, which virtually marked the end of Sumer as a
nation, made an indelible impression on its poets, who in the ensuing
years composed a whole series of lamentations commemorating the
bitter fate that had befallen their land and its cities. One of these, consisting of over five hundred lines, has been pieced together from some
forty tablets and fragments by Cyril Gadd and me. The initial lines of
this document, a translation of which will be found in the third edition
of *Ancient Near Eastern Texts,* bemoan in abundant detail the woeful
fate decreed by the leading gods of Sumer and may appropriately be
cited as a melancholy epitaph for kingship in Sumer:

> That the day be overturned, that law and order cease to exist,
> That the divine norms of Sumer be overturned,
> That a favorable reign be withheld,
> That cities be destroyed, that houses be destroyed,
> That stalls be destroyed, that sheepfolds be wiped out,
> That its (Sumer's) oxen no longer stand in their ̣ alls,
> That its sheep no longer spread wide in their sheeṇfold,
> That its rivers flow with bitter waters,
> That its cultivated fields grow weeds,
> That its steppes grow "wailing" plants,
> That the mother care not for her children,
> That the father say not "Oh my wife,"
> That the young wife rejoice not in his lap,
> That the young child grow not sturdy on his knee,
> That the nursemaid chant not a lullaby,
> That the home of kingship be changed,
> That the sought-for decisions be suppressed,
> That kingship be carried off from the land,
> That its face be directed to inimical soil,
> That the norms of Sumer cease to exist, that its rules be changed,
> That the norms of kingship and the reign of Ur be overwhelmed,
> That the princely son stretch a defiling hand on his Ekishnugal,

That Nanna show no regard for his people as numerous as yews,
That in Ur, the shrine of vast offerings, the offerings be changed,
That its people no longer inhabit its dwellings, that it be made into in-
imical soil,
That the Su-people and the Elamites, the hostile, inhabit their homes,
That its terrified shepherd in the palace be seized by the foe,
That Ibbi-Sin be brought to the land Elam in a trap,
That like a sparrow which has fled its "house," he return not to his city,
That on the banks of the Tigris and Euphrates, in their entirety, there
grow sickly plants,
That no one tread the highways, that no one seek out the roads,
That its well-founded cities and hamlets be counted as ruins,
That its teeming blackheaded people be put to the mace,
That the cultivated fields be not hoed, that no seeds be implanted in the
soil,
That the stalls provide not cream and cheese, that no dung be implanted
in the soil,
That the hum of the turning of the churn resound not in the sheepfold,
That the cattle large and small become scarce on the steppe, that all
living creatures come to an end,
That sickly headed reeds grow in the marshes, that they come to a
stenching end,
That there be no new growth in orchard and garden, that they waste
utterly away,
That Ur, the great wild ox which stepped forth confidently, which was
secure in its own strength,
My city of lordship and kingship, built on pure soil,
Like an ox be thrown instantly by the nose-rope, be fastened neck to
ground,
An, Enlil, Enki, and Ninhursag decreed as its fate,
The fate decreed by them cannot be changed, who can overturn it!
The word commanded by An and Enlil, who can oppose it!

Between the fall of Ur and the rise of Babylon as the capital of Sumer
some three centuries later flourished the dynasties of Isin and Larsa,
whose celebrated rulers included Ishme-Dagan, Lipit-Ishtar, Ur-
Ninurta, and Rim-Sin. Several dozen hymns dedicated to these rulers
have been recovered over the decades, several of which have been edited by Adam Falkenstein and his disciples. These compositions, together with those devoted to the much earlier Ur-Nammu and Shulgi of
Ur, provided a hymnal repertoire of considerable bulk and variety. As I
studied them over the years, I noticed certain features. They glorify the
ruler in hyperbolic diction and extravagant imagery; they tell us very
little about the real character and achievements of the king with whom
the hymn is concerned but are quite revealing as to the ideal, Messiah-
type of ruler that the people must have envisaged and longed for. In
1971, the Nineteenth International Congress of Orientalists that met in
Paris selected as the central theme of its sessions "Kingship in the An-

cient Near East," and this seemed an opportune occasion to present a paper in which I collected some of the more significant statements in these hymns that depict in one way or another the attributes and qualities, the powers and duties, the deeds and achievements of the ruler that should have been but never was. Below are the conclusions I reached in that study.

To start with the ideal king's embryonic beginnings, it is of interest to note that the poets who composed the royal hymns conceived of his birth on two levels, the human and the divine. But it was the latter that was close to their hearts—hardly ever do they mention the names of the real parents of the king. On the divine level, on the other hand, they rarely fail to cite the ruler's parentage, though the relevant statements are usually rather brief, and at times contradictory, or seemingly so. In the case of the kings of the dynasty of Ur, the divine parents are the deified hero Lugalbanda and his wife, the goddess Ninsun. In case of kings of the later dynasties, the parents are usually said to be the great god Enlil and his wife Ninlil, while Hammurabi of Babylon boasts Marduk as his father.

One of the more poetic stylistic features of the royal hymns consists of the use of an imaginative symbolism taken primarily from the animal kingdom, and more rarely from the world of vegetation. Thus in connection with the royal birth, a king may be described as a "true offspring engendered by a bull, speckled of head and body"; "a calf of an all-white cow, thick of neck, raised in a stall"; "a king born of a wild ox, nourished on cream and milk"; "a calf born in a stall of plenty"; "a young bull born in a year of plenty, fed on rich milk in halcyon days"; "a fierce-eyed lion born of a dragon"; "a fierce panther fed on rich milk"; "a thick-horned bull born to a big lion"; "a mighty warrior born to a lion."

The king came blessed into the world if we take literally such exalting phrases as "from the womb of my mother Ninsun a sweet blessing went forth for me"; "I am a warrior from the womb, I am a mighty man from birth"; "I am a noble son blessed from the womb"; "I am a king adored, a fecund seed from the womb"; "a prince fit for kingship from the fecund womb." But it must have been during, or following, his coronation, or when he was about to set out on a campaign against the enemy, that the poets envisaged him as receiving sundry divine blessings, most frequently from Enlil of Nippur. Usually this came about through the intervention of another deity. A concrete example of this procedure as imagined by the poets is provided by a Shulgi hymn which states that the king, "on the day he had been raised to kingship," came before Nanna, the tutelary deity of Ur, with a promise to restore joyfully his divine norms. Whereupon the god journeyed to Nippur, entered the Ekur, where he was greeted warmly by the assembly of the gods, and addressed his father Enlil thus:

> Father Enlil, lord whose command cannot be turned back,
> Father of the gods, who established the divine norms,
> You have lifted your face upon my city, you have decreed the fate of Ur,
> Bless the just king whom I have called to my holy heart,
> The king, the shepherd Shulgi, the faithful shepherd full of grace,
> Let him subjugate the inimical land for me.

According to the author of this hymn, Nanna went alone to obtain his blessing for Shulgi, while the king himself stayed in Ur. But there are hymns that depict the intervening deity taking the king along to receive the blessing directly from Enlil's mouth. Thus in a hymn dedicated to Ishme-Dagan, the king is brought to the Ekur by the goddess Bau, who asks for his blessing, which Enlil proceeds to pronounce in words that summarize succinctly everything essential for an ideal king: a throne that gathers all the divine norms, an enduring crown, a scepter that exercises firm control over the people, effective overflow of the rivers, fertility of womb and soil, a name famous and glorious, tribute from lands near and far, the sending of perennial gifts to the holy temple, the Ekur, of Nippur.

Another hymn even more representative of the realistic manner in which the poets envisioned the king's divine benediction involves the goddess Inanna and her royal husband Ur-Ninurta. This composition begins with the statement that Inanna, having determined that norms of kingship be restored and the "blackheads" be properly guided and governed, has chosen Ur-Ninurta as the shepherd over all the people. Powerful goddess though she is, she nevertheless deems it necessary first to obtain for him the blessings of An and Enlil, both of whom reside in the Ekur of Nippur. She takes the king to the two deities for their benediction. An responds with a series of blessings addressed directly to the king, and Enlil follows with his benediction. After the assembly of the gods in Nippur has said "Amen" to these blessings, Inanna turns over to Ur-Ninurta all the noble norms, and the goddess and the king leave Nippur together for their domicile, where Inanna further eulogizes him as the blessed of Enlil.

The king, however, did not always need a deity to intervene in his behalf; he could journey alone to receive blessings from various gods. Shulgi, according to one hymn, travels by boat first to Erech where, following the performance of the Sacred Marriage rite, Inanna blesses and exalts him as the one truly fit for royalty in all its aspects. From Erech he continues his journey to two other cities whose tutelary deities bless and exalt him. Finally he arrives at his capital Ur, where he presents offerings to Nanna and is further extolled and blessed.

Understandably the modern historian is eager for some information about the education and upbringing of the king-to-be. But as this is being written, there is only one hymn that intimates anything at all about the young prince's education, and that only in a very brief passage. However, its contents are, culturally speaking, invaluable. Here is what, according to this hymn, Shulgi himself has to say about his education:

> During my youth there was the academy where,
> On the tablets of Sumer and Akkad I learned the scribal art,
> No youth could write as well as I on clay,
> I was instructed in the learned places of the scribal art,
> I completed to the very end . . . , arithmetic and accounting,
> Nidaba (the patron deity of writing) . . . ,
> Had given me generously of wisdom and understanding,
> I am a dextrous scribe whom nothing impedes.

In short, the king, if we trust this hymn, was himself one of the most literate and erudite personages of the land.

A few rather vague "human interest" particulars about the life of a very young prince and the motherly love that enveloped it may be gathered from a composition that is not a hymn but a lullaby supposedly uttered by the wife of Shulgi to her ill and restless son. We read of the mother rocking her son to sleep, as it were, with wistful reassuring chants, and with promises of sweet little cheeses and well-watered lettuce, as well as with such blessings as a loving wife, beloved children attended by a joyous nursemaid, abundance of food, good angels, and a happy reign when he has ascended the throne.

But whatever his education and upbringing, the king of Sumer was the ideal man: physically powerful and distinguished-looking, intellectually without peer, spiritually a paragon of piety and probity. Ur-Nammu is described as a "comely lord," invested with grace and a halo of splendor. Shulgi has a comely mouth and a countenance most fair; his lapis-lazuli beard overlaying his holy chest is a wonder to behold; his majestic appearance qualifies him eminently for dais and throne and for the precious regalia that cover him from the crown on his head to the sandals on his feet. Lipit-Ishtar has a lapis-lazuli beard, a fair countenance, a comely mouth that makes bright the heart, a figure full of grace, lips that are the ornament of speech, fingers fair: altogether he is a virile man sweet to gaze upon. Ur-Ninurta is also a comely, virile man with fair limbs; he is full of grace, an ornament of lordship. Rim-Sin has a graceful forehead, princely limbs, a tall figure.

Even more impressive than his majestic appearance were the king's physical powers, his courage and bravery. Shulgi, for example, is a warrior from the womb, a mighty man from the day he was born; his god Nanna gave him "warriorship" and might in his temple; Enlil gave him a "noble arm"; he is a mighty king always in the forefront in battle; he is a mighty warrior born to a lion; he is a king of pre-eminent strength who exercises firmly his powers as a warrior and who glorifies in song his strength and his might.

The importance attributed to the king's physique and courage is evidenced by the rich imagery and symbolism evolved by the hymnal poets: Shulgi is a lion with wide-open mouth; a great bull with powerful limbs; a dragon with the face of a lion; he is as strong as an oak planted by a watercourse; a fertile *mes*-tree bedecked with fruit, sweet to gaze upon. Ishme-Dagan is a tall *mes*-tree thick of root and wide of branch; a lofty mountain that cannot be touched; he flashes over the land like a bright light; he is a cedar shoot planted in a cedar forest; he is luxuriant like the boxwood tree. Lipit-Ishtar holds high his head like a cedar shoot; he is a lion on the prowl that has no rival; an open-mouthed dragon, the terror of his troops; a wild bull whom none dare attack.

The powerful physique and bravery of the king were of vital importance for victory in the recurrent destructive wars that plagued the land. Many of the prayers interspersed in the royal hymns are for victory in war, and it is in connection with war that the poets evolved some of their more extravagant imagery. Shulgi is a torrent thundering against the rebellious land; his weapon grinds its teeth like a sharp-toothed beast; his fierce weapon pours out venom like a snake set for the bite; his arrows are loosed in battle like flying bats; his bow pierces the enemy like a dragon; in battle he knows no rival, a dragon whose tongue darts out against the enemy; he speeds to subdue the enemy like a lion. Ishme-Dagan is a "warrior of warriors," the wrath of weapons. Lipit-Ishtar is an attacking flood wave in battle; he flashes like lightning. Ur-Ninurta rages like a storm against the enemy; his halo of splendor covers the rebellious land like a heavy cloud.

Related to the king's prowess in war was his skill in the chase. Shulgi boasts that he hunts lions and serpents in the steppe singlehandedly, without the aid of a net or enclosure; he simply waits until the beast opens its mouth to hurl the spearpoint. He claims to be so fast on his feet that he can catch a gazelle on the run.

The king was endowed also with great wisdom and profound understanding. Virtually all the kings in the hymnal repertoire were endowed with wisdom by Enki, the god of wisdom, and with learning by Nidaba, the goddess of writing. The king was psychologically penetrating and astute: he could give wise and eloquent counsel in the assembly; he could seek and find the wise word; he could discern "the words that were in the heart" and "put an end to the heated word." He had a great love for music and song, both of which he knew proficiently and practiced diligently. At least such was true of Shulgi—a goodly part of two Shulgi hymns depict his devotion to music both instrumental and vocal, and according to the author of one of these hymns, the king himself had the "power of a poet" and composed songs and psalms.

Spiritually, the achievements of the king revolved about two major areas: religion and social behavior. In the sphere of religion, it was the ruler's devotion to the cult that primarily interested the hymnal poets; the king knew how to serve the gods, and he saw that the temple rites and rituals were properly consummated, that libations were offered daily, as well as during the various monthly holidays and on New Year's Day, when his sacred marriage to the goddess Inanna was celebrated. Shulgi also claims that he could himself interpret oracles, carry out perfectly the lustration rites, and fill the high priestly offices in accordance with the omens; he could also read the precious words of the gods before going to war by examining the entrails of a white sheep. The hymns on the whole leave the impression that the king protected the cult as celebrated in all the more important religious centers of the land. But uppermost in their minds was the Ekur, the holy temple of Nippur where virtually every king in the hymnal repertoire brought gifts, offerings, and sacrifices to Enlil.

Social justice, equity, and law, according to the hymns, were a prime concern of the ruler, since Sumerian society, not unlike our own, was polarized into rich and poor, powerful and impotent. All the kings claim to love justice and truth and hate evil and iniquity. Usually the relevant statements are brief and general, but some are more specific and detailed. Ishme-Dagan, for example, asserts that he was a judge who did not permit the powerful to oppress the weak, nor the noble to mistreat the commoner; that under his reign the poor dared talk back to the rich, there were no bribed verdicts or twisted words, and the cry of the wronged, of the widow and the orphan, was not in vain.

The society of Sumer also suffered from a generation gap, and several of the kings claim to have done something about it. Shulgi saw to it that "the mother spoke kindly to the son, the son answered truthfully to his father." Ishme-Dagan alleges that during his reign "brother spoke the truth to brother," "the father was respected," "the older sister was not contradicted," "the mother was feared."

Oriental monarchs, including those of Sumer, are often cited by the modern historian as striking examples of despotic tyrants: cruel, oppressive, ruthless. This is certainly not the way the Sumerian poets viewed their rulers. They saw all the king's activities—waging wars, constructing temples, maintaining the cult, restoring canals and digging new ones, repairing and constructing highways, promulgating law codes and morataria—all as having one supreme objective: to make the people happy, prosperous, and secure. This theme is an ever-recurring motif in the symbolism of the hymns: the king is the farmer who fills the granaries, the shepherd who enriches the stalls and sheepfolds; he is the high protecting wall of the land; the people look up to him as their father and live securely in his sweet shade. In brief, in an oft-repeated summary phrase of the poets: "He makes sweet the flesh of the people." To be sure, this was not his sole motive. There was at least one other significant source of inspiration for the ruler's brave, wise, pious, and benevolent deeds: an obsessive, ambitious drive for fame and name. Throughout their hymns, the poets, who naturally had a vested interest in the glorification of the king and the celebration of his achievements, do not tire of reiterating that as a result of his mighty deeds and unrivaled accomplishments, his sweet and noble name will be honored and exalted in all the lands unto distant days.

8
The Sages: Sumerian Wisdom Literature

The gods of Sumer may have been majestic cosmic creators, the heroes of Sumer may have been adventurous supermen, the kings of Sumer may have been redeeming Messiahs, but they would all have been forgotten, doomed to eternal oblivion, were it not for the Sumerian sages and scribes who were responsible for the invention and development of the cuneiform system of writing and the formal system of education that was its direct outgrowth. Had it not been for the inventiveness and perseverance of the anonymous, pragmatically oriented Sumerian pundits and teachers who wrote and taught during the third millennium B.C., it is hardly likely that the intellectual and scientific achievements of modern man would have been possible, for it was from Sumer that writing, learning, and education spread over the ancient Near East and gradually impregnated the civilized world. In addition to the creation and development of written communication, the Sumerian schoolmen devised a varied assortment of linguistic textbooks and dictionaries and created and preserved a vast, variegated literature. Earlier chapters concerned those Sumerian men of letters who were also poets exalting gods, heroes, and kings in legendary myths, fabulous epics, and utopian hymns. But there were also Sumerian schoolmen who observed with sharp eye and ironic temper the more mundane aspects of daily life in a Sumerian city and the not so noble pursuits of its citizens. This information comes from a varied group of rather prosaic "wisdom" compositions, most of which have been discovered in the past four decades.

In the epic tale of "Enmerkar and the Lord of Aratta," Enmerkar sends his herald three times to the Lord of Aratta with a demand for tribute, and three times the herald returns to report that his mission was unsuccessful. Enmerkar decides to send him a fourth time with an ultimatum, but the herald is unable to repeat the message to Enmerkar, who wants to be sure he has got it right. The poet continues:

> Because the herald was heavy of mouth, could not repeat it,
> The lord of Kullab patted a lump of clay, set up the words as a tablet.
> Formerly there had been no one who set up words on clay,
> But now—by Utu on this day verily it is so—
> The lord of Kullab set up words as a tablet—verily it is so.

Hence, the poet believed that Enmerkar invented the cuneiform script and that he was therefore not only a mighty hero but also an inventive sage. I cannot follow my ancient colleague. As a historian, our poet was quite as credulous and naive as the author of the King List. The cuneiform system of writing was not invented by one man, no matter how wise, nor in one day. Many generations of scribes and archivists developed the script from the first pictographic memoranda of about 3000 B.C. to the mature, effective, phonetic system of writing utilized in the thousands of documents current in later days. And this development could never have taken place had it not been for the formal system of education that evolved more or less contemporaneously, a system that included schools and academies whose teachers had become professional educators, and whose graduates had become professional scribes practicing their craft by the thousands throughout the land.

Scribes first began to appear in considerable numbers about 2500 B.C., after centuries of cuneiform pioneering and experimenting. First came the creative temple administrators who devised a pictographic script in order to record and regulate the flow of the immense quantities of material goods under their control. In this crude system of writing each sign was a rudimentary picture representing either a word or an idea whose meaning was related in one way or another to the object pictured. Realizing, however, that the pictographic signs were difficult to draw and too numerous to memorize, the more imaginative among the later temple administrators began to simplify and conventionalize the signs until their pictographic origin was no longer readily apparent. More important, they gradually "phoneticized" the script so that each sign represented a specific sound or group of sounds, regardless of its original meaning. Thus, before the end of the third millennium B.C., cuneiform had been transformed into an effective phonetic system of writing. In the centuries that followed, this system naturally underwent a number of additional changes in form and sound, but these were relatively minor.

With cuneiform writing becoming a valuable tool of communication, the scribe developed into an important trained professional. In the temple and the palace many a scribe worked not only as secretary, bookkeeper, and accountant but also as archivist, recorder, and even writer-in-residence. Others were employed to help run the large estates of the wealthy, while still others were private entrepreneurs who sat at the city gates waiting for illiterate clients to come to them for secretarial help.

Before he could practice his profession, however, the scribe had to undergo a long period of education and training in the *edubba* (literally "tablet house"), the Sumerian school that became the prototype of the educational institutions of most of the ancient world. Within its walls flourished the pedagogue and scholar, the theologian and historian, the linguist and "scientist," the writer and poet—in brief, the *edubba* was the Sumerian academe, the center of learning and culture. We know a good deal about the Sumerian school, far more than is known, for example, about the Greek and Hebrew schools of a much later day. And this knowledge is not the result of inference or surmise but comes from the excavated documents and records of the *edubba* itself: the professor's textbooks and the students' exercises, as well as from a number of revealing and perhaps even mocking essays dealing with school life.

The hopeful scribe-to-be attended school from early youth to young manhood, day after day, year after year. To be sure, he did have a vacation of six days per month: three holy days and three truly free days. Even so, the remaining twenty-four days were, to quote one ancient graduate, "long days indeed." And no wonder! The teaching was unimaginative and drab and the discipline harsh. One graduate recollects that on a single day he was caned for loitering in the street, slovenliness, talking without permission, standing up during assembly, walking out of the school yard, and failing to speak correct Sumerian, not to mention poor "penmanship."

The bane of the students and fledgling scribes was the numerous monitors and "big brothers" who watched over them like hawks, waiting gleefully, it would seem, for some lapse or misdeed that could justify the use of the cane. There were of course deeply respected and even beloved professors and headmasters. But even they sometimes resorted to severe punishment, and some only relented after receiving a substantial *baksheesh* from the well-to-do parents. Not surprisingly, some of the boys became dropouts, and there were fathers who complained bitterly about their ungrateful sons who spent their time in the public squares instead of attending school and imbibing the wisdom of the past.

But the vast majority of students did attend regularly to the day of graduation. In spite of the boring exercises and harsh punishment, they reminisced over their schooldays with the nostalgic gusto of a modern alumnus at his class reunion. After all, the *edubba* and its faculty had turned the callow schoolboy into a highly respected professional, esteemed by his fellow citizens as one who was qualified to run an estate, arbitrate between contesting parties, survey fields, settle claims, and perform many other essential services. He could indeed lay claim to being a true humanist, for in the course of his studies he had mastered and assimilated virtually all the scholarly, "scientific," and literary knowledge of his day. A Sumerian riddle concerned with the *edubba* sums up its high office: "he whose eyes are not open enters it (the *edubba*); he whose eyes are wide open comes out of it."

The scholarly discipline fundamental to all teaching and learning in the Sumerian school was language study: the control and mastery of every facet of the Sumerian and Akkadian languages in written form. (Akkadian is also sometimes called Assyrian or Babylonian.) Beginning with the most elementary syllabic exercises, the scribal neophyte went on to the writing, reading, and memorizing of hundreds of cuneiform signs and thousands of words and phrases. For pedagogical purposes, these were classified by the Sumerian teachers in the form of textbooks that gradually became standard and stereotyped over the centuries—they have been found in one version or another in virtually every important site excavated in Mesopotamia, and even in such foreign lands as Anatolia, Iran, and Palestine.

Some of these clay primers were in the area of the natural sciences and included hundreds of names of wild and domestic animals, birds and fish, trees and plants, stones and stars, as well as body parts, both animal and human. Others were geographic in character: names of lands, cities, towns, rivers, and canals. Still others were technologically oriented, itemizing innumerable artifacts made of wood, reed, clay, wool, skin, leather, metal, and stone; the wooden objects alone run into the hundreds, ranging from raw slabs to such finished products as boats and chariots. There is little doubt that these highly schematic linguistic textbooks were accompanied by explanatory comment—lectures as it were—but these were not written down and are lost forever. Bare and unappealing as these word lists are, they nevertheless demonstrate an encyclopedic, if somewhat superficial, knowledge of zoological, botanical, geographical, mineralogical, and technological lore and thus provide an invaluable source for the history of science and technology. Fortunately, the contents of most of these texts are now available to the historians of science and technology, due primarily to the dedicated labors over the past thirty years of the Finnish cuneiformist Armas Salonen. Beginning in the 1940s he has published volume after volume devoted to detailed studies of the Sumerian "scientific" and technological textbooks. His invaluable monographs cover Mesopotamian house utensils of various materials, agriculture and farming, fish and angling, birds and bird catching, bricks and brick making, and so on.

A most interesting facet of language study was provided by the bilingual syllabaries, vocabularies, and trots giving line-by-line translations from Sumerian into Akkadian. These rudimentary dictionaries came about as a result of the bilingual character of the Mesopotamian school, where the students had to learn both Sumerian and Akkadian. Among foreign peoples, these dictionaries became trilingual and even quadrilingual; there are tablets inscribed with translations of Sumerian into Akkadian and Hittite, and others with translations of Sumerian into Akkadian, Hurrian, and Canaanite. (These ancient translations of Sumerian words, phrases, and sentences into Akkadian must bear partial responsibility for my Sumerological career if only indirectly, for they had to be incorporated as basic linguistic material in the Chicago Assyrian Dictionary; the dictionary brought Arno Poebel to the Oriental Institute, and Poebel's teaching launched me on the Sumerological path.)

Mathematics was another important part of the school's curriculum. No scribe could function as a competent secretary, accountant, or administrator without a thorough knowledge of the mathematical notation current in Sumer, and its practical application. Primarily, this is a sexagesimal system—that is, its key number is 60—which, like the decimal system, made use of place notation. The student had to copy and memorize scores of tables for such operations as multiplication and factoring, and for the calculation of reciprocals, squares and square roots, cubes and cube roots, not to mention a varied assortment of calculations for volume, weight, and area. The teachers also devised a substantial number of practical problem-texts that taught the student the step-by-step operations for the calculation of the area of fields of diverse shapes, the number of bricks needed to build a wall of given dimensions, the amount of earth required to build a ramp, and so on.

Written law played a predominant role in Sumerian life, and a good part of the school curriculum was devoted to legal studies. For "lawbooks" the student had copies of numerous codes, beginning with that of Ur-Nammu; in fact all the excavated Sumerian law codes are not originals, but copies used in schools. He also had at his disposal large collections of law cases and precedents, as well as representative copies of the different types of legal documents in current use, not to mention specially compiled lists of all possible legal words, phrases, and expressions he might have occasion to utilize during his scribal career.

A striking example of a court decision that was studied in the school as part of its curriculum is a document that might be titled the "case of the silent wife." Part of the text was known as early as 1922, when Edward Chiera published his copies of a number of legal documents in the University Museum, which had been excavated by the first Nippur expedition between 1889 and 1900. The remainder of the text became available in 1950 on a clay document dug up that year by the second Nippur expedition. In 1956 I published a tentative translation of the document, and sketched its contents as follows.

Some time in the nineteenth century B.C., a murder was committed in Sumer: three men killed a temple official. The murderers, for some unstated reason, then informed the victim's wife of her husband's death. Strangely, she kept their secret and did not notify the authorities. But the arm of the law was long and sure, and the crime was brought to the attention of the then reigning king Ur-Ninurta in his capital city Isin. The king turned the case over for trial to the Citizens Assembly in Nippur, which acted as a court of justice. In this assembly, nine men arose to prosecute the accused. They argued that not only the three actual murderers but the wife as well should be executed, presumably because she had remained silent after learning of the crime and could thus be considered an accessory after the fact. Two men in the assembly spoke up for the defense of the woman. They pleaded that the woman had taken no part in the murder of her husband, and that she should therefore go unpunished. The members of the assembly agreed with the defense, arguing that the woman was not unjustified in remaining silent, since it seemed that her husband had failed to support her. Their verdict concluded with the statement that "the punishment of those who actually killed should suffice." Accordingly, only the three men were condemned by the Nippur assembly to be executed.

In 1959, Thorkild Jacobsen, who had collaborated with me in the translation and interpretation of the document in 1956, identified four new duplicating pieces which had been excavated in 1952. One of these seems to indicate that the woman was also sentenced to death. Although Jacobsen's new translation and interpretation of the text demonstrate his customary Sumerological mastery and acumen, I am still not fully convinced. There are a number of obscurities in the text that need further clarification, and, as in the case of many controversial Sumerological matters, it is advisable to take no final stand at the moment.

Another very important subject of the Sumerian curriculum dealt with agriculture and farming, for which the student had to learn hundreds of words and phrases before graduating. At least one professor deemed it necessary and useful to prepare an agricultural handbook, a forerunner, as it were, of Virgil's highly poetic *Georgica* and Hesiod's *Works and Days*. In 1951, as a result of the excavation at Nippur of a small tablet inscribed with a crucial part of this document, I published a preliminary sketch of its contents under the title "A Sumerian Farmer's Almanac." In 1960, Cyril Gadd generously made available to me his then unpublished copy of a tablet, excavated by Leonard Woolley at Ur, which was inscribed with almost the entire text of the document, and this made possible a number of improvements in its interpretation. A detailed, but still tentative, sketch of this document on farming practices, the result of a preliminary collaboration with Benno Landsberger, Thorkild Jacobsen, and Miguel Civil, appears in *The Sumerians*.

Medicine, too, was taught in the Sumerian schools, although until quite recently this could only be surmised from the hundreds of late Akkadian medical texts that utilized innumerable Sumerian medical words and expressions. But in 1940 Leon Legrain published an article in the *Bulletin* of the University Museum that brought to light a Sumerian tablet dating back to 2000 B.C., or perhaps even earlier, which had been excavated by the first Nippur expedition toward the end of the nineteenth century and had been lying in the cupboards of the museum for almost half a century.

Legrain made a brave attempt to translate part of its contents, but it was obvious to me that this was not a task for the cuneiformist alone. The phraseology of the inscription was highly technical and specialized; needed was the cooperation of a historian of science, particularly one trained in the field of chemistry. After I became curator in 1948, I was often tempted to make a new effort at translating its contents but did not succumb. One day in the spring of 1953, a young historian of science, Martin Levey, came to my office and asked if I knew of any tablets in the Museum's collection that he could help with from the point of view of the history of science and technology. I took the tablet out of the cupboard, and for several weeks Levey and I worked on deciphering its contents. I restricted myself to the reading of the signs and the analysis of the grammatical constructions, while Levey identified and interpreted the chemical and technological procedures that seemed to be involved. In 1955 we published a joint article in the *Illustrated London News* under the title "The Oldest Medical Text in Man's Recorded History: A Sumerian Physician's Prescription Book of 4000 Years Ago." But in spite of our dual effort, the translation and interpretation of the document was far from satisfactory. Miguel Civil, who was then my assistant in the museum, published a substantially improved version in 1960, and the reader interested in ancient inscriptions for poultices, remedies to be taken internally, *materia medica,* etc., will find a translation and interpretation of the document in *The Sumerians.*

Not all treatment of the sick consisted of drugs and medicines; there was a very substantial practice of psychosomatic therapy utilizing a blend of medicine, incantations, and ritual. By and large, however, this type of healing was not in the hands of the physician but of the exorcist, the psychiatrist of ancient days. He, too, got his "book" training in school, where he studied scores of incantations, spells, and conjurations, as well as rituals of sublimation, substitution, and purification, all calculated to give relief to those suffering from various mental and physical ills.

History was not neglected in the Sumerian school, though it was not understood as it is in our days in terms of underlying principles and unfolding evolutionary processes. The historical instruction given to the Sumerian student consisted primarily of lists of kings, dynasties, and brief year-date formulas. He also had at his disposal compilations of royal inscriptions prepared by some history-oriented professor. Politically and psychologically illuminating were the compilations of royal letters that the student studied and copied, for these laid bare the rivalries and intrigues behind some of the more memorable political events.

One of the most appealing subjects of the Mesopotamian curriculum was the study of literature, the large and diversified group of belles lettres composed and redacted over the centuries by the poets and bards, the direct descendants of the minstrels of preliterate days—these are the documents that provided the source material for the three preceding chapters. Another subject that must have been taught in the Sumerian school, though as yet no Sumerian textbook related to it has been uncovered, is divination, the art of reading the will of the gods and predicting the future through the interpretation of omens, dreams, the entrails of sacrificial animals, and the configuration of the heavenly bodies.

Much that we know about the Sumerian school, the *edubba,* has come to light only in the last twenty-five years, as a result of the gradual piecing together of the texts of four *edubba* essays composed by some anonymous academics. Their attitude to the school and its faculty and students seemed to be rather ambivalent: part affectionate, part deprecatory and mocking. Some of the tablets and fragments inscribed with parts of these essays were copied and published by various scholars in the first three decades of this century, but their contents were completely misunderstood even by cuneiformists. Edward Chiera, sharp-eyed and levelheaded though he was, missed the mark altogether in his attempt to interpret the contents of these documents. In his introduction to *Sumerian Religious Texts* that included his copies of four *edubba* pieces, as well as his identifications of seventeen additional pieces in the University Museum, not to mention those already published by other scholars, he misinterpreted their contents completely, assuming them to be part "of a very important legendary series that deals with the origin of Babylonian civilization, and that in its complete form must have started with a creation story." One of these *edubba* texts he even construed as "relating to the Fall of Man, as do others describing the murder of a younger brother by his elder and the invention of writing."

In 1934, when I edited Chiera's posthumous *Sumerian Epics and Myths* that included his copies of the seventeen *edubba* pieces, I was far less knowledgeable than Chiera about Sumerian literature, and in my comments to the *edubba* texts in the introduction to that volume, I could only refer to Chiera's remarks in his introduction to *Sumerian Religious Texts*. In 1938–1939, I copied more than a score of tablets of the *edubba* genre and began to have some idea of what these texts were all about. Thus in the introduction to *Sumerian Literary Texts from Nippur,* I described these texts as compositions that "elaborate in one way or another the advantages of learning the scribal art" and even recognized in a general way the nature of the contents of three of the four *edubba* essays mentioned in the preceding paragraph.

Finally, in 1949, with the help of a number of newly identified tablets and fragments in Istanbul and Philadelphia, I was able to piece together the text of the first of the four school essays and publish it as "Schooldays: A Sumerian Composition Relating to the Education of a Scribe." And what a relief it was to leave for a time the ethereal atmosphere of myth, epic, and hymn and to edit this rather simple, prosaic, earthy document that revealed how little human nature has changed over the millennia. The ancient schoolboy, not unlike his counterpart a generation ago, is terribly afraid of coming late to school "lest his teacher cane him." When he awakes, he hurries his mother to prepare his lunch. In school he misbehaves and is caned more than once by the school staff. As for the teacher, his pay seems to have been as meager then as it is now; at least he was only too happy to earn a little extra from the parents to eke out his existence.

By 1957, eight years after the publication of "Schooldays," I had pieced together the text of the second *edubba* essay, "A Scribe and His Perverse Son," from more than a score of tablets and fragments, and published a preliminary translation in the *National Probation and Pa-*

role Association Journal. This was a document even more relevant to the contemporary educational scene with its generation gap and problem children. The composition begins with an introductory question-answer dialogue between father and son but then turns into a rather diffuse monologue by the father, replete with edifying clichés and pious exhortations, as well as bitter castigations of the son's ungrateful behavior.

The third essay, "Two School Rowdies," was first brought to the attention of scholars in 1956 by Cyril Gadd, who identified and copied two tablets belonging to the document among the Ur pieces excavated by Leonard Woolley and translated and interpreted their contents for his inaugural lecture as professor at the London School of Oriental and African Studies. But these two tablets contained only the beginning and the end of the essay. In the years that followed, I identified five Nippur pieces belonging to the text, one of which was a large eight-column tablet in the Hilprecht collection, and thus a substantially more complete text of the composition became available. The major part of the document consists of a violent verbal contest between two boisterous schoolmates that is brimful of sneering, jeering insults. However, in the course of this outrageous diatribe, they reveal indirectly much about the school curriculum, as well as the rather truculent behavior of the students toward each other and toward the teacher's assistant, designated as "big brother."

The text of the fourth essay, "Colloquy between a Superintendent and a Scribe," was pieced together from a dozen tablets and fragments in the 1950s, but it was not until 1963 that I published a first tentative translation and interpretation of its contents. It consists of several verbose speeches by two school graduates who seem to be in charge of a large estate but who take pleasure in reminiscing about their education, and especially about their dedicated and devoted teachers, whom they venerate as omniscient sages.

So much for the Sumerian school and the literary essays concerned with it. Let me stress here that much of my contribution to this important facet of Sumerian culture, as indeed is true of my Sumerological researches as a whole, is of a pioneering, preliminary nature and will be modified, corrected, and amplified as additional source material is uncovered, or as new insights into long-known texts shed fresh light on their significance. Thus in recent years, Åke Sjöberg, my successor in the University Museum, has prepared three important studies concerned with the Sumerian school, two of which add some new source material, while the third provides a panoramic view of the school curriculum based on published material that I failed to utilize. In due course Sjöberg's suggestions and elaborations will trickle down to the general reader, who will then have a fuller and more accurate picture of the Sumerian school than that sketched here.

The four school essays briefly sketched above (see Chapter 5 of *The Sumerians*) constitute but a small fraction of the Sumerian wisdom genre, only that which is concerned with the observation and evaluation of contemporary educational goals and practices. They are after all but one aspect of the human scene, and it was man's behavior as a whole, his actions and reactions, his basic drives and inner motives, that interested the more observant and reflective of the Sumerian sages. Not being systematic philosophers, however, they did not produce learned tomes filled with metaphysical speculations and ontological theories. Realistic and pragmatic, they compiled the results of their observation, judgment, and meditation in the form of collections of proverbs, fables, and precepts, or as literary debates and disputations. It is the gradual uncovering of these wisdom compilations that I here briefly sketch. For while others rightly deserve the glory of harvesting this field of research, I may at least take due credit for plowing the ground and sowing the seed.

I first began to appreciate the nature and significance of Sumerian wisdom literature when preparing the introduction to *Sumerian Literary Texts from Nippur,* which included copies of quite a number of wisdom pieces. There I wrote: "Until very recent years, except for some proverb material, practically nothing was known or understood of Sumerian wisdom literature. Today we are on the threshold of realizing the complexity and variety of the Sumerian wisdom compositions. In the Nippur literary 'catalogue' of the sixty-two compositions listed, the last thirteen are all wisdom texts. To judge from the extant material, Sumerian wisdom compositions can be seen to have consisted of the following types: 1. Collections of proverbs. 2. Collections of wisdom paragraphs of various lengths. 3. Fables such as 'The Bird and the Fish,' 'The Tree and the Reed,' 'The Pickax and the Plow,' 'Silver and Bronze.' 4. Didactic compositions of considerable length."

In the early 1950s I was in a position to correct, and elaborate on, that statement primarily as a result of my stay in Istanbul in 1946 as Annual Professor of the American Schools of Oriental Research, and in 1951–1952 as Fulbright Research Professor in Turkey. Thus in 1951, I wrote that to judge from the material then available, Sumerian wisdom literature consists of five categories: proverbs; miniature essays; instructions and precepts; essays concerned with the Mesopotamian school and scribe; and disputations and debates. I characterized Sumerian proverbs as "brief pithy sayings which depend for their effect on extreme terseness of expression and the unexpected turn of phrase, on evocation and connotation rather than straight statement of fact." I also recognized at the time that from the point of view of arrangement, the Sumerian proverb collections could be divided into two types: those in which the proverbs were grouped according to an initial key word, and those in which the grouping seemed to be quite haphazard and devoid of any special guiding principle. As for the number of extant Sumerian proverbs, I noted even then that they run into the hundreds, and that "it will take the combined efforts of numerous scholars over many years before they could be fully and definitively translated and interpreted." My prediction has proven to be only too true.

On my way from Istanbul to Philadelphia in the summer of 1952, I attended the III Rencontre Assyriologique Internationale being held in Leiden. Copies of 232 tablets and fragments—including 82 inscribed with proverbs, 53 assorted wisdom texts—were in my briefcase along with the paper I was to present on "Forty-eight Proverbs and Their Translation." This report was the product of a unique experiment in cuneiform research. In my introductory remarks, I discussed the difficulty of deciphering the meaning of the Sumerian proverbs, using as an example two duplicating eight-column tablets, each originally inscribed with about 180 proverbs, that I had come upon in the course of the year's work in Istanbul. The tablets, 17×22 centimeters in size, were only partially preserved, and thus no more than about half of their contents could be restored. Even so, twenty-two additional duplicating pieces could be identified, and it was possible to recover the practically complete text of 55 of the proverbs, and a considerable part of the text of 81 more.

But copying the tablets and fragments and piecing together their contents was far simpler than ascertaining their meaning. The translation of Sumerian proverbs is difficult and unrewarding, particularly because they lack a guiding and controlling context and are extremely brief and compact in their wording. It therefore seemed advisable to enlist the help of other cuneiformists to get at their meaning, in the hope that one might hit the mark where another missed. Moreover, if two or more scholars working independently produced identical translations, their correctness would be reasonably assured. This seemed to be an experiment well worth trying, and I therefore prepared transliterations of 48 of the better preserved proverbs and mailed them to twenty cuneiformists.

Eight scholars responded: Adam Falkenstein, Cyril Gadd, Thorkild Jacobsen, Raymond Jestin, F. R. Kraus, Maurice Lambert, P. van der Meer, and Maurice Witzel. Ten of the proverbs were translated by all eight participants; of the others, the number of translations varied from one to seven. There was considerable disagreement about practically all of the proverbs, and no agreement whatsoever in the case of some. Nevertheless, it was my feeling that the experiment was by no means a failure, and that in the long run similar efforts will lead to a better understanding of the Sumerian proverb material.

On my return to Philadelphia I realized more than ever that because of my other research and commitments I could not possibly do justice, even in a preliminary way, to the vast amount of Sumerian proverb material. Fortunately, in 1953 there was a graduate student in the Oriental department of the University of Pennsylvania, Edmund Gordon, who had both the motivating drive to undertake this difficult scholarly task and the intellectual capacity to pursue it steadfastly and masterfully. Gordon's intensive research in the field of Sumerian wisdom literature that began then continued for nearly a decade and resulted in a series of groundbreaking contributions that rank among the most significant in the history of cuneiform studies. In 1955, he completed his dissertation on the proverb tablets and fragments he had identified in the University Museum and on my copies of the hundreds of proverbs in Istanbul. In the course of the next four years I put at his disposal much new proverb material from the Hilprecht collection of the Friedrich-Schiller University and from the British Museum–University Museum excavations at Ur. In addition there were now available to him several large, well-preserved proverb tablets excavated in the early 1950s at Nippur.

By utilizing all this new material in combination with that known previously, he published in 1959 a monumental University Museum monograph entitled *Sumerian Proverbs: Glimpses of Everyday Life in Ancient Mesopotamia* that is valued to this day as an outstanding contribution not only to Sumerian wisdom literature but to Mesopotamian culture as a whole. This is not to say that Gordon had resolved all problems relating to Sumerian proverbs. The Gordon monograph, for example, includes a most instructive chapter by Thorkild Jacobsen that qualified and improved not a few of Gordon's translations. But it was Gordon whose diligence and expertise laid the foundations for all future research in the area of Sumerian proverb literature.

In 1958, Gordon published another trailbreaking contribution to Sumerian wisdom literature, entitled "Sumerian Animal Proverbs and Fables," that consisted of a detailed study of 125 proverbs and sayings pertaining to animals, 38 of which could be classed as forerunners of the classic Aesopic fables. Two years later, he published a superb, sweeping survey of Sumerian wisdom literature as a whole, entitled "A New Look at the Wisdom of Sumer and Akkad," in the form of a review of *La Sagesse suméro-accadienne,* an original and stimulating book by the eminent Dutch cuneiformist J. J. A. van Dijk. In this survey, Gordon could classify Sumerian wisdom literature into eleven categories: proverbs; fables and parables; folktales; miniature essays; riddles; *edubba* compositions; wisdom disputations or "tensons"; satirical dialogues; practical instructions; precepts; and "righteous sufferer" poems—a vast improvement over my hesitant attempts at cataloguing Sumerian wisdom.

In 1961, Gordon left the University Museum and the field of Sumerian wisdom literature, with about only half of the approximately one thousand Sumerian proverbs translated. I sought and finally almost found a young scholar whom I could train to complete this task, an Iraqi graduate student at the University of Pennsylvania by the name of Hadi al-Fouadi. He loved proverbial literature in general, and Sumerian proverbs in particular. But my retirement in 1968 came too soon for fruitful collaboration with him, and he had to turn to the study of other Sumerian documents for his doctorate. Fortunately, Gordon's pioneering work is now being carried on by a recent graduate student of the University of Pennsylvania, R. S. Falkowitz, whose dissertation "The Sumerian Rhetoric Collections" is pregnant with promise.

A favorite form of the Sumerian sages was the disputation, the prototype and forerunner of the literary genre known as "tenson," which was quite popular in Europe in late antiquity and in the Middle Ages. Its major component is a an acrimonious debate, a vitriolic battle of words between two antagonists usually personifying a pair of contrasting animals, plants, minerals, occupations, seasons, or tools and implements. The argument which goes back and forth several times between the rivals consists primarily of inflating in most flattering terms one's own value and importance, and of talking down those of one's opponent. Often these compositions are rounded out formally with an appropriate mythological introduction concerned with the creation of the protagonists and with a fitting ending in which the dispute is settled in favor of one or the other of the rivals by divine decision. What is most significant about these disputations, however, is not their mythological content, important as it may be, but the fact that in the course of the arguments, the protagonists unwittingly provide us with invaluable information about the material culture and practical technological procedures of the Sumerians that is not otherwise available.

I began to study and identify the contents of several of these disputations quite early in my career, as far back as 1940. But, partly because I was immersed at the time in Sumerian mythology, I was misled by their mythological prologues and epilogues into categorizing them as myths rather than tensons. The first to define and explain their contents was J. J. A. van Dijk, who made cuneiformists aware of the true significance of these texts. Inspired by van Dijk's study, I spent considerable time during the 1950s identifying, copying, transliterating, and translating in a very preliminary way the texts of seven disputations, those between Summer and Winter, Cattle and Grain, Bird and Fish, Tree and Reed, Silver and Copper, Pickax and Plow, Millstone and *gulgul*-stone. But, as in the case of proverbs, I realized that because of other research commitments, I would not be able to do justice to these compositions that were of special significance for the technological practices and procedures of the Sumerians, aspects of culture for the study of which I was not particularly gifted. I needed help, and this time it came from abroad.

I acquired a small foundation grant in 1958 and invited Miguel Civil, a young Spanish cuneiform neophyte who had studied in France with several eminent scholars, to come to the University Museum to assist me. I soon realized that he was just the man for the disputation genre—he had an adequate understanding of tools and implements, and a psychological predilection for useful techniques and procedures. Moreover, he was endowed with a sharp eye and a photographic memory that enabled him to identify the tiniest of fragments among the University Museum pieces as well as among those I had copied in Istanbul, or those on which I collaborated with the curators in Jena and London. As for his knowledge of Sumerian, he exemplifies the student who, according to the Sumerian sage, came into the *edubba* with "unopened eyes" and left it with "eyes wide-open"—in fact, Sumerologically speaking, he is now the "sage" of the Oriental Institute. Between 1958 and 1962, the year he left the University Museum for the Oriental Institute, he prepared transliterations of the available text of the seven disputations he had pieced together from several hundred tablets and fragments.

I had now, by 1954, devoted more than two decades to highly specialized contributions in the area of Sumerian literature. For many years I was occupied in the laborious process of identifying and copying tablets while also helping others to copy hundreds upon hundreds of Sumerian literary tablets and fragments in America and abroad. In 1951–1952, for example, the curators of the Istanbul Museum of the Ancient Orient, Muazzez Çiğ and Hatice Kizilyay, and I had copied close to a thousand pieces. About to enter my sixties, the last lap of my career, I felt the need to write a book that would embody and synthesize for the general reader some of those esoteric contributions to highly specialized journals that I had been making over the years. But how could this be achieved, working from such esoteric studies as those on the prefix-forms *be-* and *bi-*, the story of Gilgamesh and the *ḫuluppu-*

The tablet room of the Istanbul Museum of the Ancient Orient in 1952. The two curators, Hatice Kizilyay (seated) and Muazzez Çiğ (standing), are in white. Examining a fragmentary tablet is Armas Salonen, the Finnish cuneiformist.

tree, and the negotiations between such exotic figures as Enmerkar and the lord of Aratta?

Gradually I began to see a solution that came to me from an unexpected source. In my position as curator of the tablet collection of the University of Pennsylvania, and as an authority on Sumerian literature and culture, I had been constantly receiving requests from fellow academics the world over who were preparing books on the history of such varied subjects as government, war, law, education, and agriculture. Would I provide them with relevant Sumerian material that they could incorporate into their introductory chapters? As I painstakingly answered each of these pleas, it became increasingly clear to me that while my Sumerian studies were narrow and seemingly far from relevant to the modern scene, they had at least one feature in common which had a popular appeal: because they dealt with the world's oldest sizable literature, they satisfy to some extent the virtually universal appeal for "firsts" in the history of civilization. I therefore prepared some twenty-five essays relating to Sumerian "firsts" as the basis for a book that might attract a more general audience, or at least be of interest to people in humanistic studies. The book began to take shape; a preliminary draft rested in my desk awaiting final formulation.

9
Birth of a Best-Seller

The years following the Second World War introduced a veritable boom in publications relating to archaeology and the history of man's ancient past. The traumatic genocidal war, and the apocalyptic atomic-bomb holocaust that ended it, made the present seem precarious and the future hopeless, leaving only the "good old days" to be remembered and cherished. The public's obsessive interest in the past became apparent with the publication of *Gods, Graves and Scholars* by the Czech journalist writing under the pen name C. W. Ceram, a book whose popular and financial success was overwhelming. There soon followed *The Dawn of Civilization,* a million-dollar project, published by Thames and Hudson with contributions by high-ranking specialists and an impressive collection of illustrations. It did not take long for German and French publishers to follow suit with similar monumental, eye-appealing publications, including some concerned primarily with the archaeology and history of Sumer. Soon American publishers realized that there was gold in "them thar tells," and I was not too surprised, therefore, when one day in 1954 there was a knock on my office door, and in came one of the editors of Doubleday & Co., a Penn alumnus, who addressed me approximately as follows: "Dr. Kramer, we are greatly interested in publishing a book on the Sumerians and believe that you are the man best qualified to do the job. We are prepared to give you an advance with the signing of the contract."

Flattered and tempted—hitherto I was accustomed to demand subsidies for my publications rather than to command advances—I was on the verge of accepting the offer immediately when I began to have second thoughts about the advisability of doing so. A book on the Sumerians in general would have to include chapters on Sumer's political history, economic structure, and social organization, and I did not feel ready at the moment to tackle these rather complex themes. Since I had devoted virtually my entire career to Sumerian literature, I would have to spend much time and effort studying what had been written by other scholars on these aspects of Sumerian culture before attempting to sketch them for the general public. Then, too, I had a manuscript lying in the drawer of my desk, or at least the preliminary version, one that embodied the results of a more than a quarter century of research and study, one that was truly mine. I explained all this to the Doubleday representative and suggested that he take my manuscript on Sumerian "firsts" back with him to New York for possible publication by his company. He seemed a bit let down by this turn of events but agreed to do as I suggested.

Some weeks later he returned with the manuscript and informed me that he and his fellow editors had read it carefully, and they all agreed that its contents were quite interesting. However, they still wanted a general book on the Sumerians, though they would not be averse to my incorporating into it part of my manuscript on the "firsts." So saying, he drew a contract from his briefcase and a check for five hundred dollars as an advance. While the advance was ludicrously small, so was my professorial salary at the time. I succumbed to the temptation and signed the contract.

Next occurred one of those minor miracles that every so often buoyed up my scholarly career. But before relating this totally unexpected event I must, in the words of Pharaoh's chief cupbearer (Genesis 41:9), "remember my faults this day," for unflattering as it may sound, it was a "sin" on my part, rather than a good deed, that set the miracle in motion. In the preface to *Sumerian Mythology,* the book I published in 1944 when I was young and more impulsive, I had the temerity to write as follows.

> It is the utilization of this vast quantity of unpublished Sumerian literary tablets and fragments in the University Museum, approximately 675 pieces according to my investigations, which will make possible the restoration and translation of the Sumerian literary compositions and lay the groundwork for a study of Sumerian culture, especially in its more spiritual aspects; a study which, considering the age of the culture involved, that of the third millennium B.C., will long remain unparalleled for breadth of scope and fullness of detail. As the writer visualizes it,

the preparation and publication of this survey would be most effective in the form of a seven-volume series bearing the general title *Studies in Sumerian Culture*. The first volume, the present *memoir,* is therefore largely introductory in character; it contains a detailed description of our sources together with a brief outline of the more significant mythological concepts of the Sumerians as evident from their epics and myths.

The five subsequent volumes, as planned by the author, will consist primarily of source material, that is, they will contain the transliterated text of the restored Sumerian compositions, together with a translation and commentary as well as autograph copies of all the pertinent uncopied material in the University Museum utilized for the reconstruction of the texts. Each of these five volumes will be devoted to a particular class of Sumerian composition: (1) epics; (2) myths; (3) hymns; (4) lamentations; (5) "wisdom." It cannot be too strongly stressed that on the day this task is completed and Sumerian literature is restored and made available to scholar and layman, the humanities will be enriched by one of the most magnificent groups of documents ever brought to light. . . .

The seventh volume, *Sumerian Religion: A Comparative Study,* intended as the last of the series, will sketch the religious and spiritual concepts of the Sumerians as revealed in their own literature. Moreover, it will endeavor to trace the influence of these Sumerian concepts on the spiritual and cultural development of the entire Near East.

Now it did not take me too long to realize that this simplistic vision of the publication of the Sumerian literary documents was a utopian pipe dream; piecing together just a single document and editing it for publication with copies, transliterations, translations, and commentary took me months of intensive, concentrated labor. In the second edition of *Sumerian Mythology,* therefore, I amended my earlier statements.

The publication of the Sumerian literary works has taken a different form than that projected at the time of the publication of *Sumerian Mythology* in 1944. I have since realized that the definitive editions of the Sumerian myths, epic tales, hymns, lamentations, essays, and proverb collections, consisting of copies or photographs of the tablets, together with transliterations, translations, and commentaries, could not possibly be produced by one man, no matter how concentrated his scholarly efforts. . . .

This more realistic view of the publication of the Sumerian literary works as a slow, ongoing, cooperative process would, I had hoped, cancel the earlier quixotic, impractical vision. But as experience teaches, once a misguided assertion has reached the printed page, it tends to remain firmly planted no matter how often it is corrected, and to stand as a constant reproach to its author. To this day, for example, when my wife, Millie, is upset with me for whatever reason, she rebukes me by saying: "Sam, so where are those seven books you promised many years ago?" Nevertheless, in this particular case, arrogance of youth paid off. The exaggerated, unrealistic, but not uninspiring, preview of the seven-volume project of 1944 led to the publication of a spurned manuscript of the Sumerian "firsts," a book that unexpectedly turned into a best-seller.

This is how it happened. One day, not long after I had signed the Doubleday contract, I received a letter from a total stranger, Dr. Charles Muses, in which he wrote that he had read my *Sumerian Mythology* and was intrigued by the projected seven-volume publication series sketched in the preface. He was a consultant editor for a newly formed publishing house, the Falcon's Wing Press, based in Indian Hills, Colorado, and he was prepared to recommend to this new publishing house, which thus far had put out but one book, a translation of the Bible, to accept virtually sight unseen any one of the seven volumes that was ready to go to press. I read and reread this letter with no little pleasure; I could hardly believe my eyes.

But the euphoria soon disappeared, for the sad truth was that though the year was now 1954, a full decade after the publication of *Sumerian Mythology*, none of the projected volumes was ready. What was worse, the publication plans for the series had been scrapped. I therefore wrote to Dr. Muses and explained in some detail the true state of affairs. But, I continued, I did have a book almost finished that was based on years of research on the Sumerian literary documents, though in a form quite other than that projected in the preface to *Sumerian Mythology*. If he were interested, I would send on the preliminary manuscript. The reply came by return mail: he was indeed interested; could I send the manuscript at once? I did so, and within a week or so, I received a proposal for a contract.

Now, however, I was confronted with a dilemma. For while this was the book I was eager to see published, I had already contracted for the general book on the Sumerians, and it was clear to me that because of this new development, I would be unable to carry out my obligation to Doubleday. I therefore asked to be let out of my contract, which the first publisher did graciously once I had returned the advance.

The next several months I devoted entirely to the preparation of the final version of the manuscript relating to Sumerian "firsts." This was no simple task, especially since I envisaged its objective as twofold: as a compilation of translations of prime source material for the comparative study of cultural origins and the history of ideas; and as a cross section of the spiritual and cultural achievements of one of man's earliest and most creative civilizations, in such sociological and humanistic endeavors as government and politics, education and literature, philosophy and ethics, law and justice, and even in such technological areas as agriculture and medicine. To achieve this twin goal, I reexamined scrupulously all my specialized publications that might have some relevance, eliminated from them all linguistic and textual comment, and reworded them in order to make them more intelligible to the general reader.

The manuscript I finally sent off to Muses consisted of an introduction that provided a brief account of the nature, scope, and restoration of the Sumerian literary documents followed by twenty-five chapters, each of which pertained to one "first" in man's recorded history. In education, I included the first example of "apple-polishing," and in the chapters dealing with politics, government, and war, the first "war of nerves," attested in the tale "Enmerkar and the Lord of Aratta"; the first "bicameral congress"; the first attempts at the writing of history, this of man's first known civil war. Along with tax reduction, the first law code, and the first legal precedent were the first pharmacopeia, evidenced by a medical prescription tablet inscribed about 2000 B.C., and a first "Farmer's Almanac." More "firsts" were in the fields of cosmogony and cosmology, literary dialogues and debates, and so on.

Muses was more than happy with the manuscript, and it went to press immediately and almost without editorial changes—except for one, the title of the book. I had suggested the title *From the Writings of Sumer,* but the editor preferred *From the Tablets of Sumer;* "tablets," he felt, was more evocative than "writings." I demurred at first, since some of the inscribed documents were on prisms and cylinders. But in spite of my characteristically literal mentality, I recognized the reasonableness of his suggestion and yielded. The full title was to be *From the Tablets of Sumer: Twenty-five Firsts in Man's Recorded History.*

One ingredient of the book I had not counted on when preparing the manuscript was illustrations. The editor, however, was convinced that illustrations would enhance the appearance and value of the book. I therefore selected eighty-one photographs and drawings, the majority of which were of tablets and fragments whose contents were relevant to the various themes treated in the book. This was hardly a choice to thrill the lay reader, since one cuneiform inscription is very like another, but it did prove to be of some value to the cuneiformist, since some of the tablets pictured provided new source material.

The book appeared in 1956, and all in all was not unattractive in appearance. Its publication was delayed several months because I wanted to study the Hilprecht collection of tablets in East Germany in order to add an appendix that sketched the contents of two rather unusual documents that hitherto had been known in part only. One of these was the historiographic "Curse of Agade: The Ekur Avenged." The other was a rare example of ancient cartography, a tablet on which was inscribed what is by all odds the oldest known city map. It consisted of a plan of Nippur, Sumer's "Jerusalem," showing several of its more important temples and shrines, its "Central Park," its walls and gates, the Euphrates River that bounded the city on the southwest, the canal that bounded it on the northwest, and the canal that flowed through its center.

The reviews of the book were unanimously very favorable, and some were raves. The public relations people of the Falcon's Wing Press succeeded in having me interviewed by several media personalities; I was interviewed for an hour, if recollection serves me, by the late Martha Dean on her radio show. The first printing of the book was thirty-five hundred copies, which sold out in a relatively short time. The publisher then printed a second run of three thousand in high expectations of continuing sales. This proved to be an error of judgment: the bubble had burst, interest in the book had waned, and there were no buyers in America. Despite its initial enthusiastic reception, *From the Tablets of Sumer* seemed doomed to oblivion.

But then, at that melancholy moment, my Sumerian *lama* (good angel) came to the rescue in a French disguise and turned gloom to cheer and failure to success. The book that seemed to be a dud became a best-seller that is still alive, though close to two decades have passed since its first appearance.

As I mentioned earlier, the 1950s were years of rich harvest for books about archaeology and the history of man's ancient past. In France, the well-known publishing house, Arthaud, realizing the potential advantages of this phenomenon, developed a project to publish a series of volumes concerned with the history of civilization. One of the consultants engaged by Arthaud was a friendly French colleague, Jean Bottéro, a noted cuneiformist deeply interested in Mesopotamian history, religion, and culture. One day in 1956 I received a letter from Bottéro informing me of the Arthaud project and requesting that I grant Arthaud permission to translate *From the Tablets of Sumer* as the first volume of the History of Civilization series. He himself, the letter continued, would prepare a special introduction to the volume for the French public and would supervise the translation. I was delighted with the proposal, and my answer was immediate and favorable. After making the necessary contractual arrangements with the Falcon's Wing Press, the book was translated and in press without delay, and appeared in 1957, less than a year after Bottéro's first letter.

For this French edition of the book I prepared two additional "firsts": the first case of juvenile delinquency and the first animal fables. The Arthaud editor changed the title of the book to *L'Histoire commence à Sumer* (*History Begins at Sumer*) and substituted for many of the tablets illustrations of statues, seals, and other archaeological artifacts, primarily from the collections of the Louvre. For whatever reasons, the edition received extravagantly favorable reviews in the French press. Some French journals reprinted impressive illustrated excerpts from it. At least one major poet, André Bréton, described it admiringly. It received a prize as the best foreign book published in France that year. And within a relatively brief span of time it sold in the neighborhood of fifty thousand copies.

But this was only the beginning. Once the French edition appeared, the publishers of virtually every European country clamored for the publication rights, and translations of the book appeared in German, Italian, Danish, Swedish, Spanish, and Portuguese. It was quite popular behind the iron curtain, with translations into Russian, Polish, Roumanian, and Czech; in Prague, one of my colleagues later informed me, the first printing of five thousand copies was sold out in a single day, with lines queuing up for hours in front of the state bookstore. It was also translated into Arabic, Hebrew, and Japanese; Chinese, so far as I know, is the only major language in which the book has not appeared. But the crowning event came in 1959, when Doubleday, the publishing house that had rejected the original manuscript, asked for the rights to publish it as an Anchor paperback, which until very recently sold several thousand copies annually.

In the preceding pages I have had occasion to mention from time to time the Hilprecht collection of the Friedrich-Schiller University. This is a collection that consists of about twenty-five hundred tablets and a number of artifacts stemming in large part from the University of Pennsylvania's excavations in Nippur during the years 1889–1900. These had been presented to Hilprecht as a gift by the Turkish government of those sultanate days, in return for his cataloguing and classifying the Assyrian and Babylonian collections of the Museum of the Ancient Orient, part of the museum complex then known as The Imperial Museum of Constantinople. Hilprecht, because of his preeminent role in the closing years of the Nippur excavations, was the bright star of the University Museum in the early 1900s. His lectures on the Assyrian and Babylonian civilizations and on the discoveries and achievements of the Nippur expedition drew immense audiences in Philadelphia, and when in 1902 the Clark Research Professorship of Assyriology was endowed, he was its first appointee. But on the way up, he had succeeded in antagonizing some of his university colleagues and even his own protégés, and he soon found himself accused of such professional misconduct as keeping for himself some of the museum finds and making a number of scholarly misstatements relating to the Nippur excavations in his writings.

The matter came to a head in the spring of 1905 when, at Hilprecht's request, the trustees of the University of Pennsylvania impaneled a court of inquiry headed by the provost and vice-provost in order to investigate the charges against him. After taking six hundred pages of testimony pro and con and conducting twenty-five hours of hearings over a three-month period, this court of inquiry cleared Hilprecht of any wrongdoing. But Hilprecht was no longer the popular and powerful figure he had been in the University Museum.

In 1910, the Board of Governors of the University Museum appointed a young anthropologist, George Byron Gordon, as its first full-fledged director, a position to which Hilprecht had aspired. He decided to challenge the authority of his new superior, who was many years his junior, and taking the keys of the Babylonian Section with him, he left for Europe. The Board of Governors upheld Gordon, and Hilprecht resigned his professorship and moved to Germany. After the First World War he returned to Philadelphia a more mellowed man. But when he died in 1925, his archaeological collection was presented by his widow, not to the University Museum, but to Hilprecht's favorite German institution, the Friedrich-Schiller University in Jena.

I had first learned of the existence of this collection in 1928 from a report in the *Zeitschrift für Assyriologie* by the German cuneiformist Heinrich Zimmern, who had made a cursory examination of its contents. Zimmern stated that about one hundred tablets in the collection were inscribed with Sumerian poems and essays. I decided that I must get to Jena to study these pieces and help make them available to the scholarly world. But what with the Nazis, the Second World War, and the East-West cold war, the years passed and I could do nothing to achieve this objective. In the early 1950s, however, East-West tensions began to relax, and my hopes rose. One day I read in the papers that President Eisenhower had been corresponding for some time with General Zhukov. This spurred me to action. If the president of the United States could write to a high government official in the Soviet Union, surely a lowly Sumerologist could try to contact someone in East Germany for permission to carry on scholarly, nonpolitical research in one of its universities. The East Germany of those early postwar years, however, was not the relatively prosperous, secure East Germany of today. Those were the days when the Berlin wall had not yet been built, when East Germans were fleeing by the thousands to West Berlin, when the East's economy was precarious and its currency far inferior in value to that of West Germany, when Russian domination was all-pervasive. Western visitors, and particularly Americans, were a rarity, and except for those officially favored, it was virtually impossible for a Westerner to obtain a visa, let alone permission to do research in an

East German institution. However, I finally succeeded in obtaining an East German visa and worked for ten weeks in the Hilprecht collection, but only after a number of rather Kafkaesque experiences with a confused and hesitant American, Russian, and East German officialdom which kept me on tenterhooks throughout my stay.

10
Journey To Jena

My campaign to get to Jena began in March of 1954. Assuming that a request to do research in a university should be made to the authorities of that institution, I wrote to the rector of the Friedrich-Schiller University, explaining in considerable detail the nature of my research and the scholarly importance of studying some of the tablets in the Hilprecht collection. By November of that year, not having received a reply, I wrote once again to the nameless rector. This also brought no response, and I could only assume that the university authorities felt that granting permission to an American scholar to work on a collection in their institution was risky business and that it was wiser, and safer, to ignore the letters altogether.

In March of 1955 I decided to try again. This time, however, I thought it best to write directly to the East German government, since it could be assumed that all cultural institutions in a Communist land were state controlled. But to whom should I address my request? Obviously, to the minister of culture if there were such an official in the East German government. It would be best, of course, to address him by name.

As fate would have it, one day the *New York Times* listed all the members of a newly formed cabinet of the East German government. Sure enough, there was a minister of culture, Dr. Johannes Becker. Taking this as a good omen, I penned a letter to Dr. Becker, dated March 17, in which I asked his help in a purely scholarly and humanistic project involving the restoration of an ancient and long forgotten literature inscribed in the cuneiform script, that of the Sumerians. I explained that the tablets and fragments recovered from Nippur, of which there was a great number in the Hilprecht collection, constitute the major source for the restoration of Sumerian literature, that these clay pieces of the early second millennium B.C. represent the oldest literature of any appreciable amount uncovered to date. Outlining the significance and influence of Sumerian belles lettres, I made it clear that it was to the piecing together and restoration of these literary remains that I had devoted my life for the past thirty years. To this end, the contents of the Hilprecht tablets were indispensable, for these fragmentary and uncertain remnants, if identified and fitted into the appropriate compositions, would most certainly be of great value in filling in lacunae in the texts; they could thus be most useful for the restoration of Sumerian literature as a whole. This, I wrote to Dr. Becker, was the reason for my request to work at the University of Jena.

I read the letter over and over again with the rather smug satisfaction that results from wishful thinking: the request seemed so "right" that it must certainly bring an immediate and favorable response. But three long months passed without a reply. Now summer was upon us, and traveling time was running out for me. On June 23 I penned a second letter to the East German minister of culture, enclosing a copy of the first. At the same time, I decided that it might be wise to get some help from other sources, and my thoughts turned to Dr. Gerhard Meyer, director of the Vorderasiatische Museum, in East Berlin, whom I had mentioned as a reference in my first letter to Becker. To be sure, Dr. Meyer and I were virtually total strangers. I knew of his scholarly contributions in the 1930s, but I had heard nothing of his work in the 1940s and had even assumed that he had died during the war years. However, in 1952, I ran into him at a congress of Assyriologists in Leiden. There I learned that he had recently become director of the Near Eastern Section of the famous Pergamon Museum in East Berlin, and that he was busy restoring its monuments and collections damaged during the war. In 1954, I saw him once again for a brief moment in Cambridge, England.

I did not know then, and do not know now, whether he was a Communist, but it seemed reasonable to assume that he was at least a scholar respected by the Communist regime of East Germany. He knew of my Sumerological contributions and of their significance for cuneiform studies, and I felt that because of our common scholarly interests he would help me get a favorable response if at all possible. So, on July 8 I sent him a note, together with yet another copy of my first letter to the minister of culture. Here I asked if Meyer would be so kind as to advise me if I might be wise in coming to Berlin to make my request in person. His answer came in less than a fortnight, informing me that my request had made some progress in the Office of the Secretary for Higher Education and that he was doing everything possible to help me. Sure enough, just two days before his encouraging letter, dated July 20, reached me, the permission arrived on a small rectangular piece of official stationery. Written on June 27, the letter was brief and to the point. Below is my English translation.

> Most Honored Mr. Kramer:
> Your letter of March 17, 1955, was turned over to us by the ministry of culture. If you wish to come to Jena for several months for purposes of research, we have nothing against it. Travel and living expenses must be borne by you, however. Moreover, you cannot make entry until September 1955. If this is not possible, the desired photographs can be sent to you at your own cost (these had been requested if permission to visit Jena was denied).
>
> Respectfully,
> Fabert, Section Director

Elated by this rather unexpected success, I nevertheless soon became aware that thus far I had cleared the first hurdle only. The piece of paper from the Office of the Secretary of Higher Education merely granted me permission to do some research in Jena for several months. First, however, I must get to Jena, and for that I needed a visa permitting me to enter the German Democratic Republic.

Now how should I go about obtaining the visa? Apply to the Russians? Or to the German Democratic Republic? And to what address? Perhaps our State Department might have suggestions. When sending for my passport, therefore, I enclosed copies of my correspondence with Dr. Becker (Exhibit A) and with the Office of the Secretary of Higher Education (Exhibit B) and asked for information and advice concerning a visa to be used in traveling in East Germany. The passport arrived in gratifyingly quick time, accompanied by a mimeographed sheet headed "Memorandum to Accompany Passport." The memorandum stated that the State Department could be of no assistance in obtaining permission to visit the Soviet zone of Germany or the Soviet sector of Berlin, but to this end the enclosed forms might be filled out in triplicate and sent, with a letter of application and two passport-size photographs, to the American consulate at Berlin, which would send them to the appropriate Soviet authorities. "It should be noted that nearly all requests for permission to enter the Soviet zone . . . have been either refused or ignored . . . and should any trouble arise during your visit, the American authorities cannot guarantee you protection in that area."

Journey to Jena

And so at least I now had something to go on. I filled out the forms in triplicate, enclosed copies of my correspondence and two freshly taken passport-size photographs, and sent them off to the American authorities in Berlin for transmission to the Soviets, together with a cover letter detailing the history of my request.

It seemed of little value to sit around Philadelphia waiting to hear from the Soviets, who had been said to almost always refuse or ignore such requests for visas. It occurred to me to write to the East German Office of the Secretary for Higher Education and ask them to try to get a visa for me, but on second thought I decided against it; it would undoubtedly take months to get results in this roundabout way, since issuing a visa was obviously the concern not of the ministry of culture but of the ministry of foreign affairs. It seemed wisest to write to the latter. This time, however, I decided against writing to the East German minister himself, for it might take a long time before the request trickled down to the appropriate lower echelons. On the assumption that there must be a special bureau in charge of passports and visas, I invented a title for this bureau, Division in Charge of Visas, and sent a letter requesting a visa, again detailing the importance of my research. I informed this Division in Charge of Visas that the American consulate in Berlin had already filed with the appropriate authorities of its government my application for a visa and asked that the visa be mailed to the American consulate, where I would pick it up on my arrival in Berlin on the twentieth of the month.

With this letter off my chest, I took off for Berlin via Lufthansa. It was only much later that I realized that asking the East Germans to send my visa to the American consulate was hardly according to protocol, for in truth my application had not been filed with the appropriate authorities of the East Germans but instead with the Russians. Worse yet, the visa division of the ministry of foreign affairs of the East Germans could hardly be expected to mail my visa to the American consulate in Berlin, which did not recognize its existence.

I arrived at the Tempelhof Airport in West Berlin on the afternoon of Wednesday, September 20, and took a room in the Hotel am Zoo, on Kurfürstendamm, Berlin's Fifth Avenue. That evening I spent walking about West Berlin in order to get reacquainted with the city, which I had not seen since 1930. Evidence of the bitter war destruction was all about. But new buildings were going up, and the West Berliners gave the impression of being reasonably optimistic and cheerful.

Early the next morning I made my first visit to the American consulate, a large building on a broad tree-lined boulevard called Kleeallee. There I learned, to my gratification and surprise, that a very real effort was being made to help me obtain the visa. Mr. S., the administrative officer of the section of the Allied commission in charge of interzonal travel, had been talking to the Russian consul, his Soviet counterpart on the Allied commission, and had actually made an appointment for the two of us to meet with him at ten o'clock the next morning. Mr. S., an American of Slovak descent, spoke optimistically about the probability of my obtaining the visa from the Russian consulate. But the reasons he gave for his rosy view did not sound very convincing, and though I could not say exactly why, I had the feeling that he was barking up the wrong tree. That afternoon, therefore, I decided to pay a visit to Dr. Meyer at the Pergamon Museum to learn what, if anything, could be done in case the meeting with the Russian consul turned out to be fruitless.

The Pergamon Museum, and its Near Eastern Section in particular, were not unknown to me. I had visited them in their heyday in 1930, not long after the impressive installation of the world-famous Ishtar Gate from Babylon. The director was then Walter Andrae, one of the best-known German excavators, who had dug in Babylon, Ashur, and Shuruppak, the city of the Sumerian Noah. At that time, I was a young scholar traveling to join the University of Pennsylvania excavations in Iraq. That was my first scientific journey and the visit to the newly installed Pergamon galleries left me breathless and with haloed memories of its impressive exhibitions.

Now, in the fall of 1955, I could not even telephone the present director, Dr. Meyer, to make an appointment, since there were no telephone connections between East and West Berlin, nor were busses or trolley cars permitted to run from one part of the city to the other. I was not aware at the time that there were an elevated and an underground train connecting the two sections of the city. Hence, I took a taxi, first making sure that the driver would be willing to risk carrying a visa-less American to the Soviet zone. On arrival at the museum I found to my disappointment that Meyer was out of the city but was expected back the next day. His secretary received me most cordially, and in the course of the conversation with her, I learned what I had strongly suspected, that it was Meyer who had persuaded the East German authorities to grant me the permission to go to Jena. This was good to know, for now I felt that I could depend on his good offices if necessary.

Getting back from the Pergamon in East Berlin to my hotel in West Berlin proved to be somewhat of a problem. I could not take a taxi even if there were one, since I had no East German money. I therefore decided to walk. The Pergamon Museum is only a stone's throw from Unter-der-Linden, the tree-lined avenue that was once the pride of Berlin. It was lovely fall weather, and I walked slowly along the boulevard to the Brandenburg Gate, where a large sign marked the boundary between East and West Berlin. There I saw East German policemen stopping all cars for questioning, and I became a bit anxious, since I had had no permission to enter any part of East Germany, including East Berlin. Soon I noted that the police did not stop any of the pedestrians, and I just kept walking, right through the Brandenburg Gate, crossing over to the Allied zone without incident.

Once in West Berlin, I did not go straight to my hotel but to the German Archaeological Institute, an institution under the control of West German scholars that also included not a few East German members. Meyer's secretary had given me a printed invitation to a lecture by Heinrich Lenzen, who had just returned from Iraq, where he was directing the German excavations at Uruk (biblical Erech). And so here I was in West Berlin on an invitation extended in East Berlin, attending a lecture of the type often given in our own museum in Philadelphia. Somehow this was reassuring.

Reassuring or not, sleep that night was rather restless for me because of the coming meeting with the Russian consul. At ten in the morning I made my second trip to the American consulate in the Kleeallee. From there Mr. S. drove me in his official car to the huge and impressive Russian embassy in East Berlin. The Russian consul received us cordially enough, and Mr. S. explained to him in Russian the nature of my request. It was soon apparent, however, that he could not, or would not, do anything to get the visa. The Russians, it seemed, were prepared to assist any accredited visitor or government representative to an officially recognized meeting or conference. My case was altogether outside that category. I was a private individual embarked on a purely personal affair, and in this case it was up to the East German government to make the decision. The consul did give us the address of the visa bureau and even telephoned ahead. Thanking him, Mr. S. drove me in the official car to nearby Louisenstrasse, where the East German passport offices were housed. Because protocol did not permit Mr. S. to enter the building, since this act would imply recognition of the existence of an East German government, he suggested that he wait for me outside in the car, in order to take me back to West Berlin.

On entering the building, I was shown to a large room where ten or twelve Germans were sitting about filling out applications for passports and visas, a dreary and depressing spectacle reminiscent of Gian-Carlo Menotti's play *The Consul,* and I came to the conclusion, which fortunately turned out to be quite mistaken, that it would take hours before my turn came. Hurrying outside, I told Mr. S. not to wait for me, since it might kill the entire day for him. As he said good-bye, it was obvious that he was in a quandary, uncertain whether to wish me luck in this offbeat enterprise.

Not long after reentering the crowded room, my name was called by a serious-looking young lady who led me to her office. There she explained that the visa was ready for me, and indeed had been ready for some time; that it would have been sent to me in America, but since I had written that I would be in Berlin on the twentieth, it was kept in the office for me to pick it up in person. There it was, a piece of paper 4 by 5⅝ inches, stating that visa, no. 5135/156, granted to Kramer, Samuel, permission for one entrance into, and exit out of, the German Democratic Republic, this entrance and exit to be at Schoenefeld, a suburb outside of Berlin.

But on the visa, above a stamped circle with a stylized hammer and sickle, was written: "Good from September 23 to October 22." This meant that I could stay in Jena one month only. I began to explain to the young lady rather vigorously that scholars are not noted for speed; that it would take me a month just to find my research bearings; that, in any case, the permit from the ministry of culture spoke of several months of research in Jena, not one. She then telephoned her chief, and after hanging up, led me up a shabby staircase to talk to Mr. Wiedemann, the man who had signed the visa.

Wiedemann was a smallish, kindly looking man, and I repeated my arguments, insisting that it was hardly fair to cut the length of my proposed stay at the Friedrich-Schiller University and thus nullify to a large extent its research value. He was not unimpressed but nevertheless hesitated to give in. Finally he consented to increase the length of my stay to six weeks, that is, to the tenth of November. Better yet, he assured me that if, after several weeks following my arrival in Jena, the rector of the university requested that my visa be renewed for another six weeks, he saw no reason why the request could not be granted.

That afternoon, elated by my success in obtaining the visa on my own, simply as a human being and scholar, I paid my second visit to the Pergamon Museum. This time Meyer was there, and we greeted each other warmly. In the course of the conversation, I learned that he had been in the United States as a prisoner of war and had spent his leisure time in captivity trying to get hold of books to keep abreast of cuneiform studies. After his return to Germany, he was taken prisoner by the Russians and then freed. Later, when Walter Andrae retired as director of the Near Eastern Section of the Pergamon Museum because of age and blindness, Meyer was appointed as his successor.

In the past five years he had done his best to restore the museum to its former glory, which meant that his time and effort went into administrative duties rather than scholarship. Still, there on his desk lay a lovely crescent-shaped electrum ornament from the eighth century B.C. which he had very recently recovered from one of the museum storerooms that had suffered considerably during the war. His face lit up as he showed me the skillfully engraved scene of a kneeling worshipper before a seated deity. The object, a precious example of the jeweler's art, had been excavated more than half a century ago in what is now Soviet Armenia and had remained uncleaned and unrecognized until now. As I watched Meyer's shining eyes and listened to his excited words, I could well understand why he had gone out of his way to help a fellow scholar. He told me that the letters which went back and forth between him and the government concerning myself and my research project formed a dossier an inch thick, but that it was worth it.

With the visa in my pocket, I was now set for the journey to Jena. All that remained was the purchase of a train ticket in East Berlin. But that was not as simple as it sounds. To purchase the ticket, I had to show not only my passport and visa but also a statement from the official *Notenbank* of East Germany that I had there exchanged American dollars into East German marks at the official rate and had not obtained them in West Berlin.

The following day, therefore, I once again trudged my weary way to East Berlin. After some inquiry, I found the official exchange bank and, as an experiment, gave the teller sixty dollars to exchange into marks. To my dismay he handed me only 132 East marks—that is, the rate was little more than 2 marks per dollar. At this rate of exchange, I was informed by all who knew, an egg for breakfast would cost more than half a dollar, and a pot of coffee close to a dollar. The cost of a regular meal would range from four to five dollars. These were prices to which research scholars are not accustomed, and for which I was unprepared.

However, there was nothing I could do about it. The ticket was finally bought for me by Dr. Meyer's secretary, who also made a reservation at Jena's leading hostel, the Hotel Am Schwarzen Baer. On Sunday afternoon a taxi picked me up with my three bags at the Hotel am Zoo. The driver brought me to the station without incident, except that he charged almost twice the usual fare. As he passed the Brandenburg Gate into East Berlin, he was stopped by the East German policemen on guard but was not detained more than a few seconds. Later, the driver explained that a certain select number of Western taxis are permitted to take passengers to East Berlin on their honor, that is, on a verbal guarantee that they have not brought in anything that was against the law.

The train, which left at 5:45 P.M. for Jena, was crowded with weekend travelers, especially the third-class coaches which constituted by far its largest part. My compartment in the second-class car was shared with only three other passengers and was quite comfortable. At Schoenefeld, just outside Berlin, the train stopped for about half an hour and was boarded for the examination of passports and other identification papers. The East German policeman assigned to our compartment looked a youngster of twenty or even less. On first seeing my American passport he seemed a bit startled. He then read the visa very carefully—it was attached with a clip to the passport, and not stamped on one of its pages—and returned the passport with a polite "Thank you."

The journey took about six hours, since the train made numerous stops before reaching Jena. It had no diner, but beer and light refreshments were served in one of the third-class coaches. There was noise and laughter coming from the third-class riders who were largely young. The passengers in my car were older professional people who, as far as I could gather from their intermittent conversations, were traveling in connection with their duties.

As the train approached the Jena station, I began to carry my bags through the aisle to the exit door, since I did not know how long the train stopped there and how much time there would be to unload. Handling three bags proved a bit awkward, and when a rather sad-looking young man who was standing in the aisle offered his help, I was quick to accept. He was a student in the Friedrich-Schiller University returning from a weekend spent in Dresden with his parents. He was amazed to hear that I was an American, for no Americans had been seen in this part of the world for many years.

The Am Schwarzen Baer was only a ten-minute walk from the station, and the young man from Dresden helped me carry my bags. On the way I got a first glimpse into the social and economic revolution going on in East Germany, and particularly of the unhappiness it brought to the merchant or bourgeois class. His father, the young man told me, was a Dresden businessman who was still trying to carry on his business as a private individual. But East Germany, he continued, was now theoretically a workers-peasants state where all major industries and enterprises were socialized and state owned. Private merchants were frowned upon and, when possible, liquidated by means of high taxes and hampering restrictions on their sources of goods and supplies. They and their children were treated as suspicious characters, possible traitors to the regime, and therefore received none of the social benefits lavished on the workers and peasants. As a university student, he was particularly bitter about the fellowship situation. Children of peasants and workers, even if they were mediocre, received fat monthly stipends which enabled them to live in relative comfort. As a merchant's son, he received no government support whatever and was having quite a difficult time. He was majoring in chemistry, a useful and practical field, but he was by no means optimistic about getting a job upon graduation in spite of his excellent grades, since the jobs were all government controlled.

At the door of the hotel the dejected young man bade me good night. Inside, a middle-aged clerk received me and showed me to a small, simply furnished room with an adjoining bath, one of the few in Jena. The next morning I rose early, eager to make my first acquaintance with the Friedrich-Schiller University. I took a continental breakfast in the hotel dining room: rolls, marmalade, and coffee. The bill was about a dollar and a quarter at the official rate of exchange. Had I ordered juice and eggs, it would have been more than double. The prices spelled trouble for the pocketbook.

As I finished breakfast, another, rather silly, matter began to bother me: what to do about tipping the waiter? This was a state-owned restaurant, and, theoretically at least, the waiters were also its owners. To leave a tip might be a serious faux pas; the waiter might take it as an offense and attribute my crude behavior to crass and ostentatious American materialism. I looked at the man who waited on me for a possible clue. He was a tall, dignified-looking individual, considerably more impressive than I was; it was rather hard to think of him accepting a pfennig or two as a gratuity. On the other hand, he was obviously working hard, taking orders and hurrying to the kitchen and back. In fact he seemed quite eager to satisfy his customers.

I looked around to see what others were doing about a tip but could come to no definite conclusion, so there was nothing to do but ask the waiter himself. I did so rather sheepishly, and the answer came back, "In my country tips are not welcome." Surprised, and a little ashamed of myself, I left no tip. But my mistake had been to ask. Later on, I learned that, owners or not, the waiters are poorly paid and look forward to the customers' tips. From that day on, I left a good 15 percent of the meal check as a tip and was a well-liked customer indeed, even by the waiter who had uttered the high-sounding but soon forgotten words that first morning.

In Berlin, Meyer had suggested that I should first contact a Professor Zucker, a Greek scholar and papyrologist of international repute who was one of the three-man curatorium responsible for the Hilprecht collection. Hence, immediately after breakfast I walked to his office in the main university building directly opposite my hotel. Zucker, a well-preserved man in his seventies, welcomed me cordially as a visiting scholar. He understood that my time was severely limited, and I was eager to get started. He had one of his students take me midway up one of the rather steep hills surrounding the city, about twenty minutes walking distance from Zucker's office, to the building which housed the collection, which was also the home of an archaeological institute

In the Hilprecht collection at Jena, 1955, with the collection's curator, Dr. Inez Bernhardt.

devoted primarily to prehistory. On the top floor, I was greeted with a most enthusiastic welcome—there was actually a sign on the wall in English, "Welcome to the Hilprecht Collection"—by Dr. Inez Bern-hardt, the assistant curator in charge of the collection.

I had first met Dr. Bernhardt in Cambridge, England, in August of 1954, during the meeting of the Twenty-Third International Congress of Orientalists. She had received her doctorate in Mesopotamian stud-ies during the war years, but knew virtually no Sumerian. Without my help she could do nothing with the Sumerian literary tablets: neither read and copy nor translate them. She was therefore overjoyed at my arrival, since I would now be in a position to guide her in preparing copies of the tablets thus making them available to scholars the world over. Then, too, the mere fact that an American professor had come all the way from Philadelphia at no cost to the Friedrich-Schiller University, in order to study a part of the Hilprecht collection, indicated that the latter must be of no little scientific importance. My visit thus brought considerable prestige to the collection whose existence had been largely unknown on the university campus. All this naturally reflected favorably on the prestige of the keeper, and brought Dr. Bernhardt out of her somewhat shadowy status.

Because of this double scholarly advantage, Dr. Bernhardt cooperated with me in every possible way and did her best to foresee and forestall any obstacles that might arise. That very first morning I found some of the tablets ready for me so that I was able to begin reading them without the delay which so frequently impedes the visiting scholar's efforts. Since photographs of the tablets would play an important role in the preparation of their publication, she took care of all the complicated official and technical details involved in getting them to and from the photographic institute so effectively that I was able to bring back to America excellent photographs of all the more important pieces. She made the necessary arrangements with the administrative officials of the university, planned the essential meetings and visits, and attended to other details as they came up. Throughout my stay in East Germany, she was a loyal assistant and constant companion, and the success of the project owes much to her wholehearted participation.

One of the more crucial meetings in the first week of my visit was with the rector of the university. Unlike the president of an American university, the rector of a German university is not appointed by trustees for an indefinite period but is elected by the faculty for a limited term. The then rector of the Friedrich-Schiller University, a physician by the name of Haemel, was a well-known dermatologist who, because of his personal popularity, had been reelected for several terms in succession. I was told that, though not a Communist, he had nevertheless managed to retain the good will and respect of the Communist government officials who controlled the budget of the university and naturally tried to influence both its curriculum and faculty. His task in these days of bitterness and tension was delicate, difficult, and at times heartrending. The Friedrich-Schiller University had a rich scholarly and humanistic tradition behind it—both Goethe and Schiller had once played significant roles in Jena—and it was the rector's immediate task to maintain this tradition.

The meeting with Dr. Haemel lasted no more than a half hour or so, but it was long enough to demonstrate that here was a sincere, straightforward, uncomplicated man, capable and energetic, who had his hands full trying to keep the university on its traditional nonpolitical path and devoted to science and the humanities. Even so comparatively unimportant an event as my visit raised political problems, and he was at first not quite sure what to do about me. Hitherto he had been accustomed to receiving scholars from Russia or the other Communist countries, all official guests of the government and the university. My case was without precedent. I was an American who had come on his own and was barely tolerated by the government. Nevertheless, he was most eager to help me wherever practical and possible, in spite of my official nonexistence. It was he who made the suggestion which quite unexpectedly changed my Jena reception from one of lukewarm tolerance to enthusiastic welcome and played no small role in the ultimate success of the project which had brought me to Jena.

In the course of our conversation I complained about the unfairness of the official dollar exchange as far as it affected me. After all, I said half jokingly, I was not a Texas oilman or an American millionaire but just a low-paid university professor who had succeeded in garnering a limited quantity of shekels for research travel abroad. How could I afford to pay some fifteen dollars per day for food alone? The rector saw the justice of these words at once. He could of course do nothing about the rate of exchange, but the university did have some funds earmarked for outside lecturers. If I would give several lectures on the Sumerians, the university would pay me their customary fee, and this would lighten my financial burden to some extent.

Here was a practical solution, and I took up his suggestion gratefully, though I could not foresee all of its favorable consequences. Preparing the lectures was a comparatively simple matter. To be sure, Sumerology is a highly specialized and esoteric field of research and does not particularly lend itself to ready-made popular lecturing. But fortunately I was carrying with me a carbon copy of the manuscript of my forthcoming book *From the Tablets of Sumer,* in order to inquire about the possibilities of the publication of a German translation. This book was written primarily for the layman rather than the scholar, and it was little trouble to prepare a series of three two-hour lectures based upon several of its more interesting chapters. Dr. Bernhardt translated them into German.

The time set for the lectures was from five to seven on three successive Thursday evenings. Announcements were posted by the rectorate in all the university institutes, and students were freed from regular classes for those hours. As a result, the first Thursday saw the Aula, the university auditorium, crowded to the doors.

The lecture, to everybody's surprise, including my own, was re-

Before his lecture in the Aula of the Friedrich-Schiller University, the author is greeted by the anthropologist Hestermann, honorary curator of the Hilprecht collection.

ceived with fervent and unforgettable enthusiasm. It dealt to a large extent with the Sumerian system of education and included the translation of the Sumerian essay "Schooldays," noteworthy, among other things, for its revelation that apple-polishing the teacher was a practice known in ancient times. The subject matter itself, therefore, though highly specialized in character, was not altogether without interest. But what lifted the hearts of the audience and expanded its spirit was the fact that at long last a professor from an American university was speaking in their midst. The great majority of the students had never seen an American in the flesh; they knew about Americans only from books and the newspapers. Here was a new and rich experience for them, and a good omen for the future. At the close of the lecture, the applause was spontaneous and prolonged. The lecture was a tremendous success, not so much because of its subject matter, but as a symbol in its small way of the unity of man and of the free exchange of ideas in a future world untroubled by passports and visas, permits and protocol.

The next two lectures were even better attended, since all of cultural Jena made sure to be on hand. Long and detailed reports of the lectures were prepared by one of the members of the history department of the university and published in full in the *Thueringer Landeszeitung,* one of the best-known East German newspapers. The University of Halle nearby invited me to deliver one of the lectures in its halls. Toward the end of my stay in Jena, the German Academy of Science, an East German organization with a good many West German scholar members, extended an invitation to repeat the lectures in East Berlin. Better yet, the research department of the Friedrich-Schiller University, which has the overall budgetary responsibility for the Hilprecht collection, became interested in my work and agreed to have copies of its Sumerian literary tablets, prepared by Dr. Bernhardt under my guidance, published under the university's auspices. There was little doubt now that my visa would be extended, as indeed it was extended when the time came, though, because of typical bureaucratic delays, there were several days during which I was without a visa. We joked about the danger of my being picked up and imprisoned as a spy, but the banter was not without certain grim overtones.

One unexpected advance in human and international communications which came about as a result of my lectures had nothing to do with Sumerology or scholarship. On leaving the auditorium after my first lecture, I was stopped by several rather attractive young female students whose spokeswoman popped a question for which I was not well prepared in spite of my professorial standing. Could I, she wanted to know, give her the names of some American college boys who would be willing to be pen pals? It took me a few seconds to recover from the shock, and even then I could think of nothing better to suggest than that they write to Haverford College for possibilities.

Another enterprise which had nothing to do with the Sumerians was a talk given before the students of the English department of the university. Though English was by no means the most popular foreign language taught there—French and particularly Russian were both in greater demand—many studied it for one reason or another. The chairman of the department was a German professor whose special field of research dealt with Americanisms in the English language. While his German assistant had spent her happiest years at Vassar College as an exchange student, the Jena students had never heard English spoken by an American, and I was therefore invited to speak before the group informally on any subject. I talked about American universities and, needless to say, was listened to with rapt attention. Later, I was told, the more advanced students prepared a list of the Americanisms I had used as part of their classwork. (Some weeks later, when I delivered the lectures in East Berlin under the auspices of the German Academy of Science, one of the professors in the linguistics department asked for special permission to record the lectures on tape since they had almost no examples of American pronunciation and speech for purposes of study.)

My daily life in Jena settled down to a rather simple scholarly routine. At seven o'clock I arose, breakfasted, and did some preliminary writing. At nine o'clock I climbed the hill to the Hilprecht collection, where I read and transliterated the contents of some of the tablets, or corrected Dr. Bernhardt's copies, until twelve. Dr. Bernhardt and I then descended the hill to the university's *mensa*, the "table" at which members of the faculty took their lunch, which was in a little building not far from my hotel. The food was good, simple, and relatively inexpensive (about half what it would cost at the hotel). The portions were small by American standards but adequate. The waiters, an elderly man and a young girl, were unusually well-mannered and responsive. The *mensa* still retained some of the old relaxed campus mood; it was free to some extent from the stress and strain of the outside world, and I looked forward with pleasure to our daily visits. After lunch we climbed once again to the Hilprecht collection. On the way up we would stop regularly at a bakery shop for some poppy-seed cakes or other cookies to go with the break for tea which took place at three-thirty in the afternoon. At five-thirty I returned to the hotel and dinner.

Sundays I usually took long walks along the tree-lined banks of the meandering Saale, which Goethe immortalized in his writings. I was rarely invited out; only two professors asked me to dinner during my stay in Jena. The attitude of the Jena professors toward me was ambivalent, for they were not quite certain how to take this unofficial, uninvited visitor from America. It was rather pleasant and even promising to see me around, but because of the political situation, it was hardly possible to relax in my presence and to feel altogether at ease. This ambivalence was poignantly illustrated one day when I was taking lunch at the *mensa,* and the rector came in with a Russian professor who was to teach in Jena that year. As an official guest of the government and the university, the rector had brought him to the *mensa* in person for his first meal and introduced him to the other members of the faculty, something he had avoided doing in my case. As he rose, however, to introduce the Russian professor, he spied me sitting at one of the tables, and was evidently a bit embarrassed, thinking of the difference in treatment accorded to the Russian and the American, although both were university professors. While on his feet, therefore, he took the occasion to introduce me also rather hesitatingly with the words, "And here in our midst is Professor Kramer from America, to prove that we have real co-existence in Jena."

Since I was rarely invited out evenings, I went to the movies rather frequently. There were three theaters in Jena, a town of about eighty thousand inhabitants, and all were state-owned, of course. The show usually began with a documentary made either in Russian or in one of the neighboring Communist countries or in East Germany itself. The subject matter ranged from a workers' vacation resort in the Thueringer mountains to Russian excavations in the land known to the ancients as Urartu; from a Romanian fair to Hungarian hunting life. Nearly all these shorts were interesting and sometimes even absorbing, in spite of their propaganda flavor.

Following the documentary came the newsreel, which was carefully edited along Communist and particularly pro-Russian lines. A good deal of it was devoted to visits by Russian and other Communist government officials to East Germany and return visits by East German government officials to Russia and the neighboring Communist countries. America was rarely mentioned, and then almost always in unfavorable terms. France and Great Britain were treated somewhat more generously and in sport scenes, even as equals. In the case of West Germany, both the Adenauer government party and the Social Democrats who were in opposition were anathema. By and large, only strikes by workers or other unfavorable developments were shown. Toward the end of my stay, however, it was noticeable that a conscious effort was being made for better East-West German cooperation, particularly in the economic field, and this was reflected at times in the West German scenes depicted in the newsreels.

The main feature brought the show to an end. Most of the films came from Russia, Italy, or West Germany. The Italian films attracted the largest crowds, and at the other extreme were the Russian productions, with their unconvincing plots and thick propaganda. They were so unpopular in fact that even the better ones played to half-empty houses.

160

For example, *Romeo and Juliet* performed in pantomime dance was excellent, but ill attended. The East Germans made uniformly mediocre films, even such an ambitious attempt as *Thaelmann: Leader of His Class,* a biographical sketch of the German Communist leader much concerned with the disintegration of the workers' strength in Germany in the thirties and the rise of the Nazis to power. Advertised all over East Germany, the film arrived in Jena preceded by a heavy fanfare. Attendance was more or less a political must; the schoolchildren were brought to see it in class formation. But I saw *Thaelmann* as one-sided and in very poor taste, with its vicious attack on the Social Democrats as craven traitors who turned the power over to the Nazis, and I suspect that it did not make much of an impression on most of its audience.

On Sunday mornings, all three theaters were turned over to the children of Jena. They showed animal and adventure films only, and at a nominal price. I was much affected by this feature of the Jena film program and the sight of the children, small and not so small, coming out beaming with delight. In this respect the socialist economy certainly showed up to advantage. It is hard to imagine American movie owners turning over their houses to the children on Sunday mornings.

Jena had no legitimate theater, but every so often the National German Theatre Company from nearby Weimar visited Jena for a guest performance, and this was usually a sellout. I managed to see only one of the productions, Tchaikovsky's *The Witch,* and found it to be a surprisingly lavish and enjoyable production. Jena also had a small but excellent orchestra; the concerts were well attended, but I succeeded in getting tickets for all of them.

In the course of my ten-week stay in Jena, I attended three public functions, all connected in one way or another with the university. On October 6, the Friedrich-Schiller University celebrated the sixth year of the founding of the republic of East Germany. Classes were suspended, and faculty and students gathered in the flower-bedecked auditorium for official exercises. The students and guests were admitted first; then the members of the faculty dressed in their varicolored robes and gowns marched in with slow and dignified steps and took their seats at the front. The program began with a few introductory remarks by the rector. A delegation of Chinese students then presented him with a bouquet of flowers—China was much beloved in East Germany at the time—and its spokesman read the usual type of laudatory congratulations. The main address was delivered by one of the theologians teaching in the university's theological faculty and dealt with the relations of the university to the central government. On the whole, it was a courageous, if soft-spoken, plea for academic and intellectual freedom, even under a totalitarian government.

The remaining two public functions were connected with the German-Russian friendship drive on which the East German propaganda mills worked zealously and constantly, with all stops pulled, so much so that the drive largely defeated its own purpose. This was particularly true during the month of October, which was designated Russian-German Friendship Month. The Friedrich-Schiller University's contribution to this propaganda talkfest was a weekend in which the thirteen Russian visiting professors who were teaching in the various universities and technological institutes throughout East Germany were welcomed. At a panel discussion on the Russian press, I had an opportunity to chat with the main speaker, a Professor Ruban from the University of Kiev, and to make conversation, I asked him whether he knew Professor Diakonoff, the curator of the Near Eastern collections in the Hermitage. His face lit up as he told me that Diakonoff and he had been students together in Leningrad some twenty years earlier but had not met since. Obviously, as a fellow Orientalist, I had more in common with Diakonoff than did his Russian colleague.

The next morning, Sunday, I attended a German-Russian friendship rally in Leuchtenburg Castle, about a half hour by car from Jena, on top of a high hill with a magnificent, sweeping view of the landscape. The guests of honor were the Russian professors, and among the participants were several hundred students from all the East German universities, including those from other Communist lands. The speeches of welcome made by student delegates from the iron curtain countries were on the whole quite temperate, without violent attacks on the West. Only the spokesman for the North Korean students denounced the United States viciously.

In Jena, I gained some insight into the bitter struggle that was going on behind the scenes between the central government and the university faculty, most of whom were not Communists. Their dissatisfaction had nothing to do with money. The East German professors were among the highest-paid personnel in the country, with salaries from four to five times those of even the more skilled workers. Translated into real wages, their salaries were about twice as high as those of the better-paid professors in American universities.

The reason for those high salaries was not only the great esteem in which the intellectual was held but also the fear that he might leave to find a position in West Germany or elsewhere. As it was, not a few of the better-known academicians had left. The East German universities thus had an unusual proportion of older men who, because of age, were no longer inclined to make a radical move. On the other hand, a good many young and comparatively inexperienced scholars found it possible to find positions, especially if they were sympathetic to the regime.

What troubled the East German professors most was the encroachment of government control on the curriculum and the textbooks. Those who still cherished the idea of academic freedom had no sense of security. They were constantly on the defensive and had to stay permanently on the alert. Never knowing how, where, and when the next blow would fall, and whether it would be possible to fend it off, many had lost the peace of mind so essential for creative intellectual activity. Of course a good deal depended on the particular field of study. There was no academic freedom at all in the social sciences and philosophy. In fact the pro-rectors—administrators somewhat similar to deans in our universities—in charge of these disciplines were active Communist theoreticians who considered the teachings of Marx and Engels as gospel, to be taught as absolute dogma. There was therefore almost no teaching of philosophy, anthropology, or sociology as these are known at Western universities—there was no need to search for social and philosophical truths, since they had already been pronounced.

One development in the field of higher education, the so-called workers-peasants college was, as far as I know, unique. It was established for the purpose of helping children of workmen and farmers to get a higher education in spite of their nonintellectual background. The students were given comparatively large fellowships (too large for their own good, according to some) and were encouraged in every way to complete their education. These new and rather admirable educational institutions were proving to be, in one respect, a thorn in the flesh of the university faculties. In order to enhance their prestige, the government tended to exert pressure to integrate these workers-peasants colleges into the university framework, in spite of their comparatively low scholastic standards.

From what I observed during my stay in Jena, the workers-peasants state was a mixed bag. Wages were adequate but no more; however there were many fringe benefits such as health care and vacations, as well as educational opportunities. The mainstay of the economy was still agriculture, and the emphasis was on the formation of farm collectives, yet many of the older farmers were deeply resentful of the government, primarily because of the very heavy taxes imposed upon them. If there was freedom of worship in East Germany and little official anti-Semitism, the government's attitude toward Israel was openly hostile, following the current Soviet line without exception, with Egypt treated as the favorite nation of the Middle East. There was of course no freedom of the press or of any other means of communication, and the many newspapers carried almost identical copy on issues of foreign affairs or domestic policy. No Western periodicals were permitted to enter the country as far as I could see.

Although the post office was under government control, as far as I could tell only one of my letters was ever opened for inspection, and this was a manuscript with photographs. I did have trouble with the Jena post office, but not because of my letters. In the course of my stay there I bought a number of beautiful and very reasonably priced art books in the university book shop, most of which were published by the Czechoslovakian press Artiae. The book shop was state-owned, and I assumed that there would be no trouble in shipping the books to America, especially since they would show both East Germany and Czechoslovakia as culture-prizing lands. The next day, however, I received an urgent telephone call at my hotel to visit the book shop. There I was informed that the Jena postal authorities would permit the mailing of only one book per month to America, and only if its cost were not over thirty marks. The book shop management, as well as the university, was quite upset, and there was a good deal of argument back and forth. But the postal authorities stuck by their guns, and I was unable to mail the books to my wife or to any of my friends.

As far as I could see, there was ample food in Jena, though there were still a few rationed items. The people, according to my own observation, were clothed well and warmly, if not in grand style—a favorite bit of apparel for the younger people was a blue, warm-looking outfit consisting of a pullover sweater and close-fitting trousers. Toward the end of my stay, all the government stores offered a large number of clothing and household items at considerably reduced prices, a state sale as it were. Only the "rentners," those who lived on pensions or on insurance payments, suffered from dire want. But even in the case of these unfortunates, it was rather surprising to note that the government was encouraging private donations to alleviate their lot.

I left Jena on December 6 in one of the official cars of the Friedrich-Schiller University. The trip to East Berlin took only about three hours and was without any untoward incident until I actually arrived in East Berlin and asked the chauffeur to take me to West Berlin, where my hotel was situated. He was unable to do this, since he was not permitted to cross from East Berlin to West Berlin without special permission. He therefore suggested that he drive to the Friedrichstrasse Station, the largest in East Berlin, and there transfer me and my bags to a taxi for West Berlin.

This however proved to be a vain hope. There were only three taxi drivers from East Berlin who had permission from the East German government to enter the West Zone. The chauffeur, a sympathetic man, then suggested that he drive me to the Brandenburg Gate, where the East Zone ends, and leave me in the car while he proceeded on foot across the boundary to find a telephone pay station and call a West Berlin taxi. After a half hour or so, the poor chap returned crestfallen; he had no West German coins to insert in the telephone box.

Fortunately I had some with me, and after taking enough for the call, he was off again to fetch the taxi. By this time, however, two East German policemen were at the car, demanding papers and questioning the contents of my bags. I had several hundred photographs of the tablets in the Hilprecht collection with me and was worried that the policemen might question their presence among my belongings. To be sure, I had permission in writing from the university authorities to take them to America, but the examination and explanation might take hours. Fortunately, on opening my bags, they saw only clothing and other personal effects—the photographs were in a special compartment. By this time the West Berlin taxi had driven up. Under the eyes of the East German policemen, and with their reluctant and somewhat bewildered permission, my three bags were transferred from one car to the other, and in less than fifteen minutes I arrived at the Hotel am Zoo. As a result of this tragicomic incident, it had taken me longer to get from the station in East Berlin to my hotel in West Berlin, a distance of two to three miles, than from Jena to Berlin, a distance of nearly one hundred fifty miles.

So ended my first stay in Jena. It was rather lonely, trying, and a bit awkward at times, but it had its scholarly reward. In the course of studying the Hilprecht collection, I identified 150 Sumerian literary pieces, about 50 of which were on well-preserved tablets. Their contents represented a cross-section of Sumerian literary categories: myths and epic tales, hymns and laments, historiographic documents and model letters, proverbs, essays, disputations. These pieces helped to fill innumerable gaps in compositions already known and pieced together in part. In the collection were also a number of hitherto unknown literary works: a hymn to the god Hendursagga, the vizier of the goddess Nanshe, who supervised man's moral conduct; a love dialogue between Inanna and Dumuzi that may be entitled "Love Finds a Way," or "Deceiving Mother"; a myth involving the underworld deity Ningishzida and the goddess Azimua; an extract of a myth relating how two brother deities had brought down barley to Sumer from the mountain where it had been stored away by the god Enlil; a pleading letter from one Gudea to his personal deity; two precious book lists, or catalogues, of the type I have already described.

In 1960 I returned to Jena for a brief stay to help Dr. Bernhardt complete the copying of the literary pieces in the collection. This time

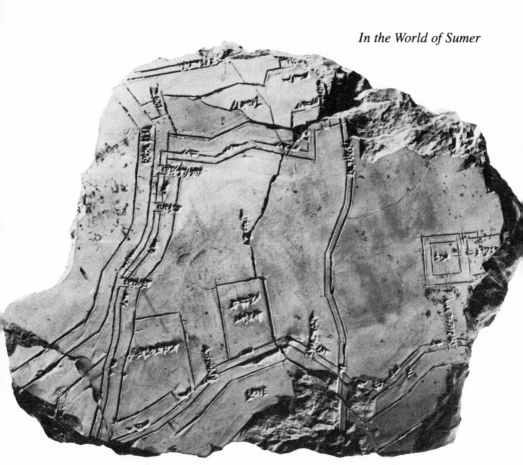

The city map of Nippur. One of the most precious clay documents in the Hilprecht collection.

the mood was less tense, and my stay more pleasant and relaxed. Dr. Bernhardt and I collaborated on several articles relating to the collection and on the publication of copies of all of the 150 literary pieces in two volumes that appeared some years later. Before publication, I made much of this material available to the younger scholars who worked with me in the ensuing decade, and since the appearance of the volumes a number of other scholars have profited substantially from them. Thus, the University Museum and Friedrich-Schiller University cooperative effort that began with little promise turned out to be one of the bright, fruitful ventures of my career.

Having had a taste of working behind the iron curtain (a designation that is resented, and not altogether unjustly, by scholars living in Communist countries), I was happy to learn one day in 1956 that F. G. Rainey, the director of the University Museum, had succeeded in negotiating a deal with the Russian authorities that would make me the first American exchange professor invited to carry on research in the Soviet Union.

Before closing this Jena chapter in my career, I may add a light-hearted note. At the end of October, after I had been in Jena for more than a month, the embassy of the USSR in Washington sent to my home in Philadelphia an application for a visa to be returned to them with three photographs, an autobiography in three copies in Russian or English, and 25¢. Upon receipt of these, they would make their decision. Evidently the decision required no lengthy deliberations, for in the same envelope, and bearing the same date, October 27, as the other enclosure was a short letter informing me that the consular service was now ready to issue the visa upon receipt of $2.50. True, I had saved the two fees, the photographs, and an autobiography in three copies, but by October 27 I was already worrying about an extension of the visa.

11
An Exchange Professor in Russia

The year 1957 was one of celebration and rejoicing for the Soviet Union. It was the fortieth anniversary of the Bolshevik Revolution as well as the year of the Sputnik. Stalin was dead, his hatchet man Beria had been liquidated, and the more amiable and amenable Khrushchev was in charge. The year before, Khrushchev had made his world-astonishing de-Stalinization speech and now, as a number of victims of the Stalinist regime were beginning to be rehabilitated, there was in the land something like a euphoria which pointed to a release of internal tensions and a desire to reach an understanding with the West. In America, too, the obdurate cold-war attitude was softening.

In that same year, the first Pugwash conference took place, when at the invitation of the American industrialist Cyrus Eaton 155 Russian scientists came to Eaton's Nova Scotia summer home to confer with some of their British and American counterparts. Following this conference, Eugene Rabinowitch, the editor of the *Bulletin of Atomic Scientists,* sent out a special issue containing a communication from the Russian scientists as well as the text of a formal resolution of the presidium of the Academy of Sciences of the USSR that read in part: "We Soviet scientists express our full readiness to participate in a common effort with the scientists of any other country to discuss any proposal directed towards the prevention of atomic war, the creation of secure peace, and the tranquility of all mankind." Rabinowitch urged that the Western scientists take up the offer and meet the Russians half-way, arguing that despite the repetition of some of the Communist propaganda demands, they undoubtedly did recognize the necessity of finding a solution to the problem of avoiding war.

Nor was this promising hope for Russian-American cooperation restricted to science and technology. That same year 1957 saw delegations of Russian farmers and journalists visiting the United States, and these witnessed for themselves that America was not on the verge of making war on the Soviet Union. The new cooperative mood had even trickled down to the humanities, at least in the fields of archaeology, anthropology, and ancient history. In 1954, at the Twenty-third International Congress of Orientalists held in Cambridge, there was a delegation of Russian Orientalists, and for the first time in decades Western Orientalists had the opportunity to communicate with their Soviet colleagues. Two years later, the Fifth International Congress of the Anthropological and Ethnological Sciences met at the University Museum in Philadelphia. Among the delegates were three Russians, including George Debetz, a leading Soviet physical anthropologist who established a close scientific relationship with the University Museum's F. R. Rainey, the president of the congress.

The following spring of 1957, Rainey, who was an "Eskimo man," that is, an anthropologist whose research related to the Eskimo peoples, and who had worked some years in Alaska, was invited to give a series of lectures in Moscow as a guest of the Institute of Ethnology and Anthropology, for the Russians were deeply interested in the culture of the Eskimos and in the archaeology of the Arctic region. While in Moscow, Rainey arranged for a professorial exchange. Debetz would come to America to study the Alaskan skeletal material in the American Museum of Natural History that Rainey had unearthed many years earlier; in exchange, I was to be invited by the Institute of Oriental Studies of the Soviet Academy of Sciences to study the archaeological collections in Moscow's Pushkin Museum and in Leningrad's Hermitage Museum, especially those relating to the ancient Near East, and more specifically to cuneiform studies. Financially, the arrangement was simple and equitable: the University Museum undertook to defray all of Debetz's expenses for his two-month stay in the United States, while the Soviet Academy of Sciences reciprocated by taking care of my expenses in the Soviet Union. Thus I became the first American exchange professor in the USSR.

I arrived in Moscow on October 20, 1957. At the airport I was met by I. S. Katznelson, an Egyptologist working primarily on the history of Nubia. Katznelson spoke French and German, and so, though I spoke no Russian, there was no language problem. It seemed a bit strange at first that an Egyptologist rather than a cuneiformist was to be my Russian connection. But this was cleared up when I was informed that the Institute of Oriental Studies had its main office in Moscow, and an affiliate in Leningrad. In order to avoid overlapping and duplication, the Moscow Institute and the University of Moscow concentrated on Egyptology, while the Leningrad affiliate and the University of Leningrad focused on cuneiform studies. The first half of my stay, Katznelson informed me, would be in Moscow, and he himself would arrange for me to deliver several lectures to be attended by his colleagues and their students.

From the airport, Katznelson drove me to the Leningradskiya Hotel, near the Leningradskiya railway station. There a room had been reserved for me. The hotel was a twenty-one-story building of typical Stalinist architectural style, stuffily furnished and, for a Westerner, a bit oppressively. After I completed the official registration at the reception desk, Katznelson led me up to a comfortable room. Before leaving me, he opened a large leather bag that he had brought from the car, and which I had eyed rather suspiciously, and out popped bedraggled rubles by the hundreds. These, he informed me, were for my meals and personal expenses while in Russia, where payment by check was then virtually unknown. He arranged to pick me up the next day for my first lecture and left.

Early next morning I put some of the rubles in my pocket and found my way to the dining room of the hotel for my first Russian breakfast. But rubles or not, I soon realized that breakfast would be hard to come by, and that I would have to wait for hours before being served. The trouble was that this was an all-out *delegatzia* year when many Communist delegations from various countries were invited to participate in the Soviet Union's celebration of the revolution. On entering the dining room, I found almost every table, adorned with a little flag at the center, occupied by the *delegatzias*. After much looking about, I spotted a small unoccupied table in a corner and sat down diffidently and not too hopefully. The waiters were very busy hurrying to satisfy the hungry Communists and paid no attention to me. Finally, as the lunch hour approached, and breakfast seemed as far away as ever, I took courage and left the hotel to forage for food in the world outside. After an hour or so of walking the Moscow streets, I came upon a cafeteria-type restaurant where the food was simple but adequate. I did not again try my luck in the hotel but ate out at restaurants, except for the meals to which I was invited by my colleagues.

The *delegatzia* epidemic proved to be somewhat embarrassing even on the scholarly level. One day I received an invitation from the president of the Soviet Academy of Sciences, Alexander Nikolayewitch

Nesmeyanov, to a reception tendered by the academy in honor of the visiting scholars and scientists who had come to celebrate the Sputnik year. On entering the long dining hall I found once again the *delegatzia* of each country—this time consisting of members of one academy of sciences or another—huddled together, with that symbolic little flag in the center, while I had to sit all alone. Following the meal, the president, as is customary in Russia, arose and toasted each delegation in turn in the name of the country and institution it represented. When he came to me, he naturally addressed me as a delegate from America, and the unbelieving eyes of the entire assembly turned to me in wonder.

In my response, I took care to point out that I was visiting the Soviet Union as an individual scholar and did not represent my government or the American Philosophical Society, which corresponds in some respects to the academies of science in other countries, or even my university. Nesmeyanov, a sensitive scientist and administrator, received these rather negative remarks with sympathy and understanding, and the ensuing applause from the congregated delegates indicated clearly that this was after all primarily a community of scholars, and not of governmental or institutional representatives.

Nesmeyanov, who, if I am not mistaken was a chemist of high repute, displayed delicacy and sportsmanship on various other occasions. When speaking of Russian scientific achievements, for example—and it should be borne in mind that these were the Sputnik days—he always took care to acknowledge the contributions made by European and American universities, with—to use his words—"their longer traditions in science and scholarship." His speeches and conversations evinced a deep desire for closer cooperation and communication among scholars and scientists the world over, unhampered by national, racial, or ideological boundaries. Nor was this desire confined to words and rhetoric. In my own case, for example, the invitation to come as an exchange professor to the Soviet Union, though offically approved, had become snarled in red tape, and for a while it looked as though I might be stranded in Berlin waiting for its arrival. I learned later that Nesmeyanov himself, upon the urgent appeal of the Institute of Oriental Studies, had taken a hand in the matter, after which the formal invitation and the visá had come through in a few days.

On one matter, to my deep regret, Nesmeyanov reneged, though I am convinced it was through no fault of his. One of the first requests I made of him as president of the Academy of Sciences was for permission to visit Zashkov, the town where I was born, and he promised to do what he could. Zashkov, as I remembered it, was more like a hamlet than a town, and I had never thought of it as having any military significance. But during the Second World War my son Daniel, who was ten years old at the time, would repeatedly bring me items from the *New York Times* reporting that the railroad station at Zashkov had passed from the Russians to the Germans and vice versa; it was therefore clear that Zashkov had somehow become of some strategic importance.

In any event I was very eager to visit it and see for myself the transformation of the town beginning with the Bolshevek Revolution, and to learn the fate of its inhabitants. After all, but for a fortunate decision on the part of my father some forty years earlier, I would have been one of them, and their fate would have been my fate. My hopes for permission to visit my old home town grew dimmer as the weeks passed. Finally I was informed that for various practical reasons, such as the absence of a hotel, the visit would be impossible. To this day I do not know the true reason for this curious reaction to my request.

I stayed six weeks in the Soviet Union, three in Moscow and three in Leningrad. My Moscow lectures were well attended and the response was enthusiastic. Except for one, all the lectures related to Sumerian history, culture, and literature. The one exception was a lecture by request on the state of Oriental studies in the United States and the names and contributions of American Orientalists, a subject of great interest to the Russian professors and students. My lectures were in English and needed the mediation of a translator except when given before smaller groups of specialists who knew enough English to follow them if I spoke slowly and clearly. Despite the warm response to the lectures, my stay in Moscow would have been relatively unfruitful had it not been for the discovery in the Pushkin Museum of a cuneiform tablet that was a literary nugget, one that set my heart thumping: a tablet inscribed with a hitherto unknown Sumerian literary genre.

It is a remarkable fact that although Russia before the Second World War had never conducted excavations in Iraq, cuneiform's home ground, it had an unbroken tradition of outstanding cuneiformists, beginning with the last half of the nineteenth century. Two of the earliest and most dedicated were N. P. Likhachov and M. V. Nikolsky, who had acquired some five thousand cuneiform tablets by purchase, many of which had been published over the years. After the Bolshevik Revolution these tablets became the property of the state and were deposited in roughly equal parts in the Pushkin Museum in Moscow and the Hermitage in Leningrad. As a guest of the Academy of Sciences, I was permitted to examine the collection of both museums and especially those tablets which were still unpublished. While examining the unpublished pieces in the Pushkin Museum I came across a well-preserved tablet which, I realized after closer study, would be the major accomplishment of my Russian stay, one totally unexpected and all the more welcome as a consequence.

The tablet, which was probably inscribed in Nippur about 1700 B.C., though its contents may have been composed much earlier, was divided by the scribe into four columns. I quickly realized that it contained two different compositions of unequal size separated by a ruled line. The first and longer one consisted of 112 lines of text, while the second had only 56 lines. Following the text of the two compositions, the scribe had drawn a double line and added a three-line colophon, giving the title of each of the compositions, consisting of its initial phrases as well as the number of lines which the compositions contain, individually and together. But all these were superficial features that were readily ascertainable; it was much more difficult to get at the meaning of the inscribed text. The first, but all-essential step, was to transcribe the text line by line, and this took a good part of my three-week stay in Moscow.

In the course of performing this task, I gradually began to apprehend the general nature of the contents of the tablet and realized that both compositions were funeral dirges, or elegies, preceded by introductory prologues. Since the elegy was a literary genre not hitherto found among the thousands of literary pieces known to me, I was very eager to edit and publish the text, and to my great joy, the Pushkin Museum authorities granted the necessary permission. However, a scholarly edition of the text would require a long period of concentrated effort that I would have to spend at my leisure in Philadelphia where I had access to the indispensable reference books and notes. The Pushkin Museum therefore generously provided me with an excellent photograph of the tablet. I devoted much of the year following my return to the United States to the translation and interpretation of the document whose contents can now be followed in *The Sumerians*.

Upon completion of the edition of the document, which included a transliteration, translation, and commentary that I titled "Two Elegies on a Pushkin Museum Tablet: A New Sumerian Literary Genre," I sent it on to the Pushkin Museum for publication. The director of the museum turned the work over to the eminent Soviet Orientalist Vasilli Vasilievitch Struve who prepared a valuable introduction. The resulting monograph, printed in English with a Russian translation, did not appear until 1960, just prior to the meeting of the Twenty-fifth International Congress of Orientalists held in Moscow that year. Needless to say it was a real pleasure to see the attractively printed little monograph in the Moscow bookstores and to receive a number of author's copies, not to mention an unexpected royalty of three hundred rubles that my wife, who had accompanied me to the meeting, had no trouble in spending in a Moscow department store.

The final three weeks of my Soviet sojourn were spent in Leningrad, where I repeated some of the lectures on the Sumerians before the Orientalists of the University of Leningrad and their students, as well as before those engaged in Oriental research in the Hermitage and the Institute for the History of Material Culture. My generous host in Leningrad was Professor Struve, who had kept Oriental studies alive and active in Russia for half a century, through revolution and turmoil, war and peace, famine and plenty. Struve, a careful epigraphist, a penetrating philologist, and an imaginative historian of the ancient world, began his scholarly contributions as early as 1912 and continued them until his death in 1965, at the age of seventy-six. His earlier publications related primarily to Egyptological research (he had studied in Berlin with the renowned Adolph Erman and Eduard Meyer) and one of his major earlier works centered on the Moscow Mathematical Papyrus. But later, as keeper of Ancient Oriental Antiquities in the Hermitage Museum, he became deeply interested in the Sumerian administrative documents, and from the 1930s on, he devoted his energies almost entirely to Sumerian history and culture, and especially to the socioeconomic features of Sumerian society.

In 1934 Struve was elected a member of the Academy of Sciences of the Soviet Union, the highest scholarly honor in the country, and materially one of the most rewarding. While I was in Leningrad he invited me to his *datcha,* his summer home, and there I met his family. I learned then that he was not only a dedicated and distinguished scholar but also a warm and generous human being. During the bitter, oppressive Stalin years he had saved more than one Jewish scholar from harassment and demotion. In 1959, my one-time assistant in the University Museum, Edmond Gordon, and I were invited to contribute to the Struve Festschrift in honor of his seventieth birthday. Gordon contributed a pioneering study relating to animals as represented in Sumerian proverbs and fables, while I took the opportunity to prepare a pioneer investigation concerned with the cultural image that the Sumerians had acquired over the centuries of foreign peoples and lands, and the variety of attitudes that had been developed toward them. Both of us deemed it a privilege to present our studies to "a devoted and creative scholar," V. V. Struve.

The Russian cuneiformist whose scholarly contributions are second only to those of Struve, and who had become the unrivaled authority on ancient Mesopotamia and some of the neighboring lands, is Igor Diakonoff, about whom I had inquired during my Jena days. I first met Diakonoff in Cambridge, when he was a relatively young man of thirty-nine, at the Third International Congress of Orientalists. Because this was the first time in decades that Russian Orientalists had been seen in the West, and Western scholars had no idea of what, if anything, was being produced in the Soviet Union in the area of ancient Near East research, it was most interesting to talk to Diakonoff. He had spent his childhood in Norway, where, if I am not mistaken, his father had been ambassador for many years, and spoke fluent English. To my great delight he brought with him a long, warm review of my *Sumerian Mythology* that he had published in a Russian scholarly journal.

It was in Cambridge that I first glimpsed the immensely productive cuneiform research that had been going on in the Soviet Union despite the problems that had at times afflicted the country. But it was not until I came to Leningrad that I became aware that there was a significant difference between Western and Russian cuneiformists in the general direction of their research, due to a contrast in viewpoints that has proved to be mutually supplementary and stimulating. While the Western scholars emphasize history, religion, and literature in their many-faceted investigations, the Russians, because of their involvement with the materialistic theory of history, focus on the socioeconomic aspects of ancient history, an area of research for which ancient Mesopotamia, with its immense quantity of written documents, is singularly suitable.

For example, I owe to Diakonoff my vision of Sumerian society that runs counter to the claim of the majority of Western scholars, who argue that the Sumerian city-state was a totalitarian theocracy dominated by the temple, which owned virtually all the land and was in absolute control of its entire economy. In 1959, Diakonoff published his challenging and illuminating work, *Sumer: Society and State in Ancient Mesopotamia,* in which he demonstrated by an imaginative utilization of the available documents that Sumerian society consisted of nobles, commoners, clients, and slaves, and that it was a society in which private property was not uncommon, though ownership was on a family, rather than individual, basis.

I also remember vividly an afternoon spent in one of the classrooms of the Hermitage Museum when one of the Sumerian legal documents utilized by Diakonoff to demonstrate his innovative theory of Sumer's socioeconomic structure was discussed in detail by Struve, Diakonoff, and me in the presence of a number of students and scholars, a discussion that was as scholarly and penetrating as any I have witnessed in the most prestigious Western universities.

If Diakonoff's original and stimulating contributions to socioeconomic history proved an inspiration to my own investigations, I, for my part, introduced him to Sumerian literature, triggering some of his research in this specialized area that was unknown in the Soviet Union

The author in Leningrad, 1957. Left to right, Igor Diakonoff, Russia's leading cuneiformist; the author; the late Soviet academician Vasily Vasilievitch Struve; Boris B. Piotrovskii, director of the Hermitage Museum.

before the appearance of my *Sumerian Mythology*. Unfortunately, except for the Pushkin Museum tablet inscribed with two elegies, there are virtually no Sumerian literary tablets in Russia. While in Leningrad, I examined the tablet collection of the Hermitage with some care and could identify only six small pieces inscribed with parts of various well-known Sumerian literary compositions. In spite of this total lack of relevant source material, two of Diakonoff's students specialized in the study of Sumerian literature, one writing her dissertation on the conjugation of the Sumerian verb in the epic texts. In 1965 I made an effort to have this woman come to the University Museum on the current cultural exchange program. But by the time I found my way through the red tape of the various governmental and semigovernmental agencies, and began to receive some positive response, I was ready to retire as curator of the Tablet collection, and there was no purpose in pursuing the matter.

In 1963, Diakonoff was a visiting professor at the Oriental Institute of the University of Chicago, and on his way to the Eastern seaboard for his return to Russia, he stayed several days in our house. In 1969, he edited *Ancient Mesopotamia,* a valuable reference book that provided Western scholars with an outstanding collection of studies by Soviet experts which were largely unknown to the world outside. In the same year, Diakonoff and I met in East Berlin, where both of us read papers relating to Mesopotamian society at a symposium sponsored by the Central Institute of Ancient History and Archaeology of the East German Academy of Sciences. In 1970, we met once again, during the sessions of the XVIII Rencontre Assyriologique Internationale that took place in Munich, where Diakonoff read a theoretical paper on "Socioeconomic Classes in Babylon and the Babylonian Concept of Social Stratification." After this, I did not run into Diakonoff for a number of years, and we were beginning to lose touch with each other. It was therefore a great pleasure to meet and talk with him once again in Leningrad in 1984 during the XXXI Rencontre Assyriologique Internationale which he helped to organize.

In the course of my visit to Leningrad in 1957 I met several of Russia's outstanding archaeologists and learned firsthand about their excavations and publications. Archaeology was big business in the Soviet Union at the time, involving budgetary outlay of several million rubles per year for excavation only, not including the salaries of the scientific personnel. The nerve center of this archaeological activity was the Academy of Sciences, functioning through its Institute of the History of Material Culture and its Institute of Ethnology and Anthropology, both of which are centered in Moscow with affiliates in Leningrad. In addition, the Academies of Sciences of the various republics of the Soviet Union, such as those of the Ukraine, Armenia, Turkmenistan, Azarbaijan, etc., make large contributions in money and personnel for excavations in their respective territories. The Hermitage and Pushkin Museum also cooperate and participate in excavations in order to add to their collections of antiquities. Finally, a large and unexpected source of income are the large scale construction projects, such as those engaged in building dams or power stations; these are required by law to call in archaeologists prior to demolishing or flooding any area where ancient tombs, villages, or buildings may be buried. With this large budget in hand, it was not surprising to learn that the year 1958 was scheduled to have forty-nine archaeological expeditions, large and small, working throughout the Soviet Union.

As an Orientalist, I was of course primarily interested in Soviet excavations in Oriental lands. In the twenty years prior to 1957, I learned, Soviet archaeologists had carried on quite a number of large-scale excavations in the region of the Caucasus, in Central Asia, and far to the east in the Altai region of Siberia.

In the outskirts of Erevan, the capital of modern Soviet Armenia, two separate expeditions had been excavating two towns dating back to the first half of the first millennium B.C. Both towns were founded by Urartu kings who had their capital in the Lake Van region of Turkey, the center of the Urartu state. The Urartu people, as is becoming ever more apparent, played a major role in the history of the Ancient Orient; Urartu was in fact responsible to a large extent for the collapse of Assyria, the scourge of the ancient Near East. It is the life and culture of this relatively little known Urartu people that the Armenian excavations were helping to resurrect. These excavations were in the charge of Boris Piotrovsky, now director of the Hermitage, but then head of the Leningrad Institute for the History of Material Culture. A red-haired, red-faced Russian, Piotrovsky, because of his many years of archaeological activity, was known with affection as the King of Armenia. In 1969, his magnificent book *Urartu* was published in English in the series Archaeologia Mundi.

In Central Asia, between the Caspian Sea and the Oxus River, Soviet archaeologists had discovered the remains of a number of peoples and cultures ranging over a period of five thousand years, from the fourth millennium B.C. to the first millennium A.D. In the now barren desert region of Khoresm, for example, S. F. Tolstov, head of the Moscow Institute of Ethnology and Anthropology, uncovered an entire civilization, including an imposing irrigation system, from the first half of the first millennium B.C. Somewhat farther to the south and east, B. A. Kuftin, B. A. Litvinsky, and V. M. Masson excavated a number of mounds that shed much light on the prehistoric peoples of the region. In Old Nisa, M. E. Masson excavated a huge area consisting of temples and palaces related to the burials of the first Parthian kings and recovered hundreds of seal impressions and ostraca covered with Parthian inscriptions.

Far to the east in the Altai region of Siberia, Russian archaeologists were fortunate enough to come upon a group of frozen tombs which during approximately twenty-five hundred years had preserved their contents almost intact: bodies of men and women, chariots, horses and their rich trappings, wooden furniture, cloth hangings and rugs, innumerable ornaments of metal. These burials, transferred and set up again in the Hermitage, afford a new insight into the life of these Russian nomads, who were probably related to the Scythians.

During my stay in Russia in 1957, I was deeply interested in the position of Soviet Jewry. In the course of discussing various aspects of Jewish life in Russia with colleagues, both Jews and non-Jews, I learned, for example, that of the approximately two dozen scholars engaged in studies related to the ancient Near East, seven were Jews, all of whom attended one or another of my lectures. These men held professorial appointments in the universities or in one of the institutes of the Academy of Sciences, or were curators in the Hermitage. Quite a number of Soviet archaeologists, ethnologists, and anthropologists were Jews, as was the associate director of the Moscow Institute of Ethnology and Anthropology. In fact, some 10 percent of Soviet intelligentsia—writers, musicians, artists, journalists, scientists, and academicians—were Jews, although Jews made up only 2 to 3 percent of the population.

Jews and non-Jews agreed that there had been a period toward the end of Stalin's life when anti-Semitism had become rampant, and Jews were in dire peril. No one with whom I spoke understood why that had come about. Since then, however, there had been a steady improvement, and almost all felt that discrimination was on the decline. Even Yiddish was making a bit of a comeback. While I was in Leningrad, I attended a Yiddish variety show called *Lachen is Gesund* (*It's Healthy to Laugh*), advertised in Russian characters, in which the actors sang Yiddish songs, recited bits from the beloved Yiddish author Sholem Aleichem, and presented skits caricaturing Russian-Jewish life. There was constant and enthusiastic applause from the middle-aged, relatively well-dressed audience.

Of course, anti-Semitism in the Soviet Union had not disappeared, but, at least on the surface, it seemed no worse than in the West. Orthodox Jews were pained by several aspects of life in Russia. First, atheism was the prevalent philosophy. Whereas in the West the Orthodox were free to live in accordance with their beliefs, in Russia Jewish groups were harassed and denigrated, and everything holy to them was ridiculed and suppressed. Another problem related to intermarriage and assimilation. Intermarriage was quite common in the Soviet Union. Among the Orientalists, for example, at least three had married non-Jewish women. Children of these marriages could designate themselves as either Russians or Jews on their identity cards, and most chose to be known as Russians. However, official Soviet attitudes toward the State of Israel changed the minds of some. In Russia, there was nothing but official hatred and warlike hostility against Israel, and the atheistic, assimilated, Communist Jew must follow the party line. By 1957 it was apparent that some of the assimilated children of these mixed marriages were reacting strongly to Soviet condemnation of Israel: the son of one of my Russian colleagues who had been a faithful Communist and had participated in the Bolshevik Revolution chose to write the word "Jew" rather than "Russian" on his identity card. But in 1957 I could not foresee the heartbreaking situation that has since developed, or that the

Soviet anti-Israel stand would bring in its wake the deadly poison of the rampant anti-Semitism of Czarist days, so that no Jew could now live in peace and security in Russia.

In 1965, my book *History Begins at Sumer* was translated into Russian, and published by the Academy of Sciences of the USSR, with an introduction by Struve. For this edition I prepared a special preface, the last paragraph of which read as follows:

> The last chapter of the Russian edition of this book is concerned with the Sumerian conception of man's "Golden Age," a speculative vision of the distant past when all mankind lived in peace and harmony free of fear, strife and want. In the four thousand years that have elapsed since the Sumerians wrote down their wistful lines about man's "lost Paradise," war and strife, poverty and hunger, fear and terror, have continued to plague mankind without rest and respite. But today fresh breezes are stirring in the strife-torn world, and a spirit of cooperation and reciprocity is beginning to break through and take hold of the hearts of men, at least on the scholarly and cultural level. To the hopeful promise of world peace and harmony, I dedicate this Russian edition of a book written by an American scholar born in Russia, about an ancient civilization, all of which helps to reveal the fundamental unity of man in time and space.

How false and overoptimistic can a prophet be?

In August 1960, Mrs. Kramer and I attended the Twenty-fifth International Congress of Orientalists in Moscow, where I read a paper entitled "The Death of Dumuzi: A Newly Restored Sumerian Poem," which corrected some errors relating to the death of this demigod that had been current for decades among cuneiformists. From Moscow we traveled to Warsaw and then to Prague. I lectured at the Oriental Institute of Charles University, where cuneiform studies had a long tradition and flourished even under Nazi and Communist domination, due primarily to the dedication and devotion of two first-rate scholars: L. Matouš and J. Klima. From Prague my wife left for Vienna, while I continued westward to Jena to assist Dr. Bernhardt with the preparation for publication of the Sumerian literary pieces in the Hilprecht collection and then to London to meet with Cyril Gadd and discuss with him our joint publication project relating to the Sumerian literary material excavated by Leonard Woolley at Ur. Mrs. Kramer joined me then, and we turned our faces east once again, first to Istanbul, where I conferred with Muazzez Çiğ and Hatice Kizilyay, the keepers of the tablet collection of the Museum of the Ancient Orient who were copying the hundreds of Sumerian literary pieces that had not been worked on for more than half a century.

Our next stop was Teheran, where I lectured at the University of Teheran, and then we traveled more than two hundred miles by car to the rock at Bisitun on whose specially prepared surface the great Darius had chiseled a trilingual inscription commemorating his victory over the Magian rebel Gaumata. It was this trilingual inscription that originally made possible the decipherment of the cuneiform script, and Bisitun is holy ground to the cuneiformist. From Teheran we flew to Karachi and for the next seven weeks roamed about in Pakistan and India. What is a Sumerologist doing in Pakistan and India? Searching for paradise, no less!

12
The Quest for Paradise

Over the past half century an ancient civilization has been uncovered in Pakistan and India which remains to this day one of the major archaeological mysteries of modern times. It flourished for a thousand years, from 2500 B.C. or earlier to about 1500 B.C., and extended from the present Pakistan-Iran border on the west to the foot of the Himalayas and the Gulf of Cambay; it was thus larger in area than ancient Mesopotamia and Egypt combined. It included scores of prosperous settlements, several of which developed into large urban centers, the best known being those unearthed near the modern villages called Harappa and Mohenjo-daro.

The people who produced this Indus civilization were farmers and cattle breeders, fishermen and boatmen, artisans and craftsmen, merchants and administrators. They were skilled in working metal, stone, and terra cotta, and made use of the wheel for transportation as well as for pottery. They were man's first known town planners. Even today it is an awesome and moving experience to walk down the broad main thoroughfares of the Mohenjo-daro ruins which divide the city into rectangular blocks separated by narrow lanes and to visit the well-preserved baked brick houses with their vestibules, porters' lodges,

---

Among the ruins of Mohenjo-daro. The chimney-like structure is the brick lining of a well, sunk through earlier building strata, now exposed.

courtyards, living rooms, well rooms, and bathrooms connected with covered street drains. They must have developed a highly centralized government: the building bricks are of uniform dimensions; there was a standardized system of weights and measures; and most significant of all, they had a uniform script consisting of some three hundred pictographic signs with conventionalized syllabic values. The reading and writing of this script had to be studied and learned by budding scribes, and thus there is every reason to assume that there were schools scattered throughout the land with a uniform system of education.

The ancient name of the land in which this highly advanced civilization took root and flourished is still unknown. It may, of course, be found mentioned in one or another of the Indus inscriptions which have been recovered on stone and copper seals, clay sealings, and potsherds. But if so there is little hope at present of recognizing it, since not a single sign of the Indus script has as yet been deciphered. As of today the hope of recovering the ancient name of this land lies not in the Indus inscriptions but in those of its neighbor to the west, the land of Sumer in southern Mesopotamia. It is a well-established fact that the Indus people had strong commercial ties with those of Sumer—some thirty Indus seals have actually been excavated in Sumer, and no doubt hundreds more are still lying buried in the Sumerian ruins. There is therefore good reason to conclude that the Sumerians had known the name of the Indus land, as well as some of its more prominent features, and that some of the Sumerian inscriptions might turn out to be highly informative in this respect.

With this in mind I searched through all the extant Sumerian literary works for possible clues and came up with the tentative hypothesis that Dilmun, a land mentioned frequently in the Sumerian texts and glorified in Sumerian myth, may turn out to be the land of the Indus or at least some part of it. The pages that follow present step by step the cuneiform evidence for this tentative identification that runs counter to the generally accepted view. But first, a brief sketch of the discovery and resurrection of the Indus civilization, whose existence had been erased from the mind and memory of man for well-nigh four millennia, and which may turn out to be Sumer's paradise.

The story begins in the year 1922 when an Indian archaeologist named R. D. Bannerji was excavating a Buddhist stupa of the first or second century A.D. at Mohenjo-daro, an ancient ruin on the Indus River, about 200 miles from Karachi. The archeological finds which so excited Bannerji had nothing to do with Buddhism but with a people and culture that could only have flourished in India long before Buddha came on the scene. Its existence, in fact, had already been surmised to some extent by Indian and British archaeologists as a result of earlier accidental finds at Harappa, a site some 350 miles to the northeast of Mohenjo-daro. The most remarkable finds from these sites were steatite seals, usually square in shape, on which were engraved what were obviously pictographic characters belonging to a totally unknown script which must have been current in ancient India over a large area comprising much of the Indus River plain.

Since Harappa and Mohenjo-daro, though hundreds of miles apart, proved to be two urban centers of a culturally identical civilization, it was not unreasonable to surmise that about them and between them had existed numerous smaller settlements, villages and towns, which belonged to the same people and culture. That this was actually the case was proved beyond doubt by the surveys and excavations of N. G. Majumdar and also by the discoveries of the noted explorer of Central Asia, Sir Aurel Stein, who in the years 1926–1928 partially excavated two settlements of the Harappa culture, one near the modern Pakistan-Iran border, the other some hundred miles northeast of Mohenjo-daro.

The results of these and other excavations and surveys did not remain hidden, as is too often the case in archaeological research, but were published, and utilized, beginning with the publication in 1931 by Sir John Marshall and his collaborators of a detailed three-volume report of the Mohenjo-daro excavations. More studies of Mohenjo-daro, Harappa, and other Indus sites were published by Ernest Mackay, Mortimer Wheeler, M. S. Vats, and Stuart Piggott in the thirties and forties.

The partition of India, however bitter its consequences, proved to be somewhat of a boon for Indus civilization archaeology. As a result of the division, almost all the known Indus sites, including Mohenjo-daro and Harappa, fell within Pakistan, and India itself was left with virtually no archaeological traces of this cultural heritage. Therefore there began a search for Harappa-type sites within India proper; now over a hundred Indus sites have been identified. In Pakistan, archaeologists from Pakistan, France, and the University Museum of the University of Pennsylvania have identified a number of additional Indus sites. The University Museum in 1960, with the close cooperation of the Pakistan Department of Archaeology, conducted under the leadership of my young colleague and former student George Dales a six-week survey of the Makran coast by boat, jeep, camel, and foot. During this survey Dales excavated at Sutkagen-dor, the site examined many years earlier by Aurel Stein, and identified a hitherto unknown Harappa settlement at Sotka-Koh, almost a hundred miles east of Sutkagen-dor.

To get some idea of the nature and character of the Indus civilization and of the people who created it, we must turn to the remains themselves, especially those uncovered at Harappa and Mohenjo-daro, the two largest and most informative Indus sites. Both Harappa and

Sealings of the Indus
civilization with the
undeciphered Indus script.

Mohenjo-daro consist of a group of irregular mounds, about three miles in circumference, the most westerly of which rises high above its neighbors. On excavation, this higher mound was found to cover the remains of a walled citadel or acropolis some 1200 by 600 feet in size, enclosing a platform about 30 feet high on which were erected the city's public buildings: the "Great Bath," a large well-drained watertight tank surrounded on three sides by a series of small rooms; the "Collegiate Building," consisting of a number of cells arranged about a cloistered court; and the "Pillared Hall," square in shape, with a roof supported by twenty pillars made of baked bricks.

The city itself, where the main population lived, lay below the citadel, in the shape of a gridiron of wide unpaved main streets running north-south and east-west which divided the city into numerous blocks of roughly equal size. The houses and shops were built of solid brick walls, mud-plastered on the inside; generally they consisted of a courtyard entered from a side alley and surrounded on two or three sides by rooms of varying size, including meticulously constructed bathrooms with elaborate drains communicating with main street drains, which could be cleaned periodically by lifting large manhole-type covers. Stairways were not uncommon and probably led to second stories, or at least to the flat roofs that covered the houses. Both cities also had what seemed to be a special workers' quarters consisting of a group of almost identically planned small two-room houses. They had very large buildings which may have been used as public granaries, as well as well-built brick platforms where the grain was pounded into flour. Everywhere throughout the city, in public buildings and private houses, were found carefully constructed brick-lined wells which provided the water supply for the inhabitants.

To judge from the skeletal remains, the majority of the Indus people belonged, anthropologically speaking, to the Mediterranean type: slender and tallish in stature and probably had brownish complexions, black hair, large brown-black eyes, and narrow, prominent noses. There seemed to have been a minority group belonging primarily to the so-called Proto-Australoid type, the predominant element among the present day aboriginal tribes in south and central India: small in stature, black of skin, with curly black hair, broad flat noses, and protruding, fleshy lips.

The mainstay of the Indus economy was agriculture, and we learn from the remains that they grew wheat, barley, the date palm, sesame, peas, a cabbage-like plant similar to that known in modern India as rai, and cotton (cotton cloth was no doubt one of the main Indus exports). The animal bones excavated at the various sites reveal that the Indus people had domesticated the long-tailed sheep, the "Kashmir" goat, the

The Great Bath at Mohenjo-daro.

pig, the buffalo, and the zebu, as well as the short-horned humpless bull. Also domesticated were the cat and two types of dogs, as well as the horse, ass, camel, and elephant.

Among the more outstanding Indus artisans and craftsmen were the architects, masons, and carpenters who planned and built the remarkably well-constructed buildings and houses, and the ubiquitous wells and drains which bespeak a regard for sanitation unique in the ancient Orient. There were the highly skilled jewelers who worked in gold, silver, and semiprecious stones fashioning the beads, armlets, necklaces, collars, girdles, and ear and nose ornaments with which the Indus people loved to bedeck their bodies. The jewelers probably prepared the steatite seals on which were engraved the Indus pictographs alongside exquisite representations of such animals as the bull, uni-

188

corn, rhinoceros, tiger, crocodile, buffalo, elephant, goat, and ante-lope. The Indus smiths and metallurgists made use of both casting and forging in manufacturing such copper and bronze implements as axes, chisels, knives, spears, razors, mirrors, fishhooks, and a varied assort-ment of pots and pans. Talented sculptors worked in sandstone, lime-stone, steatite, and bronze; the busy potters fashioned vast quantities of plain and painted clay ware and a large variety of terra cotta toys and figurines.

Merchants and tradesmen were no doubt numerous and prominent in the Indus society. Trade played a vital role in the economy, as is evi-denced by the thousands of inscribed seals used to stamp the clay labels that identified the bales of merchandise destined for local or foreign parts, as well as by the ubiquitous and uniform weights, all belonging to a system of avoirdupois in which the number 16 was the ratio unit. There was local trade between the Indus cities, towns, and villages by boat, cart, and beast; there was foreign land trade with such surround-ing regions as Baluchistan, Afghanistan, Turkestan, and perhaps Tibet; and there was foreign sea trade with such distant lands as Sumer, with stopovers in the several ports on the Makran coast. Indus seals and seal impressions have actually been found at Ur, the capital of Sumer—in fact, the dating of the Indus civilization is based largely on the exca-vations in Sumer of Indus artifacts—and it is not at all unlikely that Indus merchants settled more or less permanently in some of the more important Sumerian cities.

While much of the material culture of the far-spread Indus civiliza-tion has thus been recovered, defined, and interpreted, the intellectual and spiritual life of the people who created it remains a mystery, except for what little can be inferred about their government and religion from the all too mute archaeological finds. Thus since Harappa and Mohenjo-daro seem to be the only two relatively large cities with for-tified citadels and important public buildings, it is reasonable to infer that they were two capitals exercising a dual hegemony over a vast Indus state. Again, since the Indus culture, though found over an area of about half a million square miles in extent, was thoroughly uniform in character, and since its two major cities, Harappa and Mohenjo-daro, though occupied continuously for close to a millennium, from first to last show no significant change in their street layout and house plan-ning, it is justifiable to surmise that political and governmental power was in the hands of autocratic priest-kings surrounded by a highly cen-tralized bureaucracy. For the religious beliefs and practices of the Indus people, all we have are a few scattered clues from the seals and figu-rines, which speak for the worship of a mother-goddess, of a Shiva-like male deity, and of sacred trees and animals. There seems to have been some kind of belief in life after death, since the dead were buried in cemeteries, accompanied by a considerable number of pottery vessels, and occasionally by ornaments and toilet articles.

As of today we know nothing of the ideas and ideals of the Indus people, of the motives and values of their culture, for only literary works provide an insight into the mind and heart of a people, and none has as yet been discovered on the Indus sites. There is of course hope that some Indus literary documents will be found in the course of future excavations, for the inscribed seals prove beyond doubt that the Indus people, or rather certain sections of it, were literate. The script, to judge from the several thousand inscribed seals excavated to date, not one of which contains over twenty characters, consisted of about three hundred signs. This large number means that the signs were not alphabetic, but syllabic, that is, each character stood for a syllable rather than a single consonant or vowel. The writing was from right to left, as had been proved conclusively by the overlapping signs on potsherds unearthed at Kalibangan in the late 1950s. Unfortunately, not a single sign on the seal inscriptions has yet been deciphered with reasonable certainty. Since the seals were impressed on clay bullae attached to containers for export trade, they may include names of individuals and places, as well as words designating occupations and merchandise. While they may thus tell us something about the ethnic makeup, geography, and economy of the Indus land, there is little likelihood that they will shed any light on the intellectual and spiritual aspects of its culture. For this, the most promising hope lies not in the Indus seals but in the Sumerian documents in which references might be expected to the Indus land and people, if we could only identify the name by which these were known to the Sumerians. Which brings me back to Dilmun, the Sumerian paradise-land, and its possible identification with the land of the Indus civilization.

It was more than thirty years ago that my quest for paradise—the Sumerian paradise, that is—began. I was then in the midst of piecing together and trying to translate the epic poem "Gilgamesh and the Land of the Living," whose initial passages read as follows:

> The lord set his mind toward the "Land of the Living,"
> The lord Gilgamesh set his mind toward the "Land of the Living,"
> He says to his servant Enkidu:
> "Enkidu, brick and stamp have not yet brought forth the fated end,
> I would enter the 'land,' would establish my name,
> In its places where the names have been raised up, I would raise up my name,
> In its places where the names have not been raised up, I would raise up the names of the gods."

His servant Enkidu answers him:
"My master, if you would enter the 'land,' inform Utu,
Inform Utu, the valiant Utu,
The 'land,' it is Utu's charge,
The land of the felled cedar, it is the valiant Utu's charge,
Inform Utu."

Gilgamesh laid his hands on an all-white kid,
Pressed to his breast a speckled kid as an offering,
Placed in his hand the silver scepter of his command,
Says to the heavenly Utu:
"Utu, I would enter the 'land,' be my ally,
I would enter the land of the felled cedar, be my ally."

Heavenly Utu says to him:
"True, you are a princely warrior, but what are you to the 'land'?"

"Utu, a word I would speak to you, to my word, your ear!
I would have it reach you, give ear to it!
In my city man dies, oppressed is the heart,
Man perishes, heavy is the heart,
I peered over the wall,
Saw the dead bodies floating in the river's waters,
As for me, I too will be served thus, verily it is so.
Man, the tallest, cannot reach to heaven,
Man, the widest, cannot cover the earth.
Brick and stamp have not yet brought forth the fated end,
I would enter the 'land,' would establish my name,
In its places where the names have been raised up, I would raise up my
    name,
In its places where the names have not been raised up, I would raise up
    the names of the gods."
Utu accepted his tears as an offering,
Like a man of mercy, he showed him mercy,
The seven weather heroes, the sons of one mother,
He brings into the caves of the mountains.

Who felled the cedar, was overjoyed,
The lord Gilgamesh was overjoyed,
Mobilized his city like one man,
Mustered (its men) like twin companions. . . .

Now the literal rendering of these passages is reasonably certain; it
was the broader interpretation that troubled me at the time, and indeed
it is still not fully resolved. The difficulty centers about the motive for
Gilgamesh's journey to the place designated as the "Land of the Living," an ambiguous epithet of uncertain implication. On the surface,
the expression "Land of the Living," seems to say that it was a land of
immortals blessed with eternal life, which would suggest that Gilgamesh's journey was motivated by the quest for immortality, and this is
how I interpreted it in my first translation of the poem. However the

1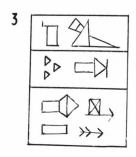

2

3

4

5

Five cuneiform passages relating to Dilmun, the Sumerian paradise-land.
Transliterations and English translations are provided on the facing page.

1   ti dingir-gin$_x$ mu-un-na-sì-mu
       zi-da-rí dingir-gin$_x$ mu-un-<na>-ab-e$_{11}$-dè
       u$_4$-ba zi-ud-sud$_x$-rá lugal-àm
       mu-níg-gilim-ma numun-lú-lu$_7$ urù-ag
       kur-bal kur-dilmun-na ki-^{d}utu-è-šè mu-un-ti-eš

       Life like a god they (the gods An and Enlil) gave him,
       Breath eternal like a god they brought down to him.
       Then, Ziusudra, the king,
       The preserver of the "name" of vegetation and the seed of mankind,
       In the land of crossing, the land Dilmun, the place where the sun rises, they
       caused to dwell.

2   uru^{ki}-kù-kù-ga e-ne ba-me-en-zé-en
               kur-dilmun^{ki}-kù-ga-àm
       ki-en-gi-kù-ga e-ne ba-me-en-zé-en
               kur-dilmun^{ki}-kù-ga-àm
       kur-dilmun^{ki}-kù-ga kur-dilmun^{ki}-šen-na
       kur-dilmun^{ki}-sikil-la kur-dilmun^{ki}-kù-ga

       The holy cities—give(?)—them to (?) him (Enki?) as his share,
               The land Dilmun is holy,
       Holy Sumer—give (?) it to (?) him as a share,
               The land Dilmun is holy.
       The land Dilmun is holy, the land Dilmun is pure.
       The land Dilmun is clean, the land Dilmun is holy.

3   má-dilmun
       kur-ta
       gú giš mu-gál

       The ships of Dilmun,
       from the foreign lands,
       brought him (Ur-Nanshe) wood as a tribute (?).

4   má-me-luḫ-ḫa^{ki}
       má-má-gan^{ki}
       má-dilmun^{ki}
       kar-ag-ge-dè^{ki}-ka
       bí-kéš

       The ships from Meluḫḫa,
       the ships from Magan,
       the ships from Dilmun,
       he made tie up alongside the quay of Agade.

5   k[u]r-má-gan^{ki}-dilmun^{ki}-bi
       ^{d}en-[ki]-me-en igi ḫé-im-da-a-du
       ^{giš}má-dilmun^{ki} giš ḫé-en-dù
       ^{giš}má-má--gan^{ki}-na an-zag ḫé-en-lá

       The lands of Magan and Dilmun
       Looked up at me, Enki,
       Moored (?) the Dilmun-boat to the ground (?),
       Loaded the Magan-boat sky high.

"Land of the Living" is depicted as "the land of the felled cedar," and Gilgamesh is designated as he "who felled the cedar," phrases which taken together with the lines: "I would enter the 'land,' would establish my name, / In its places where names have been raised up, I would raise up my name," seem to imply that Gilgamesh's journey was motivated by the drive for name and fame, the glory that would envelop him as the hero who felled the cedars in the "Land of the Living" and brought them to Erech. Be that as it may, it was my original, and probably mistaken, notion that the "Land of the Living" was a land of immortals, a kind of Elysium to which heroes and sages were translated to live in eternal bliss, that sparked my own quest for paradise, to search in the extant Sumerian documents for clues to its possible identification and localization.

First, I turned to the Sumerian Flood story that had been translated by Arno Poebel as far back as 1915. After the gods had decided to destroy mankind by means of a Flood, this myth relates, Ziusudra, a god-fearing king of the city of Shuruppak, was forewarned by Enki, the god of wisdom and man's most dependable friend and protector, to construct a huge boat in order to escape inevitable death and destruction. This Ziusudra does, and is delivered from the violent Deluge that raged on earth for seven days and nights. While still in the ark, now peacefully floating on calm waters, the grateful Ziusudra prostrates himself before the high gods and brings them sacrifices and offerings of thanks. This so pleases them that they give him "life like a god" and "breath eternal," and translate him to Dilmun, described by the poet as "the place where the sun rises." It was clear from this poem, therefore, that the Sumerian theologians had developed the concept of an Abode of the Blessed, not unlike that of the Greek Elysian plains, to which a fortunate hero or sage could be translated once he had been granted immortality by the gracious gods. Now whether this land to which Ziusudra was transplanted is to be identified with the "Land of the Living" in the Gilgamesh poem, is rather unlikely, but what is beyond doubt is that its name was Dilmun and that it was located somewhere to the east of Sumer, for the last extant line of the poem actually reads: "They (the gods) caused him (Ziusudra) to dwell in the land of the 'crossing,' the land of Dilmun, 'the place where the sun rises.'"

Once it became clear that Dilmun was the name of the Sumerian Abode of the Blessed, I began to search through the Sumerian literary documents for further clues about Dilmun and its Elysian character. And I then remembered that there was a Dilmun myth of paramount importance inscribed on a large six-column tablet in the University Museum which had been published by Stephen Langdon as early as 1915, under the title "Sumerian Epic of Paradise, the Flood, and the Fall of

Man," but which I interpreted quite differently. For this myth, too, depicts Dilmun as a land noted for purity, cleanliness, and radiance, where there is neither sickness nor death.

> The land Dilmun is pure, the land Dilmun is clean,
> The land Dilmun is clean, the land Dilmun is most bright.
> Who had lain by himself in Dilmun—
> The place, after Enki had lain with his wife,
> That place is clean, that place is bright;
> Who had lain by himself in Dilmun—
> The place after Enki had lain with Ninsikilla,
> That place is clean, that place is bright.

> In Dilmun the raven utters no cry,
> The francolin utters not the cry of the francolin,
> The lion kills not,
> The wolf snatches not the lamb,
> Unknown is the kid-devouring wild dog,
> Unknown is the grain-devouring pig,
> When a widow spreads malt on the roof,
> No bird on high devours that malt,
> The sick-eyed says not "I am sick-eyed,"
> The sick-headed says not "I am sick-headed,"
> Its old woman says not "I am an old woman,"
> Its old man says not "I am an old man."

Now though famed in myth and legend as a divine paradise to which immortalized mortals may be translated, Dilmun is not, as might mistakenly be inferred, just a literary fiction, a never-never land created by the fertile imagination of the Sumerian bards and poets. It has a long history beginning in the middle of the third millennium B.C. and continuing for some two thousand years. Thus we find Ur-Nanshe, the king who founded a powerful dynasty in Lagash about 2450 B.C., recording that the ships of Dilmun brought him wood as tribute from foreign lands. And about a century and a half later, Sargon the Great recorded on his memorial statues that the boats of Dilmun, Magan (Egypt), and Meluhha (Ethiopia) docked in his capital, Agade. Long after the Sumerians had ceased to exist, throughout the second and first millennia B.C., Dilmun is repeatedly mentioned in the cuneiform documents: there are Dilmun messengers and caravans; the Assyrian king Tukulti-Ninurta uses in his titles the epithet "king of Dilmun and Meluhha." There was a king of Dilmun by the name of Uperi who paid tribute to Sargon II of Assyria; there was another king by the name of Hundaru in whose days booty was taken from Dilmun. In the days of Sennacherib, a crew of soldiers is sent from Dilmun to Babylon to help raze that rebellious city to the ground, and they bring with them bronze spades and spikes which are described as characteristic products of Dilmun.

And so we come to the perplexing and tantalizing question of the location of Dilmun, a problem which has troubled students for over half a century. The majority of scholars identify Dilmun with the island of Bahrein in the Persian Gulf, and for well over two decades a Danish expedition has been carrying on excavations on the island in the hope of uncovering the remains of a great Sumerian civilization there, but so far in vain. Another group of scholars has defined Dilmun as a land bordering on the eastern shore of the Persian Gulf, extending from somewhere south of ancient Elam to about the Strait of Ormuz. It was for this latter localization of Dilmun which I argued some thirty years ago in a study called "Dilmun and the Land of the Living," since it seemed to me then that the description of Dilmun in the Flood story as "the place where the sun rises" indicated clearly that it should be sought not only east of Sumer, but also not south as far as the island of Bahrein lies. However in more recent years, new inscriptional material has become available which indicates that whatever its western boundary, Dilmun extended much farther to the east and included those parts of Iran, Pakistan, and India on which flourished the remarkable Indus civilization.

The new evidence is one of the cuneiform documents found at Ur, the capital of Sumer throughout much of the second half of the third millennium B.C., that were excavated more than three decades ago but for one reason or another had remained unpublished and unavailable to scholars until recent years. This new document is literary in character; in fact it is a small fragment of what was a six-columned tablet inscribed with a version of the Dilmun myth which differs to some extent from that of the Nippur tablet in the University Museum. It contains only the beginning and end of the myth, by and large identical with the beginning and end of the Nippur version of the composition. But following the goddess's complaint to Enki that Dilmun has no water and vegetation, the Ur document inserts a significant passage not found in the Nippur version. In a blessing that lists various lands, Enki includes the land of Dilmun.

> May the wide sea bring you its abundance.
> The city—its dwellings are good dwellings,
> Dilmun—its dwellings are good dwellings,
> Its barley is very small barley,
> Its dates are very large dates,
> Its harvests three . . . ,
> Its trees . . .

Thus, the Mesopotamians thought of Dilmun as a blessed, prosperous, maritime land to which were brought the world's goods by boat.

About a dozen of the administrative documents excavated with this fragment concern the seafaring merchants of Ur who brought back from Dilmun such imports as gold, copper and utensils made of copper, lapis lazuli, "fish-eyes" (perhaps pearls), beads of semiprecious stone, ivory and objects made of, or inlaid with, ivory, such as combs, pectorals, boxes, figurines, and sundry pieces of furniture. Now the fact that ivory and ivory artifacts were imported from Dilmun is fundamental and crucial for the location of Dilmun and its identification with the ancient Indus land. For this is the only large and wealthy maritime land lying to the east of Sumer which the Sumerian poets could describe as "the place where the sun rises."

But promising and intriguing as it was, the Dilmun-Indus-land hypothesis was the product of armchair scholarship, which needed corroboration from the field—that is, from the extant archaeological remains of the Indus civilization. Accompanied by my wife, I therefore journeyed to Pakistan and India in 1960, with the help of a grant-in-aid from the American Council of Learned Societies, and in the course of a seven-week stay there traveled more than four thousand miles by plane, train, bus, automobile, and a horse cart, or tonga, in order to visit the excavated Indus cites: Harappa, Mohenjo-daro, Kot Diji, Amri, Rupar, and Lothal. I studied the Indus artifacts located at the site museums, as well as the rich collections in the museums of Karachi, Lahore, and New Delhi. I met many of the archaeologists of Pakistan and India and discussed with them the various aspects of the Indus civilization. As a result of these investigations and discussions, it became apparent that there were two facets of the Indus civilization which were especially significant for its identification with Dilmun: the cult of a water deity and sea-plowing ships. First, the cult of a water deity.

One of the most striking and impressive features of the Indus cities and towns is the important role which water and cleanliness seem to have played in the life of the people, as is evident from the extraordinary number of wells and baths in both public and private buildings, as well as the carefully planned networks of covered drains built of kiln-baked bricks. It is reasonable to assume therefore—as indeed has been assumed by a number of archaeologists—that the Indus people had developed a water cult of deep religious import centering about a water god and featured by sundry rites concerned with lustration and purification. All of which seems to fit in surprisingly well with the Dilmun-Indus land hypothesis. For as is clear from the Dilmun myth, the deity most intimately connected with Dilmun is Enki, the Sumerian Poseidon, the supreme water god in charge of seas and rivers. And in the very same myth we find Dilmun described as a land that is pure and holy, adjectives which are equally applicable to such ancient Indus cities as Harappa, Mohenjo-daro, and Lothal.

Nor is the Dilmun myth the only Sumerian composition which char-

The ruins of Kot Diji, the important Indus civilization site excavated by
Dr. A. Kahn.

acterizes Dilmun as a land noteworthy for purity and cleanliness. In
"Enki and the World Order," a mythological poem of close to five hundred lines, published in 1952, we find Dilmun among the lands whose
fate is decreed by Enki as he goes about organizing the earth and its
cultural processes. The passage involving Dilmun consists of only six
lines, and only two of these are fully preserved; interestingly enough,
these read: "He (Enki) cleaned and purified Dilmun, / Placed the goddess Ninsikilla in charge of it." In fact Ninsikilla, the name of the goddess whom Enki charged with the care of Dilmun, is a Sumerian compound word meaning "the pure queen," which is probably a further
indication of the value put on purity and cleanliness in Dilmun.

The maritime character of the Indus civilization, comparable to that
of Dilmun, has been proved beyond doubt by George Dale's archaeological researches in Pakistan and India. He demonstrated that there
were at least two ancient Indus towns which were originally located on
the coast of the Arabian Sea, although as a result of coastal uplift, these
are now some distance away from the edge of the sea. The existence of
these settlements, taken in conjunction with numerous long-known
sites strung all along the Indus River, indicates clearly that the Indus

Examining potsherds from Kot Diji with Dr. Kahn.

civilization depended largely on waterborne trade, coastal and riverine. This is further corroborated by the excavations conducted by Indian archaeologists in Lothal, where what seems to be a well-planned rectangular dockyard built of baked bricks has been uncovered, complete with spillways, water locks, and loading platforms; when I visited the site in January of 1960, workmen were still trying to reach the bottom of its solid embankments.

The Dilmun-Indus land equation, if correct, would help to clarify the baffling problem of the origin and growth of the Indus civilization, if, as some archaeologists believe, the rise of the Indus cities was in the nature of a cultural explosion or revolution due to the arrival in India, early in the third millennium, of a new ethnic group which had already attained a high degree of civilization. For it is hardly likely that this people came to India from anywhere but Mesopotamia, where we first find a fully developed urban civilization with monumental architecture, a pictographic script utilized for administrative purposes, and flourishing trade relations with neighboring countries by land and sea. It is in Mesopotamia, too, that we find the worship of a water god from earliest days; his main cult was in the city of Eridu, which held his first shrine going back to the middle of the fourth millennium B.C. or even earlier.

But if so—if it was a Mesopotamian people who loaded their boats with their families and possessions, and abandoned their native land to start life afresh in distant India—who was this people? Hardly the Sumerians; the Sumerian pictographic script of the early third millennium B.C. is now well known, and it bears little resemblance to that of the Indus seals. Moreover, why should the Sumerians, who had themselves probably arrived in Mesopotamia only a few centuries earlier and made themselves lords and masters of the land later known as Sumer, leave their homes where they lived as conquerors and rulers in search for a new habitat? On the face of it, it is much more likely that it was not the Sumerians but one or another of the Mesopotamian peoples subjugated by the Sumerians who, seeing their language, faith, and way of life threatened and perhaps even suppressed, decided that home was no longer home for them and sought a new land where they were free to live with their religious convictions. This Mesopotamian people which sparked the Indus civilization most probably comprised the original settlers of Sumer, the Ubaidians, as they have come to be known from the name of the Mesopotamian site where their archaeological remains were first identified.

If this hypothesis should turn out to be correct, we then have some linguistic data which might prove valuable for the Indus language and script. For while we still know practically nothing about the grammar and structure of the Ubaidian language we do know a number of Ubaidian words denoting place names and occupations. The names of the two great Mesopotamian rivers, the Tigris and Euphrates, or *idiglat* and *buranun,* as they read in the cuneiform texts, are Ubaidian, not Sumerian, words. So too are the names of Sumer's most important urban centers: Eridu, Ur, Larsa, Isin, Adab, Kullab, Lagash, Nippur, and Kish.

Another crucial word which may turn out to be Ubaidian is Ea, one

---

Brick remains of a possible dockyard at Lothal, an Indus civilization city. Mesopotamian ships may have anchored here.

Lecturing on the interconnections between the Mesopotamian and Indus civilizations in the National Museum, Karachi (1960).

of the two names by which the Mesopotamian water god is known in the cuneiform texts, the other being Enki, the name used throughout this book. For while the latter is a typical Sumerian compound meaning "Lord of the Earth," Ea is a word whose linguistic affiliations are still uncertain; it might well be his original Ubaidian name, which the Sumerians changed to Enki when they incorporated him in their pantheon. This is corroborated to some extent by the fact that the Sumerian theologians found it necessary to stress and explain repeatedly in their hymns and myths the source of Enki's authority and power; in fact Enki often talks and acts as if he had an inferiority complex. If it is the Ubaidians who brought the water cult to India, Ea could be the name of the god about whom it centered, and it would not be too surprising to find the name in one or another of the Indus seals.

But all this is theory and hypothesis. What is urgently needed is further intensive excavations of the Indus sites, especially the larger ones which may be expected to yield not only more inscribed seals but the longer documents that may have existed and, if the gods are kinder

The Kramers with Prince Mikasa and the princess at the Imperial Palace,
Tokyo, in 1961.

than usual, even some bilingual documents written in the Indus script
and in cuneiform.

From India my wife and I continued our journey eastward to Japan
via Rangoon, Bangkok, and Hong Kong. In Japan I was a guest of the
Near Eastern Society, headed by Prince Mikasa, a younger brother of
the emperor and himself a scholar deeply interested in the archaeology
and history of the Bible Lands. We stayed several weeks in Japan,
where I delivered six lectures on the Sumerians and their literature,
three in Tokyo and three in Kyoto. From Japan we flew to Philadelphia
with stops in Honolulu, San Francisco, and Chicago. We had spent
some eight months journeying across the face of the earth, and wherever we went I planted a Sumerian seed—at least so I dare hope.

I was sixty-four years old in 1961, the year we returned from our
global pilgrimage, and the shadow of retirement was spreading its dark-
ening wings. Soon, much too soon, those rather homely clay tablets to
which I had become so devoted over the decades would be handled by
a new, younger curator; the old discolored desk on which I had written

so many thousands of words about their contents, would become *his* desk. Despite the approach of the fateful day, these pre-retirement years were among the happiest and most productive of my life. They witnessed the publication of five volumes filled with copies of more than a thousand tablets and fragments that might never have seen the light but for my guidance and collaboration, the preparation and publication of a badly needed symposium on the mythologies of the ancient world, the publication of a symposium concerned with the contributions of cuneiform studies to the history of civilization, the publication of two "popular" books—*The Sumerians* and *The Cradle of Civilization,* and last, but by no means least, the preparation and publication of a book on the Sacred Marriage rite, a theme that had been taking shape in my mind over the years as the relevant source material accumulated and fell into place, poem by poem and chant by chant.

13
Symposia, Syntheses, Summations

The first important publication to appear after my return to Philadelphia from Pakistan and India was a volume that I edited on *Mythologies of the Ancient World*. The work of ten scholars, including my contribution, this was the product of a symposium which I had arranged for the 1959 meeting of the American Anthropological Association and the American Folklore Society in Mexico City. At first glance it might seem strange that a cuneiform scholar, who had at times thought of himself as the narrowest specialist in the most highly specialized hall of learning, should have taken on this broad task. But I was not a total stranger to anthropological research. By temperament and disposition, I was attracted to the discipline of cultural anthropology; its methods and approach were often in my mind as I pursued my Sumerological studies. Not that I was fluent in anthropological jargon or an admirer of the discipline's abstractions and generalizations; I much preferred the common idiom, and felt more at home with the specific and concrete. But there is one significant aspect of cultural anthropology for which the study of Sumerian literature is both informative and illuminating, its abiding concern with the personality and character of the people who created any given culture, their psychological attitudes and emotional responses, the drives and motives that trigger and inspire their conduct and behavior.

The "personality" approach to culture had virtually never been attempted by cuneiform scholars. By and large they favored a descriptive

Miguel Civil of the Oriental Institute and the author identifying tablet fragments in the University Museum as part of a tablet copied by Kramer in 1937–1938 in Istanbul (ca. 1961).

approach; in the case of Sumerian culture, for example, they would proceed to divide it up into its various aspects—social, political, economic, legal, administrative, etc.—and then describe each of these subdivisions in as much detail as the available data permitted. I therefore found it challenging to try to fill this vital gap in Sumerological research, a task for which the Sumerian literary documents provided abundant evidence, both explicit and implicit.

My first investigative venture into the personality aspect of Sumerian culture related to the roles of love, hate, and fear as motivating emotional drives in the Sumerian behavior pattern. After collecting the relevant passages from the literary compositions, I could demonstrate that, as is true of mankind in general, love among the Sumerians was an emotion that varied in character and intensity. There was the passionate, sensuous love between the sexes that sometimes culminated in marriage; the love between husband and wife, between parents and children, and between the various members of the family; the deep platonic love between friends and companions; the divine love of the gods for the people and their rulers; the intense patriotic love for city and state.

Regarding marriage, for example, there are a number of Sumerian mythological poems indicating that there was much wooing and cooing before marriage and that it was not always, as scholars generally believed, a mere practical arrangement in which the carefully weighed shekel counted more than love's desire. There were even cases of love at first sight, and one of these ended in a violent rape that cost the passion-obsessed god his life. He was banished by his fellow gods to the Nether World, whither he was followed by his victim, who dogged his footsteps lovingly in spite of her victimization. The Bedu god, Martu, on the other hand, had no need to rape the lady of his choice. Her love was so strong that she insisted on marrying him despite the fact that he was known to all as a barbarian who "eats no cooked meat, has no house in his lifetime, and is not brought to burial when he dies." That love played a role in marriage is also indicated by the proverb, "Marry a wife according to your choice, have a child according to your heart's desire," and by such expressions as "beloved husband" and "beloved wife" that are not infrequent in the myths and hymns.

Where there is love there is hate, and the Sumerians were no exception in this respect. There was the hatred between husband and wife, and between parents and children; the hatred of the gods that brought about the destruction of the Sumerian cities and the suffering of the Sumerian people; the hatred and enmity that marked the relationship between the various deities. Not surprisingly, Inanna, the most fervent hater in Sumerian myth, was also the most passionate of lovers: she sent her overreaching husband to hell; pursued the gardener Shukalletuda relentlessly and put him to death; and to avenge an insult she sought the destruction of an entire city. In the hymnal literature this goddess who could be sweet and loving on occasion is often depicted as a venomous, thundering, tempestuous deity who brings destruction and desolation in her wake.

Fear, like hatred, strongly colored the Sumerian way of life. From birth to death the Sumerian had cause at times to fear his parent, his teachers, his friends, his fellow citizens, his rulers and superiors, the foreign enemy, the violence of nature, wild animals, vicious monsters and demons, sickness, death, and oblivion. No wonder the most desirable feature of man's Golden Age, according to the Sumerian sages, was freedom from fear.

Once upon a time there was no snake, there was no scorpion,
There was no hyena, there was no lion,
There was no wild dog, no wolf,
There was no fear, no terror,
Man had no rival.

The word "rival" brings to mind another anthropologically oriented study in which I tried to isolate and describe what seemed to me one of the major psychological incentives that motivated Sumerian behavior: the drive for superiority and preeminence, with its inevitable stress on competition and success. This obsessive drive was responsible in large part for some of the more notable achievements of the Sumerians, but it also carried within it the seed of self-destruction that helped to bring about their decline and fall. I first came upon the idea that the obsession with superiority, the driving ambition for victory over a rival, was a pervading source of motivation in Sumerian behavior in the course of piecing together and translating some of the Sumerian poems and essays which the ancient scribes themselves designated as "contests" or "disputations." Quite a number of these uninhibited and bellicose literary debates have come down to us in copies and different versions, and their very popularity indicated that they reflected a competitive behavioral pattern not unsympathetic to the Sumerian psyche. This was further corroborated by the literary compositions relating to education, which, on close study, revealed that the drive for preeminence was utilized consciously by both parents and teachers to motivate the student and to make him exert himself to the utmost in order to master the complicated and tedious curriculum that led to a career as a successful scribe and a learned scholar.

On the political scene, there are at least two epic tales celebrating the victory of the head of the Sumerian city-state Erech over a presumptuous rival who ruled the city-state Aratta. To judge from the contents of these two poems, it was the driving ambition of each of the two rulers to break down the morale of his rival by a kind of war of nerves, and to make submissive vassals of him and his subjects. The tales are full of taunts and threats carried back and forth by the messengers, as well as challenges and contests. Finally Enmerkar, lord of Erech, emerges as victor and, according to one of the poems, his defeated rival, the lord of Aratta, offered abject submission in these revealing words.

You are the beloved of Inanna, you alone are exalted,
Inanna has truly chosen you for her holy lap,
From the lower lands to the upper lands you are their lord,
I am second to you,
From the moment of conception, I was not your equal, you are the "big brother,"
I cannot compare with you ever.

Quite revealing, too, for the intensity of the Sumerian drive for victory and glory on the political front, are the numerous self-laudatory royal hymns in which the Sumerian king recounts his own virtues and achievements unblushingly and uninhibitedly in extravagant language.

This relationship between cuneiform studies and cultural anthropology was confirmed with the publication of my essay on rivalry and superiority as dominant features of the Sumerian cultural pattern in the *Selected Papers of the Fifth International Congress of Anthropological and Ethnological Sciences* in 1960. Nor was I surprised when the distinguished cultural anthropologist George P. Murdock invited me to contribute to the first volume of his journal *Ethnology*. In my introductory paragraph I attempted to explain how the long-buried Sumerian documents could reveal to a significant extent the character of an ancient culture, how they provided fresh source material for the anthropologist interested in comparative cultural studies.

Previously, in *Sumerian Mythology* I had sketched the growth and development of the science of comparative mythology—if one may use the term "science" for so inexact and elusive a discipline—that originated in the nineteenth century with the emergence and rise of comparative philology, the science devoted to language and literature. The phenomenal growth of comparative philology was itself due primarily to the recognition that Sanskrit, the language of the oldest sacred literature of the Hindu peoples, and Zend, also known as Old Persian, the language of the oldest sacred literature of the Iranian peoples, belonged to the same linguistic family as Greek and Latin. The intense study of Indo-European philology that followed was based largely on the ancient literatures of the Greeks, Hindus, and Iranians and led to the comparative study of the myths and legends related and revealed in them.

Toward the end of the first half of the nineteenth century, a new and unexpected field of study was opened for comparative mythology. For it was about this time that the Egyptian hieroglyphic and the Babylonian cuneiform scripts were deciphered, and much new mythological material was gradually recovered in the years that followed. What added impetus and excitement to this area of research was the fact that it offered a new approach to the study of the Hebrew Old Testament. For it soon became evident that some of the Old Testament contents were mythological in character, since they presented a number of clear parallels to the myths recovered from Egyptian and Babylonian sources. And so the study of comparative mythology, following in the footsteps of philology and linguistics, was no longer restricted to the ancient Indo-Europeans; it now included the ancient Semites and Egyptians.

Approximately at the same time, the new science of anthropology began to develop, a field that proved to be of fundamental importance for the study of comparative mythology. In all continents outside of Europe, hitherto unknown peoples in various stages of civilization were being discovered. Students, travelers, scientists, and missionaries studied the new languages, described the strange habits and customs, recorded the surprising religious beliefs and practices. Much new mythological material was thus recovered from these more or less primitive peoples, and the science of comparative mythology expanded accordingly.

By 1944 it was possible to divide the sources available for the study of comparative mythology into roughly two categories. The first consisted of the myths and legends of the ancient cultures such as those of the Hindus, Iranians, and Greeks on the one hand, and of the Hebrews, Babylonians, and Egyptians, on the other; these are recorded in the literatures as written down in the first millennium B.C. In this group, too, might be classed such mythologies as the Scandinavian or Eddic, Chinese, and Japanese, which are derived from the literary remains of a much later date. The second category consisted of the myths and legends of the so-called primitive peoples, as obtained by word of mouth from living members of those peoples, and reported by travelers, missionaries, and anthropologists.

With the publication in 1944 of *Sumerian Mythology*, a new, promising source for the study of comparative mythology became available to Orientalists and anthropologists alike. Over the years, however, the latter, in line with their traditional academic interests, concentrated almost entirely on the myths of the "primitives," as reported by living informants, and virtually ignored the myths of the ancients as recorded in their literatures, although these "dead informants" were often more reliable than their living counterparts. Comparative mythology was left in the hands of the philologists, psychologists, and historians of religion, and these disagreed radically in their views of the nature, scope, and significance of the ancient myths.

Some scholars looked upon the myths of the ancients as trivial, superstitious fairy tales of little intellectual and spiritual import, as infantile products of undisciplined imagination and capricious fantasy. Diametrically opposed to them were historians of religion who claimed that the myths of the ancients constituted one of the most profound achievements of the human spirit, that they were the inspired creation of gifted, unspoiled mythopoeic minds, uncontaminated by the current scientific approach and analytic mentality, and therefore open to profound cosmic insights that are veiled to modern thinking man with his inhibiting definitions and soulless logic. One renowned scholar belonging to this second group, Henri Frankfort, characterized myth as a form of poetry which transcends poetry "in that it proclaims a truth; a form of reasoning which transcends reasoning in that it wants to bring about the truth it proclaims; a form of action, of ritual behaviour, which does not find its fulfillment in the action, but must proclaim and elaborate a poetic form of truth."

There were whole schools of modern mythologists who argued that ancient myth is closely bound to rite and ritual, that myth was, as it were, nothing other than "word spoken," and that myth and ritual were two sides of the same cultic coin. On the other hand there were those who claimed that the ancient myths were primarily etiological in character: fictitious tales originated and evolved for the purpose of explaining the nature of the universe, the destiny of man, and the origin of the varied customs, beliefs, and practices current in their days, as well as of the names of holy places and outstanding, legendary individuals.

There were the psychologists who saw the ancient myths as depositories of primordial archetypal motifs revealing and illuminating man's collective subconscious. On the other hand, there were linguists and philologists who were convinced that myth was a "disease of language," the product of man's futile and misguided attempts to put into words the inexpressible.

But no matter what view one takes of the origin, character, and significance of the ancient mythologies, it seemed to me not unreasonable to expect that it be based on the actual texts of the myths as contained in the written documents of the ancients, and not on the versions surmised and improvised, transformed and recast, by some modern enthusiast with a preconceived point to make. Unfortunately, as I have indicated, the reading of the original documents is an intricate task that demands extremely specialized linguistic and philological training. Virtually all students of the ancient mythologies have to depend on the translations and interpretations prepared by others. But the available translations are sometimes outdated and misleading, and in the case of some of the ancient peoples, especially those who lived in the Near East, new documents are being discovered constantly.

All this struck me with special force on reading E. O. James's book *Myth and Ritual in the Ancient Near East* published in 1958. James, a distinguished, anthropologically oriented historian of religion with numerous works on the origin, nature, and function of religion to his credit, had made a brave attempt to be thorough, objective, and discriminating in his examination of the written documents. But often he relied on misleading translations which he could not control, and tended to take at face value secondary interpretations of the textual material and even some of the more synthetic surmises and hypotheses which pervade this area of study. I thought it high time to take a fresh look at the generally accepted, but not always trustworthy, data, at the clichés and shibboleths frequently utilized in interpreting them.

The opportunity came at the previously mentioned joint meeting of the anthropological and folklore societies, where I was able to bring to fruition the plan I had had in mind for several years: the arranging of a symposium on ten mythologies, those of Egypt, Sumer and Akkad, Anatolia, Canaan, Greece, India, Iran, China, Japan, and Mexico. (The latter I included because the meeting was to be held in that country.) Each of the contributors, a specialist in his field, was to make a determined effort to cover in the limited time available the essentials relevant to his area, utilizing the most up-to-date translations which he himself controlled.

I did not have to go far to find suitable candidates for the symposium. Six of them were colleagues at the University of Pennsylvania: the Egyptologist Rudolf Anthes, the classicist Michael Jameson, the Sanskritist Norman Brown, the Iranianist Mark Dresden, the Sinologist Derk Bodde, the Japanologist Dale Saunders. Three scholars, well known to me, came from other institutions: the Hittitologist Hans Güterbock of the Oriental Institute, the Ugaritic scholar Cyrus Gordon, then of Brandeis University, the specialist in the pre-Columbian Cultures of Central Mexico, Miguel Leon-Portilla, then assistant director of the Inter-American Indian Institute. I myself undertook to treat the mythologies of both Sumer and Akkad.

Once all these scholars had accepted my invitation to participate in the symposium, there arose the problem of financing the traveling expenses to Mexico City. It was not reasonable to expect the participants to devote weeks of research to the project and then ask them to pay their own way. I thought of a solution. Nineteen fifty-nine, the year of the symposium, was also the year in which the Doubleday-Anchor edition of *History Begins at Sumer* was published, and I could assume that my name was known to some of the Doubleday editors as the author of a kind of best-seller. Perhaps it would not be an unforgivable bit of *chutspa* on my part if I wrote to the publisher, explained the nature and scope of the symposium, and suggested that it be published as a Doubleday-Anchor book, provided Doubleday defray expenses in Mexico City. Much to my surprise, the answer was immediate: Doubleday was prepared to pay, in advance, three hundred dollars to each participant with the understanding that these were payments in full, and in lieu of royalties. I would be paid several hundred dollars more for writing the introduction to the book and for editing the manuscripts for publication. Everyone agreed, and the symposium came off according to schedule, as did *Mythologies of the Ancient World*.

The book was favorably received by scholar and student alike, and was translated into several foreign languages. In a small way it, too, became a best-seller, and Doubleday has no doubt recouped its initial outlay of thirty-five hundred dollars and made a considerable profit to boot. I mention this only because I sometimes wonder if I "sold the boys down the river" by not asking for royalties rather than a one-time payment. But who could foresee the popularity of so esoteric a volume?

In 1961, when *Mythologies* appeared, Dr. Inez Bernhardt and I jointly published a source book for Sumerian literature, the first volume of texts from the Hilprecht collection of the Friedrich-Schiller University in Jena, entitled *Mythen, Epen, Weisheitsliteratur und andere Literaturgattungen.* The second volume appeared in 1967, bringing to a happy ending a scholarly project I had begun to envision as far back as 1954, but with little hope of success.

If 1961 was a good publication year for me, it was topped by 1963 when there appeared three of my contributions that I consider to be the most important of my career. The first was a symposium on cuneiform studies and the history of civilization that I arranged for the annual meeting of the American Philosophical Society and which was subsequently published by that organization. Participating were Jacob Finkelstein of Yale, who concentrated on the cuneiform omen texts that had been inadequately exploited as historical source material, Thorkild Jacobsen of Harvard, who dealt with Mesopotamian religion from the fourth to the first millennium B.C., the eminent historian of science from Brown University, Otto Neugebauer, who demonstrated the survival of Babylonian methods in the exact sciences of antiquity and the Middle Ages, and Ephraim Speiser of Pennsylvania, who elaborated on cuneiform legal texts as a potent influence on the cultures of Mesopotamia and its neighbors. I spoke on parallels between Sumerian literary works and the biblical Song of Songs, also known as Canticles. Beginning with a brief résumé of the contents of Sumerian literature and its palpable influence on that of the Greeks and Hebrews, the paper turned to the Song of Songs and suggested that this book, which is nothing more than a loosely organized collection of sensuous love songs, reflects a Hebrew Sacred Marriage rite not unlike that current in Sumer throughout the centuries. To demonstrate this thesis, I collected and translated eleven Sumerian love songs, most of them unpublished, that are concerned in one way or another with the Sumerian Sacred Marriage rite. The detailed comprehensive article I based on this report laid the foundation for the later Patton Lectures I delivered at the University of Indiana and the book that resulted from them.

Since the Sacred Marriage rite revolved about the goddess Inanna and her unlucky lover Dumuzi, I took advantage of the opportunity offered by the symposium to include in the expanded published article three new texts found at Ur that helped to fill some of the gaps in the myth of Inanna's descent to the nether world.

But especially gratifying to me was my second major publication of 1963, the first volume of Sumerian literary texts from Ur that contained copies of 129 tablets and fragments prepared by Cyril Gadd. Here were parts of myths, epic tales, hymns, prayers, and disputations. My role in the book was limited to the introduction that identified and arranged the texts in accordance with the composition to which each piece belonged, and I therefore refused at first to be listed as a joint author. Gadd, one of Britain's leading cuneiformists for nearly half a century, was a truly modest man. He claimed that the volume might never have appeared were it not for my inspiration and collaboration, and, hence, he insisted that my name appear alongside his own.

Cyril Gadd had joined the staff of the British Museum in 1919. He was immediately attracted to the study of Sumerian language and culture, and Sumerological research continued to be an important facet of his broad scholarly interests. In 1921 he published a volume of cuneiform texts from the tablet collections of the British Museum, among which were ten elegantly copied Sumerian literary documents whose contents he summarized briefly in the introduction. In 1924 he published a *Sumerian Reading Book* that is now considerably outdated but is still one of the best little textbooks for beginners in the study of Sumerian. In the years 1923–1925, he was the epigraphist on Leonard Woolley's staff at Ur, and in 1929 he published *The History and Monuments of Ur,* a historical survey based on material then available on that all-important city. During the 1930s he copied many of the Sumerian literary tablets, which he would no doubt have published at the time but for the outbreak of the Second World War, when the antiquities of the British Museum, including all records and copies of texts, had to be evacuated because of the danger from German bombings.

In 1948, Gadd became keeper of the Department of Assyrian and Egyptian Antiquities, and his first absorbing and time-consuming task was to reinstate the antiquities and records of the museum that had been hidden away. This task took time away from his scholarly research, as did the heavy administrative duties of the department in the years that followed. In 1955, he retired as keeper and was appointed Professor of Ancient Semitic Languages and Civilization at the School of Oriental and African Studies in the University of London, a position from which he retired in 1960, when he became the principal editor of the new edition of the *Cambridge Ancient History.* In these years he had much more time for scholarly research, and he remembered the hundreds of copies of Sumerian literary texts from Ur that he had prepared two decades earlier, and which were still lying about and unavailable to cuneiform scholars. However, he no longer felt confident of his Sumerological proficiency, and it was for this reason that he invited me to join him in their publication. Needless to say I accepted joyfully, and we worked together in London for several summers on their preparation. Moreover, several years preceding the actual publication of the book in 1963, he generously made available to me Xerox copies of his autographs, and this enabled me and my assistants and collaborators in the University Museum to piece together a number of compositions that might otherwise have been too fragmentary for restoration.

Our friendship deepened as the years passed and as we collaborated on the publication of the second volume of Ur literary texts, which appeared in 1966 and contained close to three hundred copies of tablets and fragments inscribed primarily with lamentations, disputations, and proverbs. Cyril Gadd died in 1969, the year I published *The Sacred Marriage Rite,* a book I dedicated to him as the *ummia,* the savant, of London and Ur.

My third major publication of the year 1963 was *The Sumerians: Their History, Culture, and Character,* written at the invitation of the University of Chicago Press for the general public. I now felt much better qualified to produce a book of this nature than in 1954, when Doubleday had made a similar request of me. Moreover, over the years I had come to feel that *History Begins at Sumer,* my first book aimed at a wider readership, was only a torso of a book; its twenty-seven disparate essays did not give the reader any idea about how the Sumerians and their language had been discovered and resurrected, nor did it treat the political history of the Sumerian people or the nature of their social and economic institutions.

After much thought, I decided to divide the material into eight chapters. The first sketched the archaeological and epigraphical contributions that led to the development of cuneiform, presented from the point of view of the discovery and resurrection of the Sumerian people, an aspect that had not been adequately articulated by my predecessors. The second chapter was concerned with the political history of Sumer from the fifth to the second millennium B.C., introducing several new significant political events attested primarily by the Sumerian documents on which I had concentrated over the years and discussing the various types of source material available and their pitfalls. The remaining chapters surveyed the social, economic, legal, and technological aspects of Sumerian culture; religion and literature; Sumerian education and character; the key role this creative people played in the history of civilization. Only a quarter century earlier very little could have been said of these last aspects of Sumerian culture, and the relatively de-

215

tailed treatment of the education, character, and contribution of the Sumerians owed no little debt to my research and that of my collaborators in the University Museum.

The Sumerians was well received by the academic world, but I doubt that it attracted many readers from the general public, although it seems to have been used as home reading in college courses dealing with the history of civilization. It was no doubt this volume that prompted the editors of Time-Life Books to ask me to prepare the lavishly illustrated book on Mesopotamia as the cradle of civilization in their Great Ages of Man series.

Between 1963 and 1968, I published a dozen papers on various Sumerological themes. One very brief article in the *Times* of September 14, 1964, concerned the vast tablet collections of the British Museum and the rich promise they held for Sumerian research. When Cyril Gadd retired, his department was split into a department for Egyptian antiquities and one for Western Asiatic. The first keeper of the new Department of Western Asiatic Antiquities was Richard D. Barnett, a dedicated scholar of broad interests and erudite background. One of his first decisions was to attempt to make the museum's tens of thousands of unpublished tablets available to cuneiformists the world over. Not a cuneiformist himself, he succeeded in having appointed one of the leading young Sumerologists, Edmond Sollberger, of the University of Geneva. Both Barnett and Sollberger knew that the department's small staff could copy and catalogue only a tiny fraction of the thousands of unpublished tablets in the museum collections without outside help.

Hence, I was welcomed in the renowned Student's Room where in the summer of 1964 Sollberger turned over to me sixty Sumerian literary tablets that had been hiding in the cabinets of the museum for almost a century. It was some of these tablets that I had mentioned in the *Times* article. I have since had time to prepare editions of only eleven of these texts, and hope to prepare several more in the near future.

Some of the sting of retirement in 1968 was lessened by an unexpected invitation from Indiana University to deliver the prestigious Patton Lectures and to teach one semester in the anthropology department. For the lectures, whose stated purpose is to provide the opportunity for members and friends of the university to enjoy "personal acquaintance with the visiting professor," I chose as my subject the theme of the Sacred Marriage. That there had existed a fertility cult in Mesopotamia, and indeed all over the ancient world, had been known to scholars for close to a century. But until quite recently very little concrete, trustworthy data relating to it were available to the cuneiformist, and almost none at all to the anthropologist and historian of religion. Not until the 1960s, as a result of the translation and publication of an assortment of relevant Sumerian literary works scattered in museums throughout the world, did it become possible to present a fairly comprehensive and reasonably trustworthy account of the cult, and especially its central core, the Sacred Marriage rite.

My first attempt to collect and present the inscriptional data, published in the 1963 symposium on cuneiform studies and the history of civilization, was restricted by and large to the more recently published material, and did not include the texts made available in the earlier decades of the century. Moreover, I did not discuss at all the origin of the Sacred Marriage rite and its transformation over the centuries, nor did I take up the manner in which it was celebrated, all matters of anthropological and historical interest. Therefore, when I was invited to deliver the Patton Lectures, I decided to study anew all the available texts that seemed to be relevant to the Sacred Marriage rite, including several pieces still unpublished from the Museum of the Ancient Orient and the British Museum, and to present translations of those parts that were intelligible to me. At the same time, I tried to analyze their contents with a view to uncovering some plausible hypothesis to help explain the rite's origin and development and to ascertain if possible, what it was that actually took place in the course of its celebration. The Patton Lectures, in a much expanded form, were published the following year as a book entitled *The Sacred Marriage Rite: Aspects of Faith, Myth, and Ritual in Ancient Sumer,* a pioneer work that collects and analyzes all recognizable relevant material for the historian, humanist, and anthropologist. Among its more significant features are (1) an analysis of the data justifying the hypothesis that the Sacred Marriage was introduced as a local rite in the city of Erech early in the third millennium B.C., and only some centuries later was transformed into a national event; (2) a detailed sketch of the rather enigmatic contents of the available texts concerned with the ritual procedures of the Sacred Marriage ceremony; (3) a comparative treatment of some of the erotic songs related to this event and those of the biblical Song of Songs; (4) a detailed sketch of the fullest available version of the myth "Inanna's Descent to the Nether World" that ends with the death of Dumuzi and his resurrection, a poignant theme that spread from Mesopotamia to Palestine and may have been one of the prototypes of the New Testament Christ story.

The Patton Lectures were scheduled for the fall of 1968. Earlier, in May of that year, I delivered the Elizabeth James Lectures on "Sumerian Parallels to Biblical Literature" at the University of Cardiff in Wales, on the invitation of the noted British Assyriologist H. W. F. Saggs. From Cardiff I went to London, where I continued working on those sixty tablets and fragments on which I had reported in the *Times* in 1964. I also studied the large number of fragments from Ur that Cyril Gadd had left uncopied at the time of his death. From time to time I traveled up to nearby Oxford to work with the noted Hittitologist and cuneiformist Oliver Gurney on the preparation of a volume of Sumerian literary texts in the Ashmolean Museum. I also flew over to Paris in order to participate in the XVI Rencontre Assyriologique, where I read a paper on "Enki and His Inferiority Complex" that sketched the rise of Enki in the hierarchy of the Sumerian pantheon.

The year 1968, then, was well taken care, and I had little time to fret at ineluctable fate. But what of the years to follow? "Whence would come my salvation!" Of one thing I was certain: I would not stay in Philadelphia and continue to work in some office of the museum assigned to me as an act of mercy by the university authorities; this would be painfully embarrassing not only to me but also to the new curator, Åke Sjöberg, a sensitive, dedicated Sumerologist from Upsala, Sweden. But even as in earlier and happier days, my Sumerian *lama* did not now forsake me. Over the next four years I was invited as visiting professor by three illustrious foreign universities, thus becoming a migratory worker. With my wife at my side, I wandered from land to land, from city to city.

14
A Professor on the Road

My first stop was Copenhagen, the city that started the cuneiform excitement just about two hundred years ago. In 1761, the Danish government, eager to develop trade with the Orient, sent out an expedition from Copenhagen to explore Arabia, Persia, and neighboring lands. Among the members of its staff was one Carsten Niebuhr, a German by birth who was then an engineer officer in the Danish army. The expedition suffered numerous disruptive delays and hardships in the course of its journey across Egypt, Syria, Palestine, and Arabia. By the time it reached Bombay, Niebuhr and the doctor of the expedition were the sole survivors. In Bombay, the doctor, too, succumbed, and Niebuhr, now all alone, decided to return to Copenhagen via Persia and Mesopotamia. In March 1765, he arrived at Persepolis and stood in wonder among the breathtaking ruins about which he had read in the works of several earlier travelers. He spent several busy weeks sketching the monuments and copying with great exactitude a considerable number of the cuneiform inscriptions, though these were totally unintelligible to him, or to anyone else for that matter.

From Persia he journeyed to Mesopotamia, where he correctly identified the site of Babylon, as well as that of Nineveh opposite modern Mosul, and finally returned to Copenhagen in 1766. He published the results of his long journey in two volumes entitled *Reisenbeschreibung nach Arabien und andern umliegenden Ländern* between the years 1774 and 1778, and in the second of these he reproduced his admirably accurate copies of the inscriptions he had made of Persepolis. Among these were three trilinguals that formed the basis for the first successful attempts at cuneiform decipherment. To be sure, Niebuhr was not aware that the inscriptions were written in three different languages (Old Persian, Babylonian, and Elamite). But he established that they were written from left to right; that each of the three inscriptions contained three different types of cuneiform writing, which he labeled Class I, Class II, and Class III; and finally that that Class I represented an alphabetic form of writing, since it contained only a very limited number of signs.

Credit for the decipherment of the Old Persian version of the Persepolis trilinguals (Niebuhr's Class I) belongs not to a Dane but to the German Georg Grotefend. But his successful efforts were based almost entirely on Niebuhr's copies and comments. Moreover, Grotefend had the advantage of the insights of another Dane, Frederik Münter, who demonstrated that the Persepolis inscriptions belonged to the Achaemenid dynasty, a conclusion that helped to establish the names of the two kings designated in the inscriptions: Darius and Xerxes. Following Grotefend's decipherment of the Old Persian of the Persepolis inscriptions, it was the Dane Rasmus Rask, who identified the key word "Achaemenian" that the former had read incorrectly.

Now, the library of the University of Copenhagen had in its possession as early as 1820 a Nebuchadnezzar inscription from Babylon, but cuneiform research in Denmark remained at a standstill for about a century. Thanks to that university's Otto Emil Ravn, cuneiform research was revived. His first study appeared in 1909, to be followed by more than four decades of significant contributions concerned with Assyrian grammar, religion, and archaeology. Because most of Ravn's studies are in Danish, he was relatively unknown to his colleagues in other lands. But he raised at least two outstanding cuneiformists who revere his name and have spread his reputation: Thorkild Jacobsen, who left Denmark for the Oriental Institute in Chicago at the beginning of his career, and Jorgen Laessøe, now director of the Assyriological Institute of the University of Copenhagen.

I met Laessøe from time to time at Assyriological meetings and followed his career with interest, especially after studying and reviewing his major opus *The People of Ancient Assyria: Their Inscriptions and Correspondence*. One of his far-sighted achievements as director of the Copenhagen Assyriological Institute was to persuade the authorities of the university to appoint the imaginative and original Dutch Sumerologist J. J. A. van Dijk as a member of his staff in order to broaden its cuneiform base. In 1969–1970, van Dijk was called to a professorship at the Papal Institute in Rome, and I was invited by Laessøe to fill the vacated position for one year as visiting professor. There were few students in the institute that year—the University of Copenhagen was still in the throes of a student crisis—and I cannot truthfully say that I left a deep Sumerological impress there. But I did succeed in stimulating three students to become interested in Sumerian. That one of these, Bendt Alster, wrote his first monograph on *Dumuzi's Dream,* is due in large part to my stay in Copenhagen, for it was I who provided him with the identification of the basic texts and a preliminary transliteration and translation of their contents.

As the end of the Copenhagen academic year approached, and I was beginning to set my reluctant heart on returning to Philadelphia, I was surprised by a totally unexpected letter from the French cuneiformist, Jean Nougayrol, inquiring if I would agree to come for the following two years as a visiting professor of Sumerology in the École Pratique des Hautes Etudes. He was retiring that year because of age, the letter went on to say, and there was an informal understanding among his colleagues that a retiring professor would be granted any reasonable last request. His wish, the letter concluded, was to see me appointed for the next two years in his place. Needless to say, my answer was immediate and positive, and in due course I received the official notification of my appointment as visiting professor in Section V of the École Pratique des Hautes Etudes, whose faculty included some of the leading French historians of religion.

Jean Nougayrol was the French counterpart of Cyril Gadd, his close friend. Like Gadd, he was a gentle, modest scholar totally devoted to cuneiform research, copying by hand innumerable texts and translating their contents with extraordinary care and precision. I first met Nougayrol about twenty-five years ago, when he was curator of the tablet collection at the Louvre. At the time I asked for permission to collate their Sumerian literary tablets that had been copied by another great French scholar, Henri de Genouillac, and published in 1930, in order to correct some of the errors inevitably introduced by virtually all copyists, myself included. Sumerologically speaking, I was then relatively young and unknown, but Nougayrol's response was generous, and with his help I completed the task in one summer. In the years that followed Nougayrol and I met from time to time at the various Assyriological meetings, and always as friends and colleagues who understood each other tacitly, without the need of much verbiage.

Jean Nougayrol was an Assyriologist, not a Sumerologist; virtually all his contributions related to the Semitic Akkadian language and culture. But though he constantly denied it, he also had a thorough knowledge and understanding of Sumerian. A graphic illustration of this came my way in 1970, in the course of translating a poem that may be entitled "The Ideal Mother: A Sumerian Portrait." This composition was first pieced together and admirably edited in 1964 by my onetime assistant Miguel Civil. In 1967, Nougayrol published a large fragment of a tablet excavated in Ugarit, an ancient city in Syria far from Sumer, that originally contained the entire text of the poem inscribed in Sumerian, together with translations into Akkadian and Hittite, a vivid example of the pervasive influence of Sumerian literature on that of Sumer's neighbors. Nougayrol's exhaustive study of this document from Ugarit in which the Sumerian and Akkadian texts complemented each other clarified the reading and meaning of a number of obscure words and phrases in the Civil edition of the poem.

In 1970, in the course of studying the several hundred as yet unpublished Sumerian literary tablets in the Istanbul Museum of the Ancient Orient, Muazzez Çiğ, the curator of the tablet collection, and I came across a fairly well preserved duplicate of the composition that added a number of significant readings. Mme. Çiğ and I therefore prepared a new edition of "The Ideal Mother," utilizing Nougayrol's invaluable Sumero-Akkadian insights and comments. In January 1975 Jean Nougayrol died at the age of seventy-four. These few paragraphs are humbly dedicated to his memory.

The two years I spent in Paris were among the most gratifying of my scholarly career. France in some respects is the Sumerological capital of the world. Ernest de Sarzec's excavations at ancient Lagash infused the Sumerians with life; the French savant Jules Oppert gave Sumer its name; and that scholar of scholars, François Thureau-Dangin, resurrected Sumer's historic past. Thureau-Dangin dominated the cuneiform field for close to half a century, until his death in 1944 at the age of seventy-two. As I have written elsewhere, he exemplified my ideal of a productive scholar, lucid, aware of the significant, and ever ready to admit ignorance rather than to overtheorize. In 1905 he published *Les Inscriptions de Sumer et Akkad,* a milestone in the progress of Sumerian linguistic and historical studies, a superb compendium of insightful translations and tersely worded notes revealing a masterful distillation of the accumulated Sumerological knowledge of the day, much of which could be traced to Thureau-Dangin's own original contributions. To teach Sumerian language and literature in the city where Thureau-Dangin had lived and worked was for me a joyous privilege, and I tried to do it justice. My courses were well attended, and it is my hope that not a few of the students and my younger colleagues were Sumerologically stimulated and inspired.

Toward the end of the two years' stay in Paris, I received a call from the Hebrew University in Jerusalem for a visiting professorship during the academic year 1972–1973. Until quite recently, Israel was hardly noted for cuneiform research. While it is immensely rich in Palestinian and biblical antiquities, very few cuneiform tablets have been excavated there. It was not until the 1960s that an Assyriological department was established in the Hebrew University, due largely to the vision and foresight of its president, the noted archaeologist Benjamin Mazar. Even so, it first had only two cuneiformists on its staff: Chaim Tadmor, a specialist in Assyrian historiography, and Aaron Shaffer, who had obtained his doctorate at the University of Pennsylvania under my sponsorship and that of Ephraim Speiser. In the past few decades, the University of Tel-Aviv has appointed several cuneiformists in its archaeological department, and the Bar-Ilan University also has established an Assyriological department under P. Artzi, a specialist in the history of the ancient Near East. On his staff is one of my ablest ex-students, Jacob Klein, who had written in 1968 a brilliant dissertation relating to Sumer's outstanding monarch, Shulgi of Ur. Even as I write, plans are underway to augment cuneiform studies in the universities, indicating that Israel is well on its way to becoming a center for study in this field of research.

I was called to the Hebrew University to take the place of Shaffer, who was on sabbatical that year. My stay in Jerusalem was an exhilarating experience in more ways than one. To be sure, my courses were attended by relatively few students, primarily because Sumer and the Sumerians were still fairly new to Israel's students. But I spent considerable time in a working seminar attended by my younger Israeli colleagues, and this will no doubt bear rich fruit in the years to come. I also delivered a number of general lectures in Jerusalem and Tel-Aviv that should prove helpful to the future of Sumerological research in Israel. In 1975 Mrs. Kramer and I provided a fellowship at the University of Pennsylvania for young cuneiformists, Arab or Jew, male or female, to study at the University Museum and profit from its invaluable tablet collection.

At the end of the academic year in 1963, I left Jerusalem for London and Oxford to continue research on the literary pieces in the British Museum and to work with Oliver Gurney of Oxford, who had invited me to join with him in the preparation of a volume relating to the Sumerian literary tablets and fragments in the Ashmolean Museum. By this time I was rather weary of wandering from country to country and university to university, but I would have gone wherever the Sumerians were needed and wanted. However, no call came that year, and this migrant returned to Philadelphia to write and publish the results of his most recent research. Not that this aspect of my scholarly activity had been neglected during the migratory years; in fact some of my major publications appeared between 1969 and 1974: two books and some twenty articles and contributions to various handbooks and compendia.

The two books both appeared in 1969. One, the expanded version of the Patten Lectures dealing with the Sacred Marriage rite; the other, far more basic and fundamental to future Sumerological research, was published in Ankara under the title *Istanbul Arkeoloji Müzelerinde Bulunan Sumer Edebî Tablet ve Parchalari—I (Sumerian Literary Tablets and Fragments in the Archaeological Museum of Istanbul—vol. I)*. This tome consists of copies of over six hundred tablets and fragments covering the entire range of Sumerian literature: myths and epic tales, hymns and lamentations, proverbs, essays, and disputations that provide the Sumerologist with a vast treasure-house of source material for piecing together numerous Sumerian compositions, as well as with several new documents. The copies were prepared between the years 1952–1960 by the curators of the Istanbul tablet collection, Muazzez Çiğ and Hatice Kizilyay, two gracious and generous Turkish women to whom cuneiformists the world over are deeply indebted for their admirable care of the vast collection in their charge and for their abiding willingness to make its contents available to the scholarly world. I helped the two copyists prepare their autographs and wrote the introduction, published in Turkish and English, that provides a panoramic view of the identifiable and intelligible Sumerian compositions represented by one or more of the pieces published in the volume.

The second volume in this series consists of copies of almost two hundred tablets I prepared in the years 1946 and 1952 for publication by the Turkish Historical Commission. The texts of both these works were made available long before publication to my students and colleagues at the University Museum, as well as to scholars in other institutions. Many of their studies could never have seen the light of day were it not for the Istanbul Museum of the Ancient Orient and its two diligent and cooperative curators.

Of the approximately twenty papers and studies I published during my wandering years of retirement, about half consist of text copies, editions, and collations. These provide the primary material from which cuneiform specialists can work. My other papers are surveys, syntheses, and précis designed primarily for students of anthropology, comparative literature, and the history of religion. One, for example, is an essay I titled "Sumerian Similes: A Panoramic View of Man's Oldest Literary Imagery," which appeared in 1969 and is an expanded version of my presidential address delivered during the 1968 meetings of the American Oriental Society in Berkeley. This paper attempts to collect and interpret all the more intelligible similes found in twenty-odd compositions ranging over the gamut of Sumerian literary genres. It also demonstrates that though the comparisons favored by the Sumerian poets are not overly imaginative or profound, they do reflect a measure of sensitivity and sensibility relative to the world of nature as well as to man and his handiworks and are thus revealing of Sumerian culture and character.

Another rather important contribution that appeared in 1950 consisted of a group of translations of Sumerian literary documents designed primarily as basic data for the biblical scholar. Some time after the Second World War, James Pritchard, then a young, unknown biblical archaeologist, conceived the idea of publishing a compendium of translations of the more important documents excavated during the past century in "Bible Lands," in order to make them available to students of the Old Testament—a prime reference work for seminaries, divinity schools, and departments of the history of religion. To this end, he obtained the collaboration of eleven American scholars specializing in one or another of the languages of the ancient Near East who selected and prepared the relevant translations. I agreed to contribute those written in the Sumerian language. At the time, however, I felt prepared to present translations of only thirteen documents, and these appeared as a part of the vast compendium *Ancient Near Eastern Texts Relating to the Old Testament,* published in 1950 by the Princeton University Press. Several years before my retirement, Pritchard decided to add a *Supplement* to this volume designed to include many new texts and revisions of some that appeared in the first edition, providing me with the opportunity of adding more than twenty new translations, and these were published in the *Supplement* in 1969. This is still only a very small fraction of the Sumerian literary repertoire but far larger than any biblical scholar, in America or abroad, had ever had at his disposal in the English language.

One of the "retirement" articles of interest to both biblical scholars and students of comparative literature is a study of Sumerian literature and the Book of Psalms prepared jointly with Moshe Weinfeld of the Hebrew University, one of the world's leading biblical scholars whose book on Deuteronomy won wide acclaim as an outstanding example of erudition and imagination. Our joint article represents a preliminary, pioneering effort to seek out, cull, and collect a number of key passages in Sumerian literature that seem to contain significant parallels to the Book of Psalms: resemblances relating to religious thought and feeling as manifested in divine adoration and worship, in fear of god and wonder at his great deeds, in devout piety and fervent faith. For not unlike the biblical psalmists, the poets of Sumer sang of god's infinite power and glory, of his fatherly solicitude for man and his universe, of his love of justice and hatred of evil, of the righteous city and holy temple that were his sacred abode on earth; they acclaimed and exalted the idealized king of Sumer who was conceived as divinely chosen and blessed; they lamented bitterly the suffering of their people at the hands of the cruel enemy, and pronounced good tidings of hope and deliverance; they composed prayers and petitions depicting the pious Sumerian's unwavering devotion to his god and the deep longing for his presence. Admittedly, this pioneering study is neither comprehensive nor exhaustive, but it may move some future biblical scholar who is also cuneiform oriented to pursue this comparative literary research in greater breadth and with deeper penetration.

Four of my recent studies are anthropologically oriented. One, on modern social problems in ancient Sumer, is an expanded version of a paper I read before the Munich meeting of the XVIII Rencontre Assyriologique in 1970. The principal theme of that year's meetings was Mesopotamian society, and in view of today's pervading concern with the diverse ills that beset modern society, I endeavored to determine whether some of these disturbing problems troubled the ancient Sumerians as well. I combed the Sumerian literary documents to see if, though composed by visionary poets and emotional bards rather than sociologists, they might not prove revealing for this comparative inquiry, not directly of course, but inferentially and between the lines, as it were. The paper summarized the results of this quest for socioanthropological evidence from literary sources and demonstrated that, not unlike our own tormented society, the Sumerians of some four thousand years ago had their distressing shortcomings: they yearned for peace but were constantly at war; they professed such ideals as justice, equity, and compassion but abounded in injustice, inequality, and oppression; materialistic and shortsighted, they unbalanced the ecology essential to their economy; they suffered from the generation gap between parents and children, and between teachers and students; they had their drop-outs, cop-outs, hippies, and perverts; they had unisex devotees and perhaps even a "mini-maxi" controversy relating to ladies' apparel.

The second anthropologically oriented study I prepared for the Paris XIX Rencontre of Assyriologists on kingship in Sumer and Akkad, of which an expanded version was published in the official proceedings. I presented at the XXII Rencontre in Rome in 1974 a paper under the title "The Goddesses and the Theologians: Reflections on Woman's Rights in Ancient Sumer." The theme of this meeting was the subject of gods and their temples; hence, my paper addressed itself to the precarious status of women in a male-dominated society as reflected in the downgrading of several female deities by the Sumerian theologians.

Friendly adversaries: Thorkild Jacobsen and the author at Yale University (1974).

This chauvanistic manipulation I adduced from a between-the-lines reading of a number of Sumerian texts. Another study, *Sumerian Culture and Society: The Cuneiform Documents and Their Cultural Significance*, appeared as a monograph in 1975. Its purpose is to acquaint students with the nature and contents of the cuneiform documents and to demonstrate their anthropological significance with concrete examples taken from one selected group: those inscribed with Sumerian literary works.

Recently I was asked to contribute essays for two Festschriften. One is dedicated to my good friend and congenial adversary Thorkild Jacobsen, a key member of the Falkenstein-Jacobsen-Kramer Sumerological triad. I have come to realize after half a century of observing the academic scene that all kinds of scholars are necessary to advance human knowledge. There is the narrow specialist who concentrates all his work on a restricted area of investigation, and there is his opposite number who spreads his talents over varied fields of inquiry. There is the researcher who is the eternal card collector and so obsessed with minutiae that he is incapable of fusing into a coherent synthesis, or refuses to do so as a matter of principle, and there is his polar antithesis who does not hesitate to construct elaborate theories and generalizations unworried by the sparse data at his disposal. But rare indeed is the scholar who possesses these varied talents and virtues in the proper productive proportion; whose learning is deep and whose interests are broad; who assembles with patience and discrimination the multiform relevant concrete details, penetrates their contents, and comes up with a cogent synthesis that is stimulating and challenging. Thorkild Jacobsen, whose contributions and publications I have followed with intense interest and much profit for more than four decades, is a prime example of this exceptional, blessed, scholarly species. He has contributed significantly to a broad spectrum of Mesopotamian studies: philology, archaeology, cultural history, religion, mythology, government, and law among others. His syntheses and generalizations are original and perceptive, almost always grounded on discriminately selected and judiciously marshalled data, both philological and archaeological.

Nor has Jacobsen advanced Mesopotamian studies only as a scholar. During a crucial period in the history of the Oriental Institute, he was its director and chief administrator and as such was largely responsible for bringing to its faculty several eminent cuneiformists, all refugees from Nazism, who vitalized American cuneiform scholarship. During those years he conceived of and organized the Nippur expedition that made many inscriptional and archaeological discoveries and helped to clarify the perplexing excavations of the first University of Pennsylvania's expedition of 1889–1898. Add to this his role in the preparation and publication of the Chicago Assyrian Dictionary as both editor and contributor, and it is not too much to say that Mesopotamian studies, American and worldwide, would never have reached their present stage of progress but for the vision and dedication of Thorkild Jacobsen.

The Finnish scholar Armas Salonen of the University of Helsinki is the second scholar whom I saluted with a contribution to his Festschrift. To him I dedicated a study of two hitherto unknown Sumerian catalogues that list the titles of 109 poems designated as *irsheema*, "drum-accompanied laments." Only about 15 of these poems have been found; the rest await the lucky spade of a future excavator in Sumer. Armas Salonen, who passed away in 1981, six years after the appearance of his Festschrift, contributed enormously to our knowledge of the material culture of the Sumerians with books on agriculture and irrigation, hunting and fishing, hippology, tools and implements, furniture and house furnishings.

By the end of 1975 I had turned seventy-eight, and I realized that the books and articles that continued to occupy me may remain unfinished or go into print when I was no longer able to enjoy the finished results. This melancholy prospect should have dampened my enthusiasm. In practice, it did just the opposite, enhancing and intensifying my efforts to tie up loose ends, to modify and bring up to date some of my earlier translations, interpretations, and syntheses of Sumerian literature, religion, and myth. Even more pressing was the urge to translate and edit as many as possible of the British Museum tablets on the transliteration of which I had spent many a London summer. As I now see, carrying out at least part of these compelling tasks has proved to be the breath of life for me, the prolongation of my years, and has enabled me to keep writing at my desk, today, in my eighty-sixth year.

15
With the End in Sight

Nineteen seventy-six, the third year of the post-migratory phase of my retirement, proved to be especially auspicious and comforting with the publication of two major volumes of Sumerian literary documents. The first consisted of my copies of close to two hundred tablets in the Istanbul Museum of the Ancient Near East that had I had made in earlier years, published at long last by by the Turkish Historical Commission. The second, from the Oxford University Press, was authored jointly with Oliver Gurney. It includes fifty-eight Sumerian literary tablets and fragments in the Ashmolean Museum, copied by Gurney with the help of my preliminary transliterations, and an introduction that provided a detailed analysis of their contents: myths, epic tales, hymns, hymnal prayers, laments, letters, proverbs, precepts, disputations, and even incantations.

The very next year I was invited to give the Una lectures at the University of California in Berkeley. This provided me with the opportunity to begin the updating of some of my works with the idea of making their revised versions available to the academic and humanist. The modest book based on the Una lectures, *From the Poetry of Sumer: Creation, Glorification, Adoration,* consists of four chapters. The first provides a panoramic view of the recovery and restoration of the approximately six thousand Sumerian literary tablets and fragments scattered in the museums the world over, a badly needed overview that could hardly have been envisaged in earlier years.

Hubert Humphrey and the author awarded honorary degrees by President Nelson Gluek at Hebrew Union College, May 1957.

The second chapter provides a revised version of the more significant Sumerian ideas, credos, and explanations relating to the creation and organization of the universe and the creation of man. The next chapter concentrates on the role and character of the king in Sumerian society. The evidence is found in the royal hymns, a group of compositions that indirectly and quite unintentionally reveal the Sumerian vision of the ideal man; attractive, charismatic, astute, learned, eloquent, courageous, just, kind, and pious. The last chapter, which I titled "Adoration: A Divine Model of the Liberated Woman," summarizes the contents of a number of compositions relating to Inanna, the goddess whose multifaceted character is glorified in myth, epic, and hymn.

This same Inanna is the leading character in the Sumerian Sacred Marriage rite, the fertility cult that I treated in considerable detail in 1969. Now *The Sacred Marriage Rite* was out of print and no longer available. From time to time I expressed my frustration to Jean Bottéro, the French colleague who had been instrumental in converting my *From the Tablets of Sumer* into a best-seller. We agreed the best solution would be a French translation, but the French publishers shied away from the project. It was finally accepted by a rather small publishing house, Berg Internationale, and only after it had been persuaded by Bottéro's enthusiasm, his promise to translate the book himself and to prepare a special appendix that treated the related post-Sumerian Babylonian material.

The English version of *The Sacred Marriage Rite,* published more than a decade ago, had stood the test of time as a valid summation of what was known about the Sumerian fertility cult involving the shepherd king Dumuzi and his divine spouse Inanna. But in the intervening years several important editions prepared by younger scholars, all based to a large extent on my earlier contributions, had been made available. Moreover, in Israel's Bar-Ilan University, Y. Sefati, a student of my former student Jacob Klein, was in the process of preparing a definitive edition of several Sacred Marriage texts for his doctoral dissertation. The projected French publication of *The Sacred Marriage Rite,* therefore, provided me with the opportunity of making a rather thorough revision of the book, especially of its crucial last two chapters, as well as to add several hitherto unknown British Museum documents relating to the death of Dumuzi. The attractive French edition appeared in 1983. It is my hope that the French version entitled *Le Mariage sacré en Sumer et Babylone* will reach a far wider public than the English original.

The Sacred Marriage Rite is the offspring of "Inanna's Descent to the Nether World," a myth revolving about the tragic love-hate relationship between Inanna and Dumuzi. It was this tale, in whose restoration and interpretation I played a key role, that aroused my interest in the circumstances surrounding this mythical event and led me to study scores of tablets and fragments relevant to its theme. It was also responsible for the publication of another, much more popular book, *Inanna: Queen of Heaven and Earth* that has just appeared (1983), a joint work of which the principal author is Diane Wolkstein; my contribution was limited primarily to providing her with up-to-date translations of the relevant Sumerian documents. This cooperative effort began with mutual admiration and cordial harmony; I am sorry it ended on a note of disagreement and disappointment for me.

Diane Wolkstein is a gifted professional storyteller who, I learned later, had been telling the story of "Inanna's Descent to the Nether World" to a varied group of audiences, young and old, and had received from them an extraordinarily enthusiastic response. When she learned from one of my New York friends that I was scheduled to deliver the Jayne Lecture of the American Philosophical Society in late 1979, and that this would include a translation of a recently joined tablet in the British Museum that contained the very end of the myth, she came to Philadelphia, attended the lecture, introduced herself to me, and informed me about the warm response manifested by her audiences to the contents of the myth. We then agreed that if a suitable publisher could be interested, we would prepare a book that included a number of significant Inanna-related literary compositions, with "Inanna's Descent to the Nether World" as their centerpiece. What appealed to me especially about this collaborative effort was the fact that Diane Wolkstein is not only a storyteller but also a folklorist of some repute. I therefore felt that this project provided me with an opportunity to test an idea that I had frequently stressed in my publications, that the Sumerian literary documents were a veritable treasure-house of source material for the anthropologist and folklorist. Ms. Wolkstein then turned to Harper and Row, one of whose editors became intrigued with this unusual combination of Sumerology and folklore and was enthusiastic about the resulting publication.

Over the next two years I provided Diane Wolkstein with up-to-date translations of a number of Sumerian Inanna texts, and she arranged, combined, and molded their rather raw, literal contents to make them meaningful to the modern reader. On the whole she performed this delicate task with originality, ingenuity, and sensitivity, eliminating cluttering repetitions, adding explanatory words and lines when advisable, restoring broken passages when possible, and skilfully weaving the texts of selected poems into a meaningful whole. She thus succeeded in re-creating a significant group of esoteric tales and songs, long erased from the memory of man, in a form that is imaginative, evocative, and reasonably authentic. The publisher engaged a young historian of ancient art, Elizabeth Williams-Forte, to illustrate the book with relevant scenes depicted on Sumerian cylinder seals and sculptured terra-cottas. All in all, the book, which appeared in 1983, was attractive and engaging; authors and publishers were gratified with the result.

One chapter, entitled "Interpretations of Inanna's Stories and Hymns," was added without my approval. This chapter is a hodge-podge of pseudo-metaphysics, Jungian psychology, kabbalistic occultism, sexual symbolism, far-fetched midrashic interpretations, and superficial analogies. It is not a chapter to my taste, and I did not expect to have it included in a book bearing my name. But all this does not detract in any way from my high, appreciative regard for the brave, ambitious, vindictive, lovable and desirable Inanna, the goddess who helped launch me on my Sumerological career.

Another jointly authored book is to go to press in the near future, *La Mythologie suméro-accadienne.* Here also Inanna plays a major role; virtually half the texts collected in this book revolve about her deeds and misdeeds. The planning of this volume began a few years ago when Jean Bottéro and I met in Paris and agreed that the time had come for a scholarly publication directed to the humanist and academic who was not a cuneiformist, a book that included all the Sumerian and Akkadian divine tales, together with a synthesis relating to their character, purpose, and function. In the course of his long career as Professor in the École Pratique des Hautes Etudes, Bottéro had made numerous important contributions to Akkadian mythology, and therefore had the translations and interpretations readily at hand. As for the Sumerian tales, I had as a start my *Sumerian Mythology.* But this book is largely introductory in character; it provides only sketchy outlines of the more significant mythological tales, with brief citations from those that were intelligible at the time. The new book required a full annotated translation and interpretation of each and every myth, or fragment of a myth. I therefore spent the better part of two years revising, retranslating, and bringing up-to-date some twenty extant myths with the help of numerous contributions by younger scholars. All this material I then turned over to Bottéro, who translated it into French and arranged and organized it as an integral part of the Sumero-Akkadian book. There is reason to hope that it will be a standard reference work for the study of mythology and religion, and that it may prove to be a humanistic classic of sorts in the field of ancient cultural history.

While the preparation of the two French books *Le Mariage sacré en Sumer et Babylone* and *La Mythologie Suméro-accadienne* occupied much of my time and labor in the past seven years, I did not neglect my sacred trust, the newly identified Sumerian literary tablets in the British Museum. An edition of one of these tablets (BM 24975), "The *GIR₅* and the *ki-sikil:* A New Sumerian Elegy," I had published earlier in a volume dedicated to the memory of one of my former students, J. J. Finkelstein, who at the time of his unexpected death was professor of Assyriology at Yale. This unique elegiac composition is in the form of a playlet featuring two characters, an unnamed maid and her friend. It begins with the friend apprising the maid of the violent death of her beloved *GIR₅* (probably a herald in her service) who had traveled in her behalf to distant lands, and whose dead body was being returned over mountain and river. It concludes with the maid's response in which she itemizes the cult offerings she would provide for the GIR_5's ghost and the funeral rites she has prepared for his corpse.

A few years later, in 1980, I produced the edition of another unique tablet (BM 120011) entitled "Inanna and the *Numun*-Plant: A New Sumerian Myth," in a collection of essays in honor of Cyrus H. Gordon, my fellow student at the University of Pennsylvania during the late 1920s. This composition concerns the mischievous, accursed *numun*-plant to whom heaven and earth gave birth following a devastating flood sent against man because of his addiction to violence and lust, a mythological motif that at long last provides us with a moral and ethical motivation somewhat comparable with the biblical account.

The next year appeared the edition of a third tablet (BM 100046) I entitled "The Death of Dumuzi: A New Sumerian Version," in a Festschrift dedicated to the eminent Oxford Hittitologist, Oliver Gurney. This document consists of an account of the death of Inanna's spouse Dumuzi that parallels to some extent the hitherto known versions but includes a number of rather unusual themes and motifs related to sorcery, witchcraft, and burial rites which are unknown from any other source.

The very same year appeared the edition of yet a fourth tablet, "BM 29616: The Fashioning of the *gala*," dedicated to Yomokuro Nakahara on the occasion of his eightieth birthday. This scholar virtually singlehandedly pioneered and developed Sumerological research in Japan. The lamentation priest known as the *gala* is documented in one way or another from the middle of the third millennium to the very last centuries of the first millennium B.C.; many a *gala* is actually known by name from the economic, administrative, and legal documents. It has also long been known that the patron deity of the *gala* was Enki, the god of wisdom. What was not known is just how, when, and why this credo first originated. The new British Museum text demonstrates that it was current at least as far back as the Hammurabi days in the eighteenth century B.C. The theologians of that time, according to the author of this composition, believed that it was Enki who actually fashioned the *gala* and that he did so for a specific purpose, that he, the *gala*, should soothe the angry, raging heart of the goddess Inanna who was tormenting heaven and earth.

The following year saw the edition of a fifth tablet (BM 29633) I named "Lisin, the Weeping Goddess: A New Sumerian Lament" in a Festschrift dedicated to the Leyden professor F. R. Kraus, a friend and colleague of over forty years to whom all cuneiformists, and I especially, are deeply indebted for his careful and invaluable cataloguing of the Nippur tablets in the Istanbul Museum of the Ancient Orient, an impressive achievement. The rather obscure, enigmatic lament inscribed on this tablet is that of the suffering, woebegone goddess Lisin whose son had drowned in a violent tempest.

In the same year, 1982, I dedicated an edition of another "weeping-goddess" composition (BM 98396) entitled "A Sumerian Prototype of the *Mater Dolorosa*," in a Festschrift for Harry Orlinsky, one of the leading biblical and Septuagint scholars of our day. The grieving deity of this composition is the mother goddess Ninhursag, one of the four principal gods of the Sumerian pantheon. According to the poet, Ninhursag's comely son had disappeared, and she went about searching for him, carrying reeds and rushes, lamenting among the canebrake, a melancholy quest that was interfered with by "something like a heavenly star" (perhaps a meteor) which had turned noon to dusk and set the earth atremble. The search ends tragically when the goddess is informed that her son is in Arali (the nether World) and the officials in charge will not surrender him to her.

Also in 1982, my edition of three Sumerian literary catalogues inscribed on three small cylinders (BM 23612, 85564, 23249) appeared in a Festschrift dedicated to my Russian friend and colleague, Igor Diakonoff, the scholar who introduced the study of Sumerian literature in the Soviet Union. Ancient catalogues inscribed with the titles of Sumerian literary works, most of which are still lying buried in the ruins of Sumer, are invaluable for the information they provide on the nature and scope of Sumerian literature. To date some fifteen catalogues from the first half of the second millennium B.C. are known, listing several hundred titles. The newly uncovered cylinders are inscribed with more than thirty titles of compositions by the ancient scribes as *balag*-songs, that is, songs to be accompanied by a lyre.

In the fall of 1982 I was invited to join the faculty of Dropsie College as visiting adjunct professor to conduct a biweekly seminar devoted to the translation and interpretation of Sumerian literary texts. Only two students were sufficiently advanced to participate in this seminar, in the course of which I prepared editions of two more British Museum tablets. One of these (BM 88318) I published in the newly launched Canadian journal *Receuil de travaux et communications de l'Association des Études du Proche-Orient Ancien*. This remarkable composition of fifty-two lines, which may be entitled "The Ascension of Dumuzi to Heaven," provides us with an unexpected ending to the bittersweet Dumuzi-Inanna love affair. For according to the author of this poem, Dumuzi, though inevitably doomed to sickness and suffering for daring to love and have intercourse with the holy Queen of Heaven, does not die. Rather, he journeys to heaven in a richly-laden boat where he is stationed as a planet or star, with the help of Inanna's mother Ningal and his own mother Zertur.

The edition of the other tablet (BM 23631) presented in the Dropsie seminar is for the J. J. van Dijk Festschrift. Van Dijk is one of the leading cuneiformists of our day, a scholar whose perceptive insights, penetrating judgment, and discerning deductions combined with epigraphic expertise have done much to illuminate Sumerian religion and mythology. He recently published two magnificent volumes in which he pieces together and restores a complex, multifaceted composition of over seven hundred lines from two hundred tablets and fragments scattered in museums here and abroad, translating and interpreting the contents masterfully—a fitting climax to a lifetime of devoted cuneiform research. Even to write a review of that work for the *Journal of the American Oriental Society* took me several months!

To return to the tablet, prepared for the van Dijk Festschrift, which is inscribed with two compositions in four columns which together may be called "Bread for Enlil, Sex for Inanna," here the scribe had designated the compositions as songs dedicated to the sun god Utu, Inanna's brother and mentor. The first composition, rather poorly preserved, concerns in large part the god Enlil rather than Utu; it depicts a ritual involving a temple priest, a worshipper called the "righteous man" or the "most righteous of men" (perhaps the king), the god Enlil, and his vizier, the god Nusku. As the poet envisioned in his imagination, the worshipper has come into the temple with bread, flour, beer, and wine as offerings for his lord Enlil. Thereupon Nusku turns to Enlil and pleads with him to accept the food and liquor and to eat and drink these offerings so that plants and grains may grow luxuriously in the field and the rivers may team with fish.

But it is the content of the second composition that is most surprising and unexpected, since it portrays Inanna, the goddess of love and passionate desire, as one who knew not how to perform the sexual acts. Inanna, according to the poet, had left her temple, her mother, her mother-in-law, and her sister-in-law presumably because she was unable to consummate her marriage to Dumuzi. On her way, the wandering goddess encounters her brother in a tavern. Having satisfied her thirst with beer provided by her brother, she pleads with him to let her accompany him to his divine dwelling, the cedar mountain, since she knew not such "womanly things" as kissing and copulating. Then, her plea continues, after she has eaten of the herbs and cedars of the mountain, he is to send her back home. It would seem, therefore, that the eating of plants growing on the sun god's mountain would endow the goddess with the sexual knowledge of which she was ignorant. But such is not stated explicitly in the text, nor are we informed how Inanna had learned that the herbs and cedars would educate her sexually.

In addition to the books and specialized articles cited above, I found it useful to prepare a number of brief syntheses of a more general nature. The first of these, "Poets and Psalmists, Goddesses and Theologians," appeared in 1976 in *The Legacy of Sumer,* a collection of essays by different scholars edited by Denise Schmandt-Besserat, an anthropologist whose studies have shed much light on the origins of the cuneiform system of writing. This paper presents some of the results of two comparative studies relating to Sumerian literature, religion, and society. The first concerns the Sumerian parallels to the Book of Psalms. The second is an anthropologically oriented study relating to the role of women in a male dominated society. Beginning with an account of the deterioration of women's rights in Sumer, as evidenced by the relevant legal and administrative documents dating from the second half of the third millennium B.C., it concludes with a sketch of the partially successful victimization of the female deities by the Sumerian theologians who tried to reduce them in status and to transfer some of their powers to male deities.

In November 1979, I delivered the Jayne Lecture before the American Philosophical Society, later published in an expanded version in the *Proceedings* of the Society. This paper sketches the contents of some of the more important Sumerian literary tablets "excavated" from the British Museum drawers and includes an edition of the third tablet of the Ur version of "Inanna's Descent to the Nether World" which provided the very end of the myth.

Several of the tablets in the British Museum were inscribed with laments by a goddess for her lost son, or for the destruction of her city and temple, and the death of her spouse as well as her son. Two of these laments I published in 1982, and I had prepared transliterations and translations of three more. Moreover, forty years before I had published a monograph, *Lamentation Over the Destruction of Ur,* in which a "weeping goddess," in this case Ninlil, the tutelary deity of Ur, played a major role. The time seemed ripe for an analytical synthesis of all the more important laments related to the weeping goddess and her agony, a melancholy theme that had begun to haunt my imagination. When, therefore, I was invited by the new editor of the *Biblical Archaeologist* to contribute to this journal, I took it as a favorable omen for exorcising the weeping goddess obsession and proceeded to comb the Sumerian literary documents in order to select and collect all the more significant and intelligible passages that portray in one way or another the role, character, and behavior of the weeping goddess as envisioned by the Sumerian poets and bards. In the resulting study, "The Weeping Goddess: Sumerian Prototypes of the *Mater-Dolorosa,*" I analyzed and interpreted the contents of several compositions in which this suffering and compassionate deity played a major role.

I continued my integrative surveys at the Jerusalem meeting of the International Congress of Biblical Archaeology in 1984 with a paper which discussed some of the results of my probing of extant Sumerian myths. Myth by myth, I illustrated the methods by which the authors began and developed their plot scenarios in order to explain the sources and backgrounds of some important theological credo current in their days. Later in the year I went to the Assyriological meeting in Leningrad with a paper on the various mythological passages which shed light on Sumerian relations with such ancient lands as Dilmun and Elam, with such regions as that of the Cedar Mountain and Mt. Ebih.

Finally, I may mention two studies relating to texts I edited years ago which I have prepared in response to publications by fellow scholars. One concerns that very important tale in the Sumerian repertoire, that of the Deluge, preserved only in part on a fragment in the University Museum. It was first published by Arno Poebel in 1914; in 1950 I published a new translation of the text which, except for a few modifications, was based entirely on Poebel's edition. In more recent years Miguel Civil and Thorkild Jacobsen have made serious attempts to retranslate and reinterpret the text. Both scholars made a number of significant lexicographical, grammatical, and interpretative suggestions, but neither has resolved the difficulties and obscurities that abound in the extant text. Much of its contents remains puzzling and enigmatic, especially the first part of the myth relating to the events leading up to the divine decision to destroy mankind by sending a devastating flood. My paper "The Sumerian Deluge Myth: Reviewed and Revised" appeared in the volume *Anatolian Studies* dedicated to Richard Barnett, whose broad vision and informed foresight at the British Museum inspired the hope that one day its rich tablet collection will restore and illuminate many Sumerian literary compositions, including the fragmentary Deluge myth, that edifying tale of mankind's creation, destruction, and preservation.

My second paper was on the prologue of a law code that I edited in 1954 under the title "The Ur-Nammu Law Code." At the time I assumed that the author of the code was Ur-Nammu, since his was the only royal name mentioned in the text. Twenty-one years later, Oliver Gurney and I published a joint article in honor of Benno Landsberger that included copies, transliterations, and translations of two fragments excavated by Leonard Woolley at Ur that belong to the Ur-Nammu Law Code and which provided the partial text of what were estimated to be thirty-nine laws, of which sixteen were quite well preserved. Four years later, J. J. Finkelstein, who toward the end of his life had devoted much effort to Mesopotamian law, presented new, improved translations of the extant portion of the prologue and thirty-one laws. And in

1981, Fatma Yildiz, one of the curators of tablet collection of the Istanbul Museum of the Ancient Orient, in close association with J. J. van Dijk, published a most important article based on the identification of a tablet whose contents fill in the gaps of the second half of the prologue and provide the complete text of the first ten laws, some of which were missing or fragmentary. Moreover it provides a clue to the identity of the author of the code. This new tablet makes it evident that the author of the code was certainly not Ur-Nammu, and while its author is still uncertain, the likelihood is that it is Ur-Nammu's son, Shulgi. But this raises a number of problems relating to the translation and interpretation of the prologue of the code, and it is to offer a possible solution to these problems that I prepared a paper entitled "Who Wrote the Ur-Nammu Law Code?" for the journal *Orientalia*.

So much for my efforts during the past seven years. And what of the future? Now that the kur-nu-gi₄a, the "Land of No Return," is almost within sight, I confess that the future is not my favorite province of concern. A more appropriate note on which to close this book is a very brief summary of my scholarly past.

I see my more enduring contribution to cuneiform research as threefold. First, and most important, is the role I played in the recovery, restoration, and resurrection of Sumerian literature, or at least of a representative cross section. To be sure I was by no means the first to be concerned with this humanistic endeavor, nor have I brought it to fruition. But through my efforts several thousand Sumerian literary tablets and fragments have been made available to cuneiformists, a basic reservoir of unadulterated data that will endure for many decades to come. Second, I endeavored, consciously and purposefully, and with a fair degree of success, to make available reasonably reliable translations of many of these documents to the academic community, and especially to the anthropologist, historian, and humanist. Third, I have helped to spread the name of Sumer to the world at large, and to make people aware of the crucial role the Sumerians played in the ascent of civilized man.

As the academic title Clark Research Professor of Assyriology indicates, research was always my main interest and concern. But I did not neglect teaching altogether, especially in the form of seminars where I guided younger colleagues and graduate students in the copying, restoring, and translating of one or another of the Sumerian compositions. In my pre-retirement years, for example, I had as many as seven graduate students in close succession who went on to obtain their doctorates with me or my successor, Aåke Sjöberg, not to mention one volunteer of mature age, Jane Heimerdinger, who has devoted much of her time to the preparation of copies of hundreds of small fragments that will make many a future Sumerologist happy by filling in a missing sign, word, or phrase in the text of the composition he happens to be piecing together.

From time to time I also gave courses in Sumerian mythology designed for undergraduates, but I must admit that these were not overly successful. Often the class would start with as many as twenty or more students, but the number would be considerably reduced as the weeks passed. This is one failure, however, of which I am by no means ashamed. For, as I realized in due time, many of these students came to this course with extravagant notions about the profound cosmic insights of the ancients, and even with some hope of psychiatric therapy for their own troubled minds and hearts. Instead, they found a rather hard-nosed, common-sense agnostic and skeptic who offered them the disturbing ambiguities and uncertainties of historical truth, rather than the reassuring and consoling words of salvation they had come to hear. Much as I would have liked to help and heal these troubled spirits, I could not think of compromising my scholarly integrity, and so I had to content myself with the few students who persisted, either for credit or because they were temperamentally attuned to my non-oracular, non-kabbalistic approach to the study of myth.

Throughout this book I have mentioned the Sumerian *lama,* the good angel that came to my rescue in time of need. In two matters dear to my heart, however, I must sadly report he has failed me. One concerns the hope, or rather the vision, of the establishment of an American Institute of Sumerology, preferably on the campus of the University of Pennsylvania, that would promote research and teaching on all aspects of Sumerian language, history, and culture. But though I have done much to publicize the Sumerians and their crucial role in the history of civilization, I have lacked the charisma to attract and inspire American "angels" to help make this dream a reality, and the *lama* seemed unable to help.

Nor did he serve me better in a more personal matter that I had cherished over the years: to have my ashes buried in Ur, the Sumerian city where—so at least the Bible tells us—Father Abraham was born, as a symbolic reminder of Arab-Jewish fellowship and fraternity. This, I fear, is now quite impossible; the political struggle between the two related peoples has become so embittered that even a well-meaning, innocent Sumerian *lama* cannot bridge the gap sufficiently to make this metaphoric wish come true. But as one Sumerian sage put it, "Friendship lasts a day, kinship lasts forever," and I will not give up the hope that sooner or later ancient Sumer and Ur, resurrected out of dust and ashes by the spade of the modern archaeologist, will help to revive the spiritual and familial bond between Arab and Jew.

Abbreviations

AASOR	*Annual of the American Schools of Oriental Research*
ActaOr	*Acta Orientalia*
AfO	*Archiv für Orientforschung*
AJA	*American Journal of Archaeology*
AJSL	*American Journal of Semitic Languages and Literatures*
AnBi	*Analecta Biblica*
AnOr	*Analecta Orientalia*
ArOr	*Archiv Orientální*
AS	*Assyriological Studies,* Oriental Institute, University of Chicago
BASOR	*Bulletin of the American Schools of Oriental Research*
BIN	*Babylonian Inscriptions in the Collection of James B. Nies,* Yale University
BiOr	*Bibliotheca Orientalis*
CRRAI	*Compte rendu de la . . . Rencontre Assyriologique Internationale*
IEJ	*Israel Exploration Journal*
JAOS	*Journal of the American Oriental Society*
JBL	*Journal of Biblical Literature and Exegesis*
JCS	*Journal of Cuneiform Studies*
JNES	*Journal of Near Eastern Studies*
JQR	*Jewish Quarterly Review*
OECT	*Oxford Editions of Cuneiform Texts*
OIP	*Oriental Institute Publications*
Or	*Orientalia*
PAPS	*Proceedings of the American Philosophical Society Held at Philadelphia for Promoting Useful Knowledge*
RA	*Revue d'assyriologie et d'archéologie orientale*
RSO	*Rivista degli Studi Orientali*
YOS	*Yale Oriental Series, Babylonian Texts*
ZA	*Zeitschrift für Assyriologie*

Works by the Author

A. Books and Monographs

1. *The Sumerian Prefix be- and bi- in the Time of the Earlier Princes of Lagaš. AS* 8. Chicago, 1936.
2. *Gilgamesh and the Huluppu-Tree: A Reconstructed Sumerian Text. AS* 10. Chicago, 1938.
3. *Lamentation over the Destruction of Ur. AS* 12. Chicago, 1940.
4. *Sumerian Literary Texts from Nippur in the Museum of the Ancient Orient at Istanbul. AASOR 23.* New Haven, 1944.
5. *Sumerian Mythology: A Study of Spiritual and Literary Achievement in the Third Millennium B.C.* Memoirs of the American Philosophical Society 21. Philadelphia, 1944.
6. *Enki and Ninhursag: A Sumerian "Paradise" Myth. BSAOR,* Supplementary Studies 1. New Haven, 1945.
7. *Schooldays: A Sumerian Composition Relating to the Education of a Scribe.* Museum Monographs, University Museum, University of Pennsylvania (reprinted from *JAOS* 69 [1949]). Philadelphia, 1949.
8. *Enmerkar and the Lord of Aratta: A Sumerian Epic Tale of Iraq and Iran.* Museum Monographs, University Museum, University of Pennsylvania. Philadelphia, 1952.
9. *Biblical Parallels from Sumerian Literature: Handbook on the Special Exhibit in Honor of American-Jewish Tercentenary, 1654–1954.* University Museum, University of Pennsylvania. Philadelphia, 1954. Co-author, E. I. Gordon.
10. *From the Tablets of Sumer: Twenty-five Firsts in Man's Recorded History.* Indian Hills, Colo., 1956.
11. *L'Histoire commence à Sumer.* Paris, 1957.
12. *History Begins at Sumer.* Garden City, N.Y., 1959.
13. *Two Elegies on a Pushkin Museum Tablet: A New Sumerian Literary Genre.* Moscow, 1960.

14. *Mythologies of the Ancient World.* Edited and with Introduction by S. N. Kramer. Chap. 2. "The Mythology of Sumer and Akkad." Garden City, N.Y., 1961.
15. *Sumerische literarische Texte aus Nippur. Vol. 1, Mythen, Epen, Weisheitsliteratur und andere Literaturgattungen.* Berlin, 1961. Co-author, I. Bernhardt.
16. *Sumerian Mythology.* New York, 1961.
17. *The Sumerians: Their History, Culture, and Character.* Chicago, 1963.
18. *Literary and Religious Texts.* Ur Excavation Texts 6/1. London, 1963. Co-author, C. J. Gadd.
19. *Literary and Religious Texts.* Ur Excavation Texts 6/2. London, 1963. Co-author, C. J. Gadd.
20. *Cradle of Civilization.* New York, 1967.
21. *Sumerische literarische Texte aus Nippur. Vol. 2, Hymnen, Klagelieder, Weisheitstexte und andere Literaturgattungen.* Berlin, 1967. Co-author, I. Bernhardt.
22. *The Sacred Marriage Rite: Aspects of Faith, Myth, and Ritual in Ancient Sumer.* Bloomington, 1969.
23. *Istanbul Arkeoloji Müzelerinde Bulunan Sumer Edeb, Tablet ve Parchalari (Sumerian Literary Tablets and Fragments in the Archaeological Museum of Istanbul.)* Vol. 1 by M. Çiğ and H. Kizilayay with Introduction and Catalogue by Samuel Noah Kramer. Ankara, 1969. Vol. 2, Ankara, 1976.
24. *Sumerian Culture and Society: The Cuneiform Documents and Their Cultural Significance.* Cummings Modules in Anthropology 58. Menlo Park, Calif., 1975.
25. *L'Histoire commence à Sumer.* Rev. ed. Paris, 1975.
26. *Sumerian Literary Texts in the Ashmolean Museum. OECT* 5. Oxford, 1976. Co-author, O. Gurney.
27. *From the Poetry of Sumer: Creation, Glorification, Adoration.* Una's Lectures 2. Berkeley, 1979.
28. *History Begins at Sumer: Thirty-nine Firsts in Man's Recorded History.* 3d rev. ed. Philadelphia, 1981.
29. *La Mariage sacré en Sumer et. Babylone.* Rev. ed. with Translation and Addenda by Jean Bottéro. Paris, 1983.
30. *Inanna, Queen of Heaven and Earth: Her Stories and Hymns from Sumer.* New York, 1983. Co-author, D. Wolkstein.

B. Articles

1. "The Verb in the Kirkuk Tablets." *AASOR* 9 (1929–1930 [1931]), 62–119.
2. "New Tablets from Fara." *JAOS* 52 (1932), 110–132.
3. "A Matter of Method in Sumerology." *AJSL* 49 (1934), 229–247.
4. "Dr. Chiera's List of Duplicates to De Genouillac's *Textes religieux sumeriens.*" *JAOS* 54 (1934), 407–420.
5. "Introduction to the Texts with Complete Lists of Duplicates." In E. Chiera, *Sumerian Epics and Myths. OIP* 15. Chicago, 1934, 1–8.
6. "Introduction to the Texts, with Complete Lists of Duplicates." In E. Chiera, *Sumerian Texts of Varied Contents. OIP* 16. Chicago, 1934, 1–8.
7. "Studies in Sumerian Phonetics." *ArOr* 8 (1936), 18–33.
8. "Gilgamesh and the Willow Tree." *The Open Court* 50 (1936), 100–106.
9. "Inanna's Descent to the Nether World: The Sumerian Version of 'Ištar's Descent.'" *RA* 34 (1937), 93–134.
10. "Additional Material to 'Inanna's Descent to the Nether World.'" *RA* 36 (1939), 68–80.
11. "*Langdon's Historical and Religious Texts from the Temple Library of Nippur:* Additions and Corrections." *JAOS* 60 (1940), 234–257.
12. "Ishtar in the Nether World According to a New Sumerian Text." *BASOR* 79 (1940), 18–27.

13. "Sumerian Literature: A Preliminary Survey of the Oldest Literature in the World." *PAPS* 85 (1942), 293–323.
14. "The Oldest Literary Catalogue: A Sumerian List of Literary Compositions Compiled about 200 B.C." *BASOR* 88 (1942), 10–19.
15. "The Slaying of the Dragon." *The University of Pennsylvania General Magazine and Historical Chronicle* 44 (1942), 358–364.
16. "Man's Golden Age: A Sumerian Parallel to Genesis 11: 1." *JAOS* 63 (1943), 191–194.
17. "The Oldest 'Book' Catalogue." *University of Pennsylvania Library Chronicle* 9 (1943), 5–14.
18. "Sumerian Literature." In J. T. Shipley, ed., *Dictionary of World Literature*. New York, 1943, 559.
19. "The Epic of Gilgameš and Its Sumerian Sources: A Study in Literary Evolution." *JAOS* 64 (1944), 7–23.
20. "The Death of Gilgamesh." *BASOR* 94 (1944), 2–12.
21. "The Oldest 'Book' Catalogue." *University of Pennsylvania General Magazine and Historical Chronicle* 46 (1944), 164–170.
22. "Corrections to 'The Epic of Gilgameš and Its Sumerian Sources.'" *JAOS* 64 (1944), 83.
23. "The Quest for Immortality." *Cathedral Age* 19 (1944), 18–19.
24. "Immortality on Clay." *University of Pennsylvania General Magazine and Historical Chronicle* 46 (1944), 222–226.
25. "A Sumerian 'Paradise' Myth." *Crozer Quarterly* 22 (1945), 207–220.
26. "Heroes of Sumer: A New Heroic Age in World History and Literature." *PAPS* 90 (1946), 120–130.
27. "Immortal Clay: The Literature of Sumer." *The American Scholar* 15 (1946), 314–326.
28. "Sumerian Literature." In J. T. Shipley, ed., *Encyclopedia of Literature*. Vol. 1. New York, 1946, 1–3.
29. "Accadian Literature." In J. T. Shipley, ed., *Encyclopedia of Literature*. Vol. 2. New York, 1946, 914–917.
30. "Interim Report of Work in the Museum at Istanbul (to October 16, 1946)." *BASOR* 104 (1946), 8–12.
31. "Gilgamesh and the Land of the Living." *JCS* 1 (1947), 3–46.
32. "The Harmal Geographical List." *Sumer* 3 (1947), 48–83. Co-author, S. J. Levy.
33. "Report on the Collection of Unpublished Texts in the Iraq Museum." *Sumer* 3 (1947), 112–118. Co-authors: T. Baqir and S. J. Levy.
34. "Immortal Clay of Sumer." *Sumer* 3 (1947), 202–216. Translated into Arabic by B. Francis.
35. "Second Interim Report on Work in the Museum at Istanbul." *BASOR* 105 (1947), 7–11.
36. "Excerpts from Report as Annual Professor of the Baghdad School." *BASOR* 106 (1947), 2–4.
37. "The Tablet Collection of the University Museum." *JAOS* 67 (1947), 321–322.
38. "Fragments of a Diorite Statue of Kurigalzu in the Iraq Museum." *Sumer* 4 (1948), 1–39. Co-authors, T. Baqir and S. J. Levy.
39. "New Light on the Early History of the Ancient Near East." *AJA* 52 (1948), 156–164.
40. "Iraqi Excavations During the War Years." *University Museum Bulletin* 13/2 (1948), 1–29.
41. "Gilgamesh and Agga." *AJA* 53 (1949), 1–18. With Appendix by Thorkild Jacobsen.
42. "A Blood-Plague Motif in Sumerian Mythology." *ArOr* 17/1 (1949), 399–405.
43. "Schooldays: A Sumerian Composition Relating to the Education of a Scribe." *JAOS* 69 (1949), 199–215. See also Books and Monographs, no. 7.
44. "Schooldays 4000 Years Ago." *Parents Magazine* 24 (1949), 46–47, 87–88.

45. "The Restoration of Sumerian Literature: An example of Turkish-American Cultural Cooperation." *Türk Tarih Arkeologye ve Etnografye Dergisi* 5 (1949), 32–44.
46. Translation of Sumerian texts in J. B. Pritchard, ed., *Ancient Near Eastern Texts Relating to the Old Testament*. Princeton, 1950; 2d ed. 1955; 'Sumerian Myths and Epic Tales," 37–59; "Lipit-Ishtar Lawcode," 159–161; "Sumerian Petition," 382; "A Sumerian Lamentation," 455–463; "A Sumerian Letter," 480–471; "Sumerian Love Song," 496.
47. "Sumerian Religion." In V. Ferm, ed., *Forgotten Religions*. New York, 1950, 45–62. Later titled *Ancient Religions*.
48. "Inanna's Descent to the Nether World, Continued." *PAPS* 94 (1950), 361–363.
49. "New Discoveries in Nippur." *Pennpix* 6 (1950), 14–15, 28.
50. "Inanna's Descent to the Netherworld Continued and Revised." *JCS* 4 (1950), 199–214; 5 (1951), 1–17.
51. "Mercy, Wisdom and Justice; Some New Documents from Nippur." *University Museum Bulletin* 16/2 (1951), 28–39.
52. "Sumerian Wisdom Literature: A Preliminary Survey." *BASOR* 122 (1951), 28–31.
53. "Bref aperçu concernant les restes littéraires sumériens." *Scientia* 45 (1951), 99–109.
54. "A Sumerian 'Farmer's Almanac.'" *Scientific American* 185 (1951), 54–55.
55. "The Sumerian School: A Pre-Greek System of Education." In G. E. Mylonas, ed., *Studies Presented to David Moore Robinson*, vol. 1. St. Louis, 1951, 238–245.
56. "A Fulbright in Turkey." *University Museum Bulletin* 17/2 (1952), 3–56.
57. "Preliminary Report on the Unpublished Sumerian Literary Tablets from Nippur in the Museum of the Ancient Orient (Istanbul)." *Or,* n.s. 21 (1952), 249–250.
58. "Five New Sumerian Literary Texts." *Belleten* 16 (1952), 345–365. Co-authors, H. Kizilyay and M. Çiğ. In Turkish.
59. "Selected Sumerian Literary Texts: Final Report of a 'Fulbright' Research Year in the Istanbul Museum of the Ancient Orient." *Or,* n.s. 22 (1953), 190–193. Co-authors, H. Kizilyay and M. Çiğ.
60. "The Myth of Inanna and Bilulu." *JNES* 12 (1953), 160–188. Co-author, T. Jacobsen.
61. "Sumerian Historiography." *Eretz-Israel* 3 (1953), 51–57 [In Hebrew.] Cassuto Memorial volume.
62. "The Oldest Laws." *Scientific American* 188 (1953), 26–28.
63. "The First Farmer's Almanac." In *The Book of Knowledge Annual* (1953), 54–55.
64. "Old World Archaeology." In *The American People's Encyclopedia Year Book: Events and Personalities for 1952* (1953), 055–056.
65. "Sumerian Historiography." *IEJ* 3 (1953), 217–232.
66. "Ur-Nammu Law Code" *Or* n.s. 23 (1954). 40–51. With Appendix by Adam Falkenstein.
67. "Enmerkar and Ensukussiranna." *Or,* n.s. 23 (1954), 232–234.
68. "Forty-eight Proverbs and Their Translation." *CRRAI* 3 (1954), 75–84.
69. "Four Firsts in Man's Recorded History: School-Law-Taxes-Wisdom." *Archaeology* 7 (1954), 138–148.
70. "First Pharmacopoeia in Man's Recorded History." *American Journal of Pharmacy* 126 (1954), 76–84. Reprinted in *The New York Physician and American Medicine* 43 (1954), 16–24.
71. "Schooldays 4000 Years Ago." In *Book of Knowledge Annual 1954*, 51–52.
72. "Archaeology: Old World Archaeology." In *The American People's Encyclopedia Year Book: Events and Personalities in 1953*. Chicago, 1954, 153–155, 157–158.
73. "Man and His God: A Sumerian Variation on the 'Job' Motif." In M. Noth, ed., *Wisdom in Israel and in the Ancient Near East Presented to Professor Harold Henry Rowley. Supplement 3*. Leiden, 1955, *Vetus Testamentum*, 170–182.

Works by the Author

74. "Tales of Sumer: Man's Oldest Myths" *University Museum Bulletin* 19/4 (1955), 1–29. With painting by Hellmuth Schubert.
75. "The Oldest Medical Text in Man's Recorded History: A Sumerian Physician's Prescription Book of 4000 Years Ago." *Illustrated London News* 3045 (Feb. 26, 1955), 370–371. Co-author, M. Levey.
76. "Archaeology: Old World Archaeology." In *The American People's Encyclopedia Year Book: Events and Personalities of 1954.* Chicago, 1955, 131–135.
77. "Sumerian Theology and Ethics." *Harvard Theological Review* 49 (1956), 45–62.
78. "Recht, Medizin und Landwirtschaft bei den alten Sumerern." *Das Altertum* 2 (1956), 131–140.
79. "Sumerische Ethik und Weisheitssprüche." *Wissenschaftliche Annalen* 5/10 (1956), 767–774.
80. "Sumerische literarische Texte in der Hilprecht-Sammlung." *Wissenschaftliche Zeitschrift der Friedrich-Schiller-Universität Jena, Gesellschafts- und Sprachwissenschaftliche Reihe* 5/6 (1955–56), 753–763. Co-author. I. Bernhardt.
81. "Götter-Hymnen und Kult-Gesänge der Sumerer auf zwei Keilschrift-'Katalogen' in der Hilprecht-Sammlung." *Wissenschaftliche Zeitschrift der Friedrich-Schiller-Universität Jena. Gesellschafts- und Sprachwissenschaftliche Reihe, 6/7 (1956–1957), 389–395. Co-author, I. Bernhardt.*
82. *"Die sumerische Schule." Wissenschaftliche Zeitschrift der Martin-Luther-Universität Halle Wittenberg. Gesellschafts- und Sprachwissenschaftliche Reihe* 5 (1955–1956), 695–704.
83. "A Father and his Perverse Son." *National Probation and Parole Association Journal* 3 (1957), 169–173.
84. "The Sumerians." *Scientific American 197/4 (1957), 70–83.*
85. *"Corrections and Additions to SRT." ZA* 52 (1957), 76–90.
86. "Hymn to the Ekur." In *Scritti in Onore di Guiseppe Furlani: RSO* 32 (1957), 95–102.
87. "Le Plus petit manuscrit du monde." *Les Nouvelles littéraires artistiques et scientifiques* 1576 (Nov. 14, 1957), 1 and 8.
88. "Love, Hate and Fear: Psychological Aspects of Sumerian Culture." *Eretz-Israel* 5 (1958), 66–74. Mazar volume.
89. "First Pharmocopoeia in Man's Recorded History." *May and Baker Pharmaceutical Bulletin* 7 (1958), 114–117.
90. "Sumerian Literature and the Bible." *Studia Biblica et Orientalia* 3: AnBi 12 (1959), 185–204.
91. "New Sumerian Literary Fragments." *Türk Arkeoloji Dergisi* 8 (1959), 3–4. Co-authors, M. Çiğ and H. Kizilyay.
92. "A Sumerian Document with Microscopic Cuneiform." *Expedition* 1/3 (1959), 2–3.
93. "The Ancient Empires of the Middle East." In *The Book of Knowledge.* Vol. 1, 649–660.
94. "The World's Oldest Known Prescription." *The CIBA Journal* 12 (1959), 16–21.
95. "Gilgamesh: Some New Sumerian Data." *Cahiers du Groupe Francois-Thureau-Dangin* 1 (1960), 59–68.
96. "Rivalry and Superiority: Two Dominant Features of the Sumerian Culture Pattern." In *Selected Papers of the Fifth International Congress of Anthropological and Ethnological Sciences.* Philadelphia, 1960, 287–291.
97. "Enki und die Weltordnung: Ein sumerischer Keilschrift-Text über die 'Lehre von der Welt' in der Hilprecht-Sammlung und im University Museum of Pennsylvania." *Wissenschaftliche Zeitschrift der Friedrich-Schiller-Universität Jena. Gesellschafts- und Sprachwissenschaftliche Reihe* 9, 1/2 (1959–1960), 231–256. Co-author, I. Bernhardt.
98. "Sumero-Akkadian Interconnections: Religious Ideas." *CRRAI* 9 (1960), 272–283.
99. "Death and the Netherworld according to the Sumerian Literary Texts." *Iraq* 22 (1960), 59–68.

100. "Sumerian Literature, A General Survey." In G. E. Wright, ed., *The Bible and the Ancient Near East*. New York, 1961, 249–266.
101. "New Literary Catalogue from Ur." *RA* 55 (1961), 169–176.
102. "The Sumerians and the World about Them." In *The Ancient World*. Moscow, 1962, 291–299. B. P. Struve Festschrift.
103. "Cultural Anthropology and the Cuneiform Documents." *Ethnology* 1/3 (1962), 299–314.
104. "The Biblical Song of Songs and the Sumerian Love Songs." *Expedition* 5/1 (1962), 25–31.
105. "Dilmun: Quest for Paradise." *Antiquity* 37 (1963), 111–115.
106. "Literary Texts from Ur VI, Part II." *Iraq* 25 (1963), 171–176.
107. "Cuneiform Studies and the History of Literature: The Sumerian Sacred Marriage Texts." *PAPS* 107/6 (1963), 485–527.
108. "Die Suche nach dem Paradies, Dilmun und die Indus-Zivilization." *Wissenschaftliche Zeitschrift der Martin-Luther-Universität, Halle Wittenberg* 12 3/4 (1963), 311–317.
109. "The Indus Civilization and Dilmun, the Sumerian Paradise Land." *Expedition* 6/3 (1964), 44–52.
110. "Sumerian Literary Tablets from Ur." *CRRAI* 11 (1962), 93–101.
111. "Sumerische literaire teksten uit Ur." *Phoenix* 10/1 (1964), 99–108.
112. "CT XLII: A Review Article." *JCS* 18 (1964), 35–48.
113. "New Light on Old Myths." *Times* (London, Nov. 14, 1964).
114. "Sumerian Literature and the History of Technology." In *Ithaca. Proceedings of the Tenth International Congress of the History of Science*. Paris, 1964.
115. "Sumerians." In *The World History of the Jewish People*. 1st series. Vol. 1, 149–156.
116. "'Vox Populi' and the Sumerian Literary Documents." *RA* 58 (1964), 149–156.
117. "Two Fragments of Sumerian Laws." In *Studies in Honor of Benno Landsberger*. *AS* 16. Chicago, 1965, 13–19. Co-author, O. R. Gurney.
118. "Shulgi of Ur: A Royal Hymn and a Divine Blessing." In A. Neuman and S. Zeitlin, eds., *The Seventy-fifth Anniversary Volume of the Jewish Quarterly Review*. Philadelphia, 1967, 369–380.
119. "Musical Tablet." *Museum Newsletter* 5/2 (1967).
120. "Reflections on the Mesopotamian Flood." *Expedition* 9/4 (1967), 12–18.
121. "The World of Abraham." In *Everyday Life in Bible Times*. National Geographic Book Service. Washington, 1967, 39–55.
122. "The Babel of Tongues." *JAOS* 88 (1968), 108–111.
123. "Lamentation over the Destruction of Nippur: A Preliminary Report." *Eretz-Israel* 9 (1969), 89–93.
124. "Death of Ur-Nammu and His Descent to the Netherworld." *JCS* 21 (1969), 104–122.
125. "Sumerian Similes: A Panoramic View of Some of Man's Oldest Literary Images." *JAOS* 89 (1969), 1–10.
126. "Inanna and Šulgi: A Sumerian Fertility Song." *Iraq* 31 (1969), 18–23.
127. Translations of Sumerian Texts in J. B. Pritchard, ed., *The Ancient Near East: Supplementary Texts and Pictures Relating to the Old Testament* (1969) and/or *Ancient Near Eastern Texts Relating to the Old Testament*, 3d ed. with Supplement (1969). "Sumerian Hymns," 573–586; "Sumerian Wisdom Texts," 589–591; "Sumerian Lamentations," 611–619; "Sumerian Sacred Marriage Texts," 637–645; "Sumerian Miscellaneous Texts," 646–652.
128. "Sumerian Sacred Marriage Songs and the Biblical 'Song of Songs.'" *Mitteilungen des Instituts für Orientforschung* 15/2 (1969), 262–274.
129. "u$_5$-a a-u-a: A Sumerian Lullaby." *Estratto da Studi in Onore di Edoardo Volterra* 6 (1969), 191–205.
130. "Collations to CT XLII." *JCS* 23 (1970), 10–16.
131. "From the Poetry of Sumer, Preview of a Supplement to ANET." *The Israel Academy of Sciences and Humanities Proceedings* 4/2 (1969), 14–28.

Works by the Author

132. "Enki and His Inferiority Complex." *Or*, n.s. 39 (1970), 103–110.
133. "The Dumuzi-Inanna Sacred Marriage Rite: Origin, Development, Character." *CRRAI* 12 (1969), 135–141.
134. "La Rite de mariage sacré Dumuzi-Inanna." *Revue de l'histoire des religions: Annales du Musee Guimet* (1969), 121–146.
135. "Sumerian Epic Literature." In *La Poesia epica e la sua formazione*. Accademia Nazionale dei Lincei. Rome, 1970, 825–837.
136. "Keš and Its Fate: Laments, Blessings, Omens." In *Gratz College Anniversary Volume* (1971), 165–175.
137. "CT XV: Corrigenda et Addenda." *RA* 65 (1971), 23–26.
138. "Aspects of Mesopotamian Society, Evidence from the Sumerian Literary Sources." In H. Klengel, ed., *Schriften zur Geschichte und Kultur des Alten Orients*. Vol. 1. Berlin 1971, 1–13.
139. "Kingship in Sumer and Akkad: The Ideal King." *CRRAI* (1971), 163–176.
140. "Modern Social Problems in Ancient Sumer: Evidence from the Sumerian Literary Documents." *CRRAI* 18 (1972), 113–121.
141. "The Jolly Brother: A Sumerian Dumuzi Tale." *The Journal of the Ancient Near Eastern Society of Columbia University* 5 (1973), 243–253. Gaster Festschrift.
142. "Prologomena to a Comparative Study of the Book of Psalms and Sumerian Literature." *Bulletin of the Israel Society for Biblical Research* 56 (1973), 8–24.
143. "CT XXXVI: Corrigenda and Addenda." In *Iraq* 36 (1974), 93–102. Mallowan Festschrift.
144. "Prologomena to a Comparative Study of the Book of Psalms and Sumerian Literature." *Beth Mikra* 56 (1974), 136–159. Co-author, M. Weinfield. In Hebrew.
145. "Die Tempel und Götterschreine von Nippur." *OR* 44 (1975), 96–102. Co-author, I. Bernhardt.
146. "Thorkild Jacobsen: Philogogist, Archaeologist, Historian." In *Sumerological Studies in Honor of Thorkild Jacobsen on His Seventieth Birthday. AS* 20. Chicago, 1975, 1–7.
147. "Two British Museum *iršemma* 'Catalogues.'" *Studia Orientalia* 46 (1975), 141–166. Salonen Festschrift.
148. "Poets and Psalmists: Goddesses and Theologians." In Denise Schmandt-Besserat, ed., *The Legacy of Sumer*. Bibliotheca Mesopotamica 4. Malibu, 1976, 3–21.
149. "Commerce and Trade: Gleanings from Sumerian Literature." *Iraq* 39 (1977), 59–66.
150. "The *GIR₅* and the *ki-sikil:* A New Sumerian Elegy." In *Essays on the Ancient Near East in Memory of Jacob Joel Finkelstein*. Connecticut Academy of Arts and Science Memoir 19. Hamden, Conn., 1977, 139–142.
151. "The Ur Excavations and Sumerian Literature." *Expedition* 20 (1978), 41–47.
152. "Die sumerische Literatur: Der Menscheit älteste Belletristic." In *Der Garten in Eden*. Berlin: Museum für Vor und Frühgeschichte, 1978.
153. Preface to H. Frankfort, *Kingship and the Gods: A Study of Ancient Near Eastern Religion as the Integration of Society and Nature*. Phoenix edition. Chicago, 1978, v–viii.
154. "Sumerian Literature: Recovery and Restoration." In *Essays on the Occasion of the Seventieth Anniversary of the Dropsie University*. Philadelphia, 1979, 307–315.
155. "Sumerian Literature and the British Museum: The Promise of the Future." *PAPS* 124/4 (1980), 295–312.
156. "Inanna and the *Numun*-Plant: A New Sumerian Myth." In *The Biblical World: Essays in Honor of Cyrus H. Gordon*. New York, 1980, 87–97.
157. "The Death of Dumuzi: A New Sumerian Version." *Anatolian Studies* 30 (1981). 5–13. Oliver Gurney Festschrift.
158. "BM 29616: The Fashioning of the *Gala*." *Acta Sumerologica* 3 (1981), 1–11. Yokomuro Nikahara Festschrift.
159. "Lisin, the Weeping Goddess: A New Sumerian Lament." In *Zikir Šumim: Assyriological Studies Presented to F. R. Kraus*. Leiden, 1982. 133–144.

160. "Binning 3." In C. B. F. Walker and S. N. Kramer, "Cuneiform Tablets in the Collection of Lord Binning." *Iraq* 44 (1982), 71–86.
161. "Three Old Babylonian *Balag*-Catalogues from the British Museum." In *Societies and Languages of the Ancient Near East*. Warminster, 1981–1982, 206–213. Diakonoff Festschrift.
162. "BM 98396: A Sumerian Prototype of the *Mater-Dolorosa*." *Eretz-Israel* 16 (1982), 141*–146*. Orlinsky Festschrift.
163. "The Weeping Goddess: Sumerian Prototypes of the *Mater-Dolorosa*." *Biblical Archaeologist* (Spring, 1983), 69–80.
164. "The Sumerian Deluge Myth: Reviewed and Revised." *Anatolian Studies* 33 (1983), 115–121. Barnett Festschrift.
165. "BM 88318: The Ascension of Dumuzi to Heaven." *Receuil de travaux et communications des etudes du Prache-Orient ancien* 2 (1984), 5–10.
166. "The Urnammu Law-Code: Who Was Its Author?" *Or* 52 (1983), 453–456.
167. "Bread for Enlil: Sex for Inanna." Forthcoming in *Orientalia* (1985). Van Dijk Festschrift.
168. "Sumerian Mythology: Reviewed and Revised." Forthcoming in the proceedings of the International Congress of Biblical Archaeology.
169. "The Marriage of Martu." Forthcoming in the volume commemorating the founding of the Assyriological Institute of Bar-Ilan University.
170. "Sumer and Its Neighbors: Gleanings from Sumerian Mythology." Forthcoming in the volume celebrating the ninetieth anniversary of Gratz College.

C. Reviews and Review Articles

1. D. E. Faust. *Contracts from Larsa Dated in the Reign of Rim-Sin. YOS* 8. New Haven, 1941. Reviewed in *AJA* 47 (1943), 133–135.
2. H. M. Orlinsky, ed. *An Indexed Bibliography of the Writings of William Foxwell Albright*. New Haven, 1941. Reviewed in *AJA* 47 (1943), 135–136.
3. A. Heidel. *The Babylonian Genesis: The Story of Creation*. Chicago, 1942. Review article in *JAOS* 63 (1943), 69–73.
4. C. H. Gordon. *The Loves and Wars of Baal and Anat*. Rome, 1945. Reviewed in *AJA* 50 (1946), 423–424.
5. Henri and H. A. Frankfort, J. A. Wilson, T. Jacobsen, and W. A. Irwin. *The Intellectual Adventure of Ancient Man*. Chicago, 1946. Short reviews in *American Anthropologist* 50 (1948), 313–314; and in *Jewish Social Studies* 10 (1948), 281–282.
6. Review article in *JCS* (1948), 37–70.
7. B. Hrozny. *Histoire de l'Asie anterieure, de l'Inde et de la Crete (jusqu'au debut du second millenaire)*. Paris, 1947. Reviewed in *BiOr* 6 (1949), 81–83.
8. A. L. Oppenheim. *Catalogue of the Cuneiform Tablets of the Wilberforce Eames Babylonian Collection in the New York Public Library. AOS* 32. New Haven, 1948. Reviewed in *JQR* 41 (1950), 221–224.
9. W. von Soden. *Das akkadische Syllabar. AnOr* 27. Rome, 1948. Review article in *BiOr* 7 (1950), 76–78.
10. R. Weill. *La Cité de David: Compte rendu des fouilles executée à Jerusalem sur la site de la ville primitive, campagne de 1923–24*. 2 vols. Institut francais d'archeologique et historique 44. Paris, 1947. Reviewed in *Jewish Social Studies* 13 (1951), 73–74.
11. A. Poebel. *Miscellaneous Studies. AS* 14. Chicago, 1947. Reviewed in *JAOS* 73 (1953), 51–53.
12. N. Glueck. *Explorations in Eastern Palestine IV*. 2 vols. Pt. I: *Text;* Pt. II: *Pottery Notes and Plates. AASOR* 25–28 (for 1945–1949). New Haven, 1951. Reviewed in *Jewish Social Studies* 15 (1953), 66–67.

Works by the Author

13. L. Braidwood. *Digging Beyond the Tigris*. New York, 1953. Reviewed in *Scientific Monthly* 77 (1953), 271–272.
14. A. Falkenstein and W. von Soden. *Sumerische und akkadische Hymnen und Gebete*. Zürich, 1953. Review article in *BiOr* 11 (1954), 170–176.
15. V. E. Crawford. *Sumerian Economic Texts from the First Dynasty of Isin. BIN 9.* New Haven, 1954. Review article in *JAOS* 75 (1955), 128–130.
16. E. L. Bennett, Jr. *The Pylos Tablets: Texts of Inscriptions Found 1939–1954.* Princeton, 1955. Reviewed in *United States Quarterly Book Review* 12 (1956), 164 ff.
17. H. Gross. *Die Idee des ewigen und allgemeinen Weltfriedens im alten Orient und im Alten Testament.* Trier, 1956. Reviewed in *JBL* 27 (1958), 386–388.
18. E. O. James. *Myth and Ritual in the Ancient Near East: An Archaeological and Documentary Study.* New York, 1958. Reviewed in *American Anthropologist* 61 (1959), 532–533.
19. S. Moscati. *The Face of the Ancient Orient: A Panorama of Near Eastern Civilizations in Pre-Classical Times.* Chicago, 1960. Reviewed in *Science* 131/3415 (1960), 1728–1729.
20. J. Fontenrose. *Python: A Study of Delphic Myth and its Origins.* Los Angeles, 1959. Reviewed in *AJA* 65 (1961), 405.
21. A. Parrot. *The Temple of Jerusalem.* New York, 1955. *Samaria, the Capital of the Kingdom of Israel.* New York, 1958. *Babylon and the Old Testament.* New York, 1958. Reviewed in *Jewish Social Studies* 24 (1962), 50–51.
22. J. Finegan. *Light from the Ancient Past: The Archaeological Background of Judaism and Christianity.* Princeton, 1959. Reviewed in *Jewish Social Studies* 25 (1963), 230–231.
23. H. W. F. Saggs. *The Greatness That was Babylon: A Sketch of the Ancient Civilization of the Tigris-Euphrates Valley.* New York, 1962. Reviewed in *Archaeology* (June 1963), 134.
24. J. Læssøe. People of Ancient Assyria: Their Inscriptions and Correspondence. New York, 1963. Reviewed in *Archaeology* 18/1 (1965), 70.
25. C. H. Gordon. *Before the Bible: The Common Backgrounds of the Greek and Hebrew Civilizations.* New York, 1963. Reviewed in Archaeology 18/1 (1965), 75–76.
26. E. Anati. *Palestine Before the Hebrews: A History from the Earliest Arrival of Man to the Conquest of Canaan.* New York, 1963. Reviewed in *Jewish Social Studies* 28 (1966), 34.
27. A. L. Oppenheim. *Ancient Mesopotamia: Portrait of a Dead Civilation.* Chicago, 1965. Reviewed in *Archaeology* 19/2 (1966), 138–139.
28. C. Wilcke. *Das Lugalbandaepos.* Wiesbaden, 1969. Reviewed in *ActaOr* 33 (1971), 363–378.
29. F. H. Taylor. *Babel's Tower: The Dilemma of the Modern Museum.* New York, 1945. Reviewed in *Crozer Quarterly* 22 (1945), 268–271.
30. E. Porada. *Seal Impressions of Nuzi.* New Haven, 1947. Reviewed in *Crozer Quarterly* 25 (1948), 268–269.
31. T. Jacobsen. *Toward the Image of Tammuz and Other Essays on Mesopotamian History and Culture.* Cambridge, 1970. Reviewed in *Catholic Biblical Quarterly* 33 (1971), 266–268.
32. W. H. Ph. Römer. *Das Sumerische Kurzepos 'Bilgameš und Akka.' Alter Orient und Altes Testament* 209/1. Neukirchen-Vluyn, 1980. Reviewed in *JAOS* 102 (1982), 655.
33. Review of J. J. van Dijk. *UD-ME-LAM-bi-NIR-GAL: Traduction et Introduction.* Leiden, 1983. *JAOS* 105 (1985), 135–139.

Other Works Cited

Albright, W. F. *The Archaeology of Palestine*. Harmondsworth, 1949.
———. *From the Stone Age to Christianity: Monotheism and the Historical Process.* Baltimore, 1940.
Ceram, C. W. *Gods, Graves and Scholars: The Story of Archaeology*. Translated by E. B. Garside. New York, 1951.
Chadwick, H. M., and N. K. Chadwick. *The Growth of Literature*. 3 vols. Cambridge, 1932–1940.
Chiera, E. *Sumerian Epics and Myths. OIP* 15. Chicago, 1934.
———. *Sumerian Religious Texts*. Crozer Theological Seminary. Babylonian Publications 1. Upland, Pa., 1924.
———. *Sumerian Texts of Varied Contents. OIP* 16. Chicago, 1934.
Childe, V. Gordon. *The Dawn of European Civilization*. Rev. ed. London, 1947.
Cooper, J. S. *The Curse of Agade*. Baltimore, 1983.
Diakonoff, I., ed. *Ancient Mesopotamia: Socio-Economic History: A Collection of Studies by Soviet Scholars*. Wiesbaden, 1973.
———. *Sumer: Society and State in Ancient Mesopotamia*. Moscow, 1959. In Russian, with English résumé.
Gadd, C. *A Sumerian Reading Book*. Oxford, 1924.
———. *History and Monuments of Ur*. London, 1929.
Gordon, E. I. *Sumerian Proverbs: Glimpses of Everyday Life in Ancient Mesopotamia*. Philadelphia, 1959.
Gray, L. H., and G. F. Moore, eds. *The Mythology of All Races*. 13 vols. Boston, 1916–1932.
Hastings, J. *Encyclopedia of Religion and Ethics*. Edinburgh, 1908–1927.
James, E. O. *Myth and Ritual in the Ancient Near East: An Archaeological and Documentary Study*. London, 1958.
Laessøe, J. *People of Ancient Assyria: Their Inscriptions and Correspondence*. Translated by F. S. Leigh-Browne. London, 1963.
Langdon, S. H. *Sumerian Epic of Paradise, the Flood, and the Fall of Man*. Museum of the University of Pennsylvania. Publications of the Babylonian Section 10/1. Philadelphia, 1915.

Other Works Cited

Mackay, E. J. H. *Further Explorations at Mohenjo-daro.* 2 vols. Delhi, 1938.

——. *The Indus Civilization.* London, 1935.

Majumdar, N. G. *Explorations in Sind.* Delhi, 1934.

Mallowan, Sir M. "Noah's Flood Reconsidered." *Iraq* 26 (1964), 68–83.

Marshall, Sir J. H., ed. *Mohenjo-daro and the Indus Culture.* 3 vols. London, 1931.

Niebuhr, C. *Reisenbeschreibung nach Arabien und andern umliegenden Ländern.* 2 vols. Copenhagen, 1774–1778.

Piggott, S. *Some Ancient Cities of India.* Calcutta, 1945.

Piotrovsky, B. *Urartu.* Archaeologia Mundi. Geneva, 1969.

Poebel, A. *Grundzüge der sumerischen Grammatik.* Rostock. 1923.

——. *The Sumerian Prefix Forms e- and i- in the Time of the Earlier Princes of Lagaš.* Chicago, 1931.

Pritchard, J. B., ed. *Ancient Near Eastern Texts.* 2d ed. Princeton, 1955; 3d ed. 1969.

Saggs, H. W. F. *The Greatness That Was Babylon.* New York, 1962.

Speiser, E. A. "The Epic of Gilgamesh." In Pritchard, ed., 72–99 (see above).

Thureau-Dangin, F. *Les Inscriptions de Sumer et Akkad.* Paris, 1905.

van Dijk, J. J. A. *La Sagesse suméro-accadienne.* Leiden, 1953.

Vats, M. S. *Excavations at Harappā.* 2 vols. Delhi, 1940.

Wheeler, Sir R. E. M. "Harappā, 1946: The Defences and Cemetery R 37." *Ancient India* 3 (1947), 58–130.

Woolley, Sir C. L. *Excavations at Ur.* London, 1954.

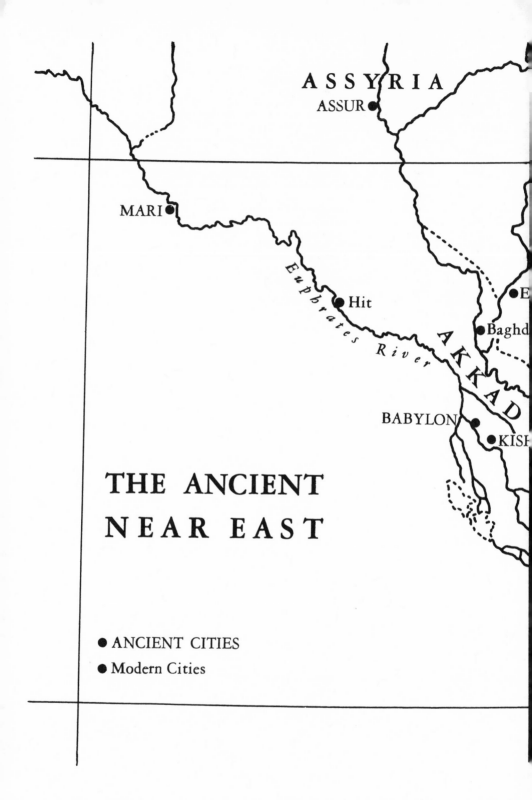

ASSYRIA

ASSUR

MARI

Euphrates River

Hit

E

Baghd

AKKAD

BABYLON

KISH

THE ANCIENT
NEAR EAST

● ANCIENT CITIES
● Modern Cities

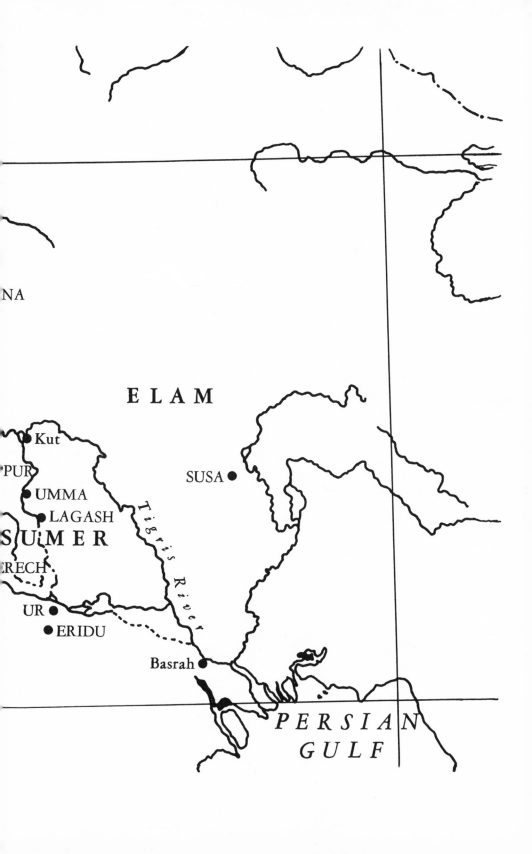

NA

E L A M

● Kut

PUR

● UMMA

● LAGASH

SUSA ●

S U M E R

RECH

Tigris River

UR ●

● ERIDU

Basrah ●

P E R S I A N
G U L F

Samuel Noah Kramer in his later eighties is curator emeritus of the Babylonian tablet collection of the University Museum, University of Pennsylvania, Clark Research Professor emeritus of the University of Pennsylvania Graduate School, and visiting professor, The Dropsie University, Philadelphia. He has shared Sumerian wisdom with his students at the universities of Indiana and Copenhagen, at the Sorbonne, and at Hebrew University. Among his publications, ranging from the most technical to the popular are Sumerische literarische Texte aus Nippur, Sumerian Literary Texts in the Ashmolean Museum, History Begins at Sumer, *and* The Sumerians. *He is still hard at work.*

The manuscript was edited for publication by Carol Altman Bromberg and Bernard Goldman. The book was designed by Don Ross. The typeface for the text is Times Roman, designed under the supervision of Stanley Morison about 1932, and the display face is Mistral. The book is printed on 60-lb. Glatfelter text paper and is bound in Holliston's Roxite vellum over binder's boards.

Manufactured in the United States of America.